Time, Existential Presence, and the Cinematic Image

Ethics and Emergence to Being in Film

Sam B. Girgus

EDINBURGH
University Press

To
Judith Ann Elizabeth Scot-Smith Girgus
Our daughters Katya, Meighan, and Jennifer
Jeff and Ali
Our grandchildren Arielle Gianni, Zachary Isaac, Mia, and Max

Edinburgh University Press is one of the leading university presses in
the UK. We publish academic books and journals in our selected subject
areas across the humanities and social sciences, combining cutting-edge
scholarship with high editorial and production values to produce academic
works of lasting importance. For more information visit our website:
edinburghuniversitypress.com

Edinburgh University Press Ltd
The Tun—Holyrood Road
12 (2f) Jackson's Entry
Edinburgh EH8 8PJ

First published in hardback by Edinburgh University Press 2018

Typeset in 11/13 Monotype Ehrhardt by Servis
Filmsetting Ltd, Stockport, Cheshire, and
printed and bound in Great Britain.
by CPI Group (UK) Ltd, Croydon, CR0 4YY

A CIP record for this book is available from the British Library

ISBN 978 1 4744 3623 6 (hardback)
ISBN 978 1 4744 3624 3 (paperback)
ISBN 978 1 4744 3625 0 (webready PDF)
ISBN 978 1 4744 3626 7 (epub)

Contents

List of Figures iv
Acknowledgements v

Introduction – Time, Existential Presence, and the Cinematic
Image: Ethics and Emergence to Being in Film 1

**Part I The Otherness of Existence and "Spacious Temporality":
Delayed Cinema and Freedom**
1 Delayed Cinema and "This Space-Time of Freedom": De Sica's
Bicycle Thieves (1948) 33
2 *La Demora* (2012) 56
3 Existence and Ethics in the Dardenne Brothers' *Two Days, One
Night* (2015) 78

**Part II Western Spaces:
Landscapes of Denial, Death, and Freedom**
4 *El Viaje:* Tommy Lee Jones and the Violent Times of the Mission
to Mexico 101
5 The American Way: Time, Death, and Resurrection in Iñárritu's
Western Masterpiece 127

Epilogue – Time, Spacing, and the Body in Martin Scorsese's *The
Age of Innocence* (1993) 153

Index 188

Figures

I.1 *Mr Smith Goes to Washington*: Jimmy Stewart as Mr. Smith
carries time and infinite responsibility on his shoulders   18

1.1 *Bicycle Thieves*: A mysterious maternal gaze as a young boy seeks
paternal guidance and care   51

1.2 *Bicycle Thieves*: A young girl suddenly changes the ethical and
existential dynamic in a crowded urban setting   52

1.3 *Bicycle Thieves*: An exchange of looks and the gaze suggests
existential revelation and encounter   53

2.1 *La Demora*: Struggling with age and infirmity   57

2.2 *La Demora*: Dutifully bathing her elderly father   58

3.1 *Two Days, One Night*: Marion Cotillard appeals for support   89

3.2 *Two Days, One Night*: Cotillard striving for identity, dignity, and
power   97

4.1 *The Three Burials of Melquiades Estrada*: Tommy Lee Jones makes
Barry Pepper his prisoner   106

5.1 *The Revenant*: Leonardo DiCaprio struggles for survival and
regeneration in the wilderness   130

5.2 *The Revenant*: Searching for meaning and understanding   150

E.1 Michelle Pfeifer in *The Age of Innocence*   181

Acknowledgements

Ever since I ventured into the area of film and philosophy, Sarah Cooper has been a source of great support and encouragement. Just as important, she serves as a model for the best of the scholarship and criticism in this field. I also would like to thank Kyle Stevens for making it possible to have a special Laura Mulvey issue of the peer-reviewed *New Journal of Film and Television Studies* 15:4 (December 2017) in which a briefer version of the introductory chapter to this book appeared. Since overhearing him more than a dozen years ago talking about Levinas and phenomenology while working out at a local gym, philosopher Aaron Simmons has been a deep reservoir and a perpetual energy force for me with ideas and insights about ethics, religion, and philosophy. His collegiality represents the best of the ideal of a community scholars. I learn from him as both a professor and a person. Similarly, J. Douglas Macready has engaged in a continuous dialogue with me about issues of ethics and political philosophy for nearly a decade since he wrote to me about my first essay on Levinas, ethics, and film. I have learned regularly from him and gained from the extraordinary depth and range of his knowledge and expertise as a true modernist and humanist. Jerry Christensen also remains at my side in spirit if not always in physical presence as a best friend and colleague. As Jerry once said of a colleague, he is always there not only as a source of encouragement and support but also as an academic and scholarly conscience insisting upon the highest standards of academic and critical excellence.

Regarding this work, my relationship and association with Laura Mulvey has been one of the highlights of my career of nearly half a century. I met her first in London at a scheduled time that was sandwiched in between also seeing two former students I also would like to thank for their friendship and support, Charles Walker, a member of Parliament for many years, and April Yanicelli, a former Vanderbilt student. As a result of that meeting with Laura Mulvey in London, she visited Vanderbilt, arriving on election day 2016 for a week-long series of events that were made possible by generous support from Dana Nelson in the Department of English, Jennifer Fay from Cinema and Media Arts, and Katherine Crawford of Women's and Gender Studies. The emotion of that historic political moment helped to hasten and cement our relationship as we shared our sense of alarm and concern. Her warmth, generosity, charm, and quiet charisma made her presence a wonderful event for the students and faculty who immediately warmed to her qualities of sympatico and graciousness. Introduced regularly during her visit as a woman who changed modern consciousness and as the inspiration for what could be called the Age of Mulvey in film, media, and women's and gender studies, her openness and humility made her visit memorable for those who met her and heard her and saw her various presentations.

Much of what has been attempted and achieved over the past two years in the form of this book, the Laura Mulvey visit, the special journal issue, the completion of rigorous research in several inter-connected fields, and the building of the foundation for a special project on renewing the American story was made possible to a considerable extent through the graduate assistance of Lara Casey. Her steady professionalism, sharp intelligence, consistent efficiency, and creative imagination were evident and felt in these various endeavors. I could not have asked for or imagined a better or stronger graduate assistant. Her sense of responsibility, personal initiative, and commitment to excellence made her impact upon and contribution to these projects of great significance. I would like to thank Dana Nelson for the support from the Department of English for these various projects. Also in the department, Sandra Bohn has been a source of special assistance along with Janis May, Jeffrey Cooper, and Jeana Poindexter.

I have been fortunate to be at Vanderbilt when two extraordinary leaders have served in the position of chancellor. Gordon Gee was a pioneer in introducing change at the university while Nick Zeppos stands as an influential force and figure in modern higher education, articulating and executing a philosophy of unbridled intellectual investigation, academic freedom, and civic discourse in a time of historic change. His work at Vanderbilt with Pulitzer Prize-winning historian Jon Meacham exemplifies such leadership. Meacham occupies a distinguished place in a great tradition of modern American historians who have brought the American narrative of tragedy and redemption to life through the strength of their academic scholarship, their critical and intellectual integrity, and their sharp and effective creativity. He has been similarly distinguished for his crucial role as a public intellectual at the forefront of the on-going fight for democracy, equality, and freedom in our challenging times. I thank them for their encouragement and friendship to me in my own work.

When it comes to technology, computers, and digital operations, the help and time of Michael McAllister has proven indispensable to the work of this dinosaur who remembers the days of newspaper city desks with the reverberating sounds of pounding Royal typewriter keys, telephones ringing alarms, and pinging teletypes. He has proven to be a man of near infinite patience and kindness, qualities that make him an excellent teacher. Ellis Dews, Mark Swain, and Jon Bates also have been available for consistent help in the area of media and technology.

It has been a delight and pleasure both professionally and personally to work with the folks at Edinburgh University Press beginning with Gillian Leslie and Richard Strachan who initially supported and encouraged this work. I also would like to thank for their work and help Laura Booth, Eddie Clark, Rebecca Mackenzie and Emma Rees.

Friends, colleagues, current and former students remain crucial all along the way for their intellectual engagement and their spirited encouragement. These include Brian and Judy Jones, Martha Matzke, Cynthia Lucia, Colleen Glenn, Thomas Schatz, Dudley Andrew, John Belton, Hans Ulrich Gumbrecht, Jennifer Smyth, Brian Bergen-Aurand, Kathryn Hearst, Joe Kickasola, Negi and Jean and family, Danny and Emily and Family, Audrey Shapiro, Cammie Nichols, Joci Straus, Rochelle Mann, Claire Darling, Peter Bailey, Rebecca Bell-Metereau, Thadious Davis, Bridget Orr, Jonathan Lamb, Colin Dayan, John Lachs, Mark Schoenfield, Michael Kreyling, Carol and Keith Hagan, Carol Burke, Anne Kern, J. Delayne Ryms, Haerin Shin, Alex Dubilet, Kate Ferguson, Henry Hill Perot, Peter Dale, Katie McCall, Melanie Shepard, Fabiani Duarte, Shayna Humphrey, Alexa Simon, Trey Harwell, Benjamin Grimwood, Emma Noyes, Peter Burke, Rachel Young, Isabel Turley, Claire Hagney, Laiba Fatima, George Miller, Carsen Smith, Caroline Volgman, Phil Burnham, Catherine Prater, Jane Dorsey Taylor, Mary Dachille, Emily Mathewson, Ean Pfeiffer, Aviel Ginzburg, Agnieszka Supel, Sedrissa Veal, Magda Zaborowska, Karen Stenard, Eddie O'Neill, Ginia McPhearson, "Brittwick" Strottman, Nicole Crane, Colleen Weatherford, Alison Barnes, Melanie Griffith, Ben Scott, Mandy Dake, Amity Wang, Jacqui Leitzes, Nancy Cain Marcus, Dawn Ferguson, Kelli Fuery, Tasha Brennan, Benjamin Grimwood, Jen Graham-O'Brien, Chad Gervich, Cindy Lyle, Nikki Mack, Robert Mack, Rory McTurk, Emily Blackledge, Cliff Richmond, Brooke Lyle, Risa Arnold, Ruth Banes, Fred Blankfein, Willie Geist, Marietta Parrish, Molly Moreau, Eddie Michaels, Ashley Peak, Gurjeet Birdee, Cynthia Allen, Chad Given, Steve Ladd, Dr "Skip" Daube, Clay Bailey, Ralph Schueller, Cheryl Dalton, Mary Ellen Pethel, and Robert and Marguerite Jones.

For more than fifty years, Scottie has been there every step of the way at the center of our family universe with love, understanding, patience, and a good measure of forgiveness, soon followed by our daughters Katya, Meighan, and Jennifer, and then Jeff and Ali, and our grandchildren Arielle Gianni, Zachary Isaac, Mia, and Max. With each passing moment, their brightness and force as guiding stars grow ever greater and more vibrant.

Introduction – Time, Existential Presence, and the Cinematic Image: Ethics and Emergence to Being in Film

For years now, digital and computer technologies have been redefining and transforming cinema and media. Digital and computer-generated images have tended to supplant traditional film that relies on photography and chemistry, thereby sparking controversy over the putative "death of cinema." The new digital technologies can readily vary and alter temporal fluctuations and rhythms of film. Such technologies have enabled Laura Mulvey to articulate her own version of the slow cinema movement of recent years.[1] Dubbed "delayed cinema," the fresh idea of cinema Mulvey proposes in her seminal study, *Death 24x a Second: Stillness and the Moving Image* (2006), exploits digital and computer technological operations for rethinking not just slow cinema but time in cinema.

Delayed cinema as conceptualized and articulated by Mulvey creates possibilities for a fresh discussion of cinematic time in a new philosophical context. Specifically, new thinking about time in delayed cinema can contribute to recent discussions of emerging presence by philosophers committed to the existential challenge for authenticity, immediacy, and intensity in contemporary thought and experience. The sustained tension in film between, in Mulvey's phrase, "stillness and the moving image" enacts an existential drama that directs access not only to the Freudian "uncanny"—the *unheimlich*—but to the existential coming of being and presence.[2] Mulvey's project of delayed cinema opens new territory in cinema and media studies by concentrating on the stillness of the image in relation to the flow of images that all together constitute a film from the framed image to the launching of the audio-visual trajectory of a film's images and signs. Mulvey's epistemology and method can be used to study the emergence of existential presence in film as a new time and ontology of cinema.

Following Mulvey's theory, it becomes clearer how the tension between stillness and movement in film gives birth to presence. The stillness of the framed film image in relation to the moving image creates the spatial and temporal conditions for an expanded existential presence. Thus, in film, stillness alone turns presence into the living dead; movement alone fails to hold presence, making it a fugitive. The interaction between the two, stillness and the moving image, spawns a new spatio-temporal dimension for emerging existential presence in film.

Philosopher Jean-Luc Nancy presciently analogized the existentialism of emerging presence and the emerging cinematic and media image. Nancy says of the body, "it's *the coming to presence,* like an image coming on a movie or a TV screen—coming *from* nowhere behind the screen, *being* the spacing of this screen."[3] As a film scholar and filmmaker himself as well as a philosopher, Nancy recognized the parallelism between emerging existential presence and the production of screen images. Moreover, Nancy's notion of emerging presence and the existential as a kind of shock of recognition also works for the shifting and fluid times of delayed cinema. Speaking of transcendence and existence, Nancy writes of the "here and now, as a presence that would be the singular presence of a strike, of a spring, of a free leap in existence and of existence."[4] Similarly, delayed cinema could be seen and heard as operating existentially in time with strikes, springs, and leaps into a new existence.

The shifting fluidities of cinematic time in delayed cinema also generate emerging existential presence in the production of previously sub-surface images or in holding exposed images in prolonged examination for fresh life and meaning. Slowing, reversing, stopping, stalling film in delayed cinema reveal depths of previously invisible moving images. Altering temporalities for the images of delayed cinema exposes a bounty of semiotic signs for study as potential events of emerging being and presence. These temporal and spatial shifts realize what Mulvey describes as "stretching out the cinematic image" (*D24*: 183, 146). Such "stretching out" becomes a spatio-temporal dimension for the emergence to presence, what philosopher and cultural historian Hans Ulrich Gumbrecht terms "this expanding present."[5]

Accordingly, delayed cinema of stillness and movement reinforces the efforts of contemporary thinkers who expound the importance of existential presence in lived experience, critical thought, and ethical engagement. Delayed cinema speaks directly to the theme of emerging existential presence in the work of Nancy, Gumbrecht, and George Steiner. It informs Nancy's existential togetherness, Gumbrecht's expanded presence in modern lifestyles, and Steiner's "real" presence in art and thought. Delayed cinema facilitates and expresses the philosophical, ethical, and aesthetic search for existential presence. Interestingly, Asbjørn Grønstad has suggested connecting Nancy and Gumbrecht on ethics and slow cinema.[6]

In addition, the writings of other modern thinkers on the phenomenology of time and ethics also can render insight into the temporal relationship of delayed cinema to existential presence and the ethical imperative, a relationship that provides a basis for new thinking about time in film. Such modern philosophers include Paul Tillich on the idea of "*kairos*" or "the eternal now," Emmanuel Levinas's non-synchronic diachronic time of responsibility to the other, and Julia Kristeva's development of the Freudian *zeitlos* or "lost time."

The intellectual and ethical investment of these thinkers in the idea of a transcendent temporal dimension, of a time beyond conventional linear regimes, suggests comparison to delayed cinema's changing temporalities involving stillness and the moving image. Emerging existential presence often occurs with the disruption of controlled, conventional temporal regimes that define, categorize, and essentialize being. Similarly, for delayed cinema, breaking from the prescribed temporal regime for film of twenty-four frames a second creates a new temporal order and experience. Such a break also suggests the possibility in film for expressing a transcendent temporal dimension of developing ethical subjectivity that counters ordinary, linear, chronological time involving narrative, character, and meaning. The pertinence and significance of disjunctive temporal regimes for these ethical and philosophical projects give a sense of ethical and artistic urgency to the innovations of delayed cinema.

The work of presence thinkers comes at a time of great change in the idea and experience of presence in both the culture at large and among scholars and critics concerned with presence. Interestingly, without much expressed concern for existential thought, Mulvey also considers delayed cinema as related to the modern thrust toward presence. She says that "delayed cinema gains further significance as outside events hasten the disappearance of the past" (*D24*: 23). As an example of such an event, she believes that for many the world and our conception of time were "irrevocably changed" by "the events of September 2001 in New York and Washington, DC." She suggests that today a "newly configured present" prompts a rapid recession of the last century into a kind of void (*D24*: 23, 24). Mulvey's interpretation of the significance of 9/11 intimates a broad change in cultural attitudes about time: a move away from belief in historical progress and a meaningful future and toward a sense of time as a disappearing past and an extended present.

Also for Gumbrecht, the movement toward presence indicates a growing change in how people today tend to think about time to help them understand events and live their lives. Gumbrecht writes, "Today we increasingly feel that our present has broadened, as it is now surrounded by a future we can no longer see, access, or choose and a past that we are not able to leave behind" (*OBP*: 20). He believes this new "configuration" of time—a "chronotope"—compels a new existential encounter and challenge.

Gumbrecht's and Mulvey's thoughts on presence reflect not only general shifts in social and cultural attitudes toward time in everyday life, but they also are consistent with movements and trends in the humanities and the sciences.

For some in academia, a commitment to presence represents a response to years of obscure critical theory and convoluted hermeneutical analysis. Thus, Steiner, an esteemed philosopher and public intellectual, contrasts the felt experience of existential presence with the ambiguities involving the rupture between the word and the thing in modern discourse and experience. Steiner bemoans modernity's revolutionary rejection of "the covenant between word and object, the presumption that being is, to a workable degree, 'sayable' and that the raw material of existentiality has its analogue in the structure of narrative." He writes, *"It is this break of the covenant between word and world which constitutes one of the very few genuine revolutions of spirit in Western history and which defines modernity itself."*[7] Thus, in art, thought, and experience, Steiner maintains the indispensable centrality of "aesthetic presence" and "the irreducible autonomy of presence" as a salve to the open wound of the break between the word and the thing that constitutes a crisis of mind and spirit in modernity.[8] For Steiner, existential presence emphasizes experience over the interpretation of experience and avoids repetitious hermeneutical argument about meaning. Also, Nancy, in his strong call for presence, proposes an emerging presence in the form of a regenerative "birth to presence." Nancy sees such an emerging "birth to presence" as "a *coming* and a *passing,* an *extending* and a *penetrating"* that challenges and subverts "a stable, fixed being."[9]

Gumbrecht and others deem epiphanic resonances of existential immediacy and intensity an important part of the movement toward presence. Thus, Gumbrecht's argument that at least since James Joyce and high modernism *"literature can be the place of epiphany"* for the existential subject also obtains for film (*OBP*: 6; emphasis in the original). Noting that "epiphany within aesthetic experience is an event because it undoes itself while it emerges," Gumbrecht sees the fleeting epiphany as vital for existential presence. He welcomes "epiphanies that, for moments at least, make us dream, make us long for, and make us perhaps even remember, with our bodies as well as with our minds, how good it would be to live in sync with the things of the world."[10]

Nancy in turn speaks of "divine epiphany" that "is revealed immediately" (*BP*: 54). He experiences music as an epiphanic moment of existential presence that conveys the possibility of emotional and spiritual transcendence. Like Steiner, Nancy believes that music conveys a "hope" and a promise of "a touch of eternity" that can "come and come again."[11] For Nancy and Steiner as well, the unique structuring of time and sound in music creates the possibility of experiencing intense existential clarity in a multi-temporal dimension that transforms the meaning of now.

Also, taking an original approach of "otherness" and "togetherness" to his unique existentialist world view, Nancy writes, "The otherness of existence happens only as 'togetherness.' . . . Community is the community of *others"* (*BP*: 155; emphasis in the original). Saying "Being is being-with," Nancy continues, "The *with* is the most basic feature of Being, the mark [*trait*] of the singular plurality of the origin or origins in it." He continues, "Presence is impossible except as copresence."[12] He relates presence to the immanence of transcendence.[13]

Steiner's case for presence recalls the language of other philosophers who bet or wagered on belief and meaning. He simply says of presence and transcendence in language, thought, and art, "This essay argues a wager on transcendence. It argues that there is in the art-act and its reception, that there is in the experience of meaningful form, a presumption of presence."[14]

To a certain extent, the intersection of existential presence, including the relationship to transcendence and ethics, with theories of cinema should seem a natural outgrowth of the concern of existentialism and cinema with time. The intrinsic connection between film and time has long been established and studied. For example, Mary Ann Doane describes film as a literal time "machine."[15] Similarly, Andrei Tarkovsky, the great director and philosopher of film, proposes that "the virtue of cinema is that it appropriates time." He asks and answers, "What is the essence of the director's work? We could define it as sculpting in time."[16] Tarkovsky goes so far as to assert that time becomes the actual material of cinema.

Thus, as a unique temporal art form, film suggests a special readiness for making an aesthetic and ethical purpose of enacting existential coming into presence and being. Viewed through the perspective of an existential analytic, cinematic time, as the interaction between stillness and the moving image, becomes a force for dramatizing a broadening and deepening presence experience. Defined in part by its special relationship to time, film can be viewed and studied for its potential dramatic realization of, in Gumbrecht's terminology, a "presence culture" of existentially grounded being that engages what he deems a "meaning culture" inundated and overburdened with criticism and hermeneutics (*OBP*: 3).

In fact, it can be argued that cinema has a vital role to play in what apparently for Gumbrecht constitutes a program for promoting "the production of presence" in all aspects of modern life, especially the academic. Gumbrecht maintains that "in a world so saturated with meaning," it becomes crucial to realize *Erleben* or "the immediacy of lived experience . . . under layers of meaning" (*PP*: 105, 43). Film provides a crucial arena and culture for balancing presence with meaning. Birth to presence in a film implies a search for meaning.

Thus, Mulvey's model of delayed cinema in conjunction with the work of other thinkers such as Nancy can provide the basis for new thinking about time in cinema in relation to emerging existential presence and the ethical imperative. Indeed, elements of Nancy's theory of time, presence, and being as expressed in his most salient and intellectually creative concepts of the spacing of time, happening, co-presence and co-appearance, and the transposition of inner and outer spaces for otherness promise to be quite compatible with the paradigm of delayed cinema for cinematic study. The spacing of time, for example, suggests similarities with the stretching out of the image in Mulvey's delayed cinema, while the idea of the phenomenological and psychological fluidity of the boundaries between inner and outer spaces can be visualized and enacted in the stillness and movement of mobile framing in cinema.

Similarly, Nancy's rethinking of time and space in terms of "with" and "us" and "we" challenges cinema to dramatize the ethical encounter of otherness and togetherness. Nancy's existential imperative of the otherness of existence as togetherness becomes a drama on film in shared temporal space over the ethical imperative of the encounter with otherness.

While Nancy's philosophical terms extend to thinking and studying cinema, Mulvey's conceptualization of time and space in film helps to imagine a temporal regime for emerging existential presence. Delayed cinema opens the possibility for new seeing and thinking for film and experience. Delayed cinema enacts the encounter with existential presence.

MULVEY ON STILLNESS AND THE MOVING IMAGE

Accordingly, this study of time and the coming of presence in film proceeds along two theoretical and philosophical tracks that regularly intersect and meld across a variety of films of aesthetic and cultural interest. The first track conveys the crucial conceptual and critical apparatus of Mulvey's paradigm of stillness and movement that can be employed to examine emerging existential presence in film. The second explores emergence and birth to presence as a movement toward and for being, especially as proposed in the work of contemporary thinkers such as Nancy, Gumbrecht, and Steiner, among others. The two tracks in the films in this study merge in the drama of the existential struggle to be, as Nancy says, "in touch with *ourselves* and in touch with the rest of beings." Nancy writes, "We are in touch with ourselves insofar as we exist. Being in touch with ourselves is what makes us 'us,' and there is no other secret to discover buried behind this very touching, behind the 'with' of coexistence" (*BSP*: 13; emphasis in the original).

Considering her intellectual journey of "discovery," Mulvey readily notes that delayed cinema was around before her book. Like Freud with the unconscious and psychoanalysis, for Mulvey delayed cinema was available for study and use for some time, hiding in plain sight, so to speak, but available for those inclined to see film that way for closer, slower readings of images in relation to moving images. With the advent of new digital film and media, Mulvey composed an original theory for the new situation and times. Her theory and criticism encourage reviewing old films to recover lost images, happenings, and insights while instituting new ways for watching, studying, and making cinema, including computer-generated work.

Thus, for Mulvey, new digital and computer technologies have transformed the experience of viewing and studying film since the time when a character in Jean-Luc Godard's *Le Petit Soldat* (1960) [The Little Soldier] remarks, "To photograph a face is to photograph the soul behind it. Photography is truth. And the cinema is truth, twenty-four times a second."[17] Mulvey maintains, "My point of departure is an obvious, everyday reality: that video and digital media have opened up new ways of seeing old movies" (*D24*: 8). This new technology, as she describes it, has enabled the creation of a "new kind of ontology" of cinema—a "delayed cinema" of "stillness" (*D24*: 12, 8). She says, "Needless to say, there is nothing fundamentally new here. To see cinema through delay is to discover a cinema that has always been there, either overtly in the experiments of the avant-garde or more covertly in the great range of fiction film" (*D24*: 8). Nevertheless, Mulvey renews cinema by inventing a new way of looking at it. She writes, "Delayed cinema works on two levels: first of all it refers to the actual act of slowing down the flow of film. Secondly it refers to the delay in time during which some detail has lain dormant, as it were, waiting to be noticed." Also, demonstrating her particular focus on the Freudian unconscious and the *unheimlich*, she adds, "There is a loose parallel here with Freud's concept of deferred action (*nachtraglichkeit*), the way the unconscious preserves a specific experience, while its traumatic effect might only be realized by another, later but associated, event" (*D24*: 8).

Now positioning film in the Mulvey-presence paradigm provides a coherent theoretical structure for what previously for some had been something of an improvised methodology for stilled and slow film viewing based at times on informed instinct and critical impulse. As Mulvey states, her paradigm explains what had been going on all along. Her work now positions delayed cinema on a solid critical foundation for future study.

In the preface to her book, Mulvey emphasizes how in delayed cinema, stillness, slowness, and movement transform temporal and spatial dimensions to create a new aesthetic for film. She focuses on one particular seminal film, Dziga Vertov's *Man with a Movie Camera* (1929), to illustrate and elaborate upon her theory. She notes how Vertov famously invented his own delayed cinema by freezing the frame of his movie after a dynamic sequence of movements by horse and carriage and train. Mulvey writes, "This accumulation of movement had carried forward the movement of the film and of time itself, so when the image froze another temporal dimension suddenly emerged. While movement tends to assert the presence of a continuous 'now', stillness brings a resonance of 'then' to the surface" (*D24*: 13). She cites this sequence in Vertov's seminal documentary film as evidence of an original understanding by the director and his editor, Elizaveta Svilova, of the significance of the relationship of stillness and movement to the multiple temporalities of film.

For Mulvey, the Vertov documentary becomes a primary exhibit of how the multiple temporalities of stillness and movement incorporate a sense of the power to end and renew life into the structure of film. Film, as Vertov demonstrates, can stop and go, suggesting life and death by freezing and then continuing temporal and spatial movement. Throughout her book, Mulvey reiterates André Bazin's crucial association of the photograph with time and death. For Bazin, the photographic image engages life and death in its very nature and form. Bazin famously claims in "The Ontology of the Photographic Image" that the photograph "embalms time."[18] In the context of such a theory of photography, Mulvey writes, "The reality recorded by the photograph relates exclusively to its moment of registration; that is, it represents a moment extracted from the continuity of historical time" (*D24*: 13). In her work, Mulvey assiduously elaborates upon Bazin's signature theme of stopping time and life in the photographic image.

In another example of how delayed cinema complicates issues of time that originally had been raised by photography, Mulvey alludes to the idea of presence in a way that suggests the potential for lengthier discussion of the relationship between delayed cinema and existential presence. In this example, Mulvey picks up on a discussion by two students of modern film, Chris Petit and Manny Farber, about a seemingly insignificant moment in the Howard Hawks classic *The Big Sleep* (1946), starring Humphrey Bogart, which Petit includes in his video *Negative Space* (1999). In his video, Petit slows down the movement of a particular scene from the regular twenty-four frames a second, concentrating, according to Mulvey, on a moment in *The Big Sleep* when "Bogart is crossing the street and, unmotivated by plot, glances up at the sky and then touches the fire hydrant as he arrives at the other side. Various extras, including a young girl, walk past him" (*D24*: 194). Mulvey then elaborates upon the discussion about the girl. She says,

> When the commentary draws attention to the young woman walking past in the background, at that moment her presence suddenly becomes more significant than the presence of the star. After all, Bogart is known, familiar. The hierarchy of star and extra shifts. The young woman, a cinematic document as mysterious as an unidentified photograph, has a presence that would be impossible to perceive at 24 frames per second and can only be discovered in the "playful" process of repetition and return. (*D24*: 194)

Mulvey's use of the word "presence" in her discussion of the girl in *The Big Sleep* proves especially illuminating in the context of the theme of existential presence in film and the insights of such presence thinkers as Nancy and Gumbrecht. At first, presence as used by Mulvey for the unidentified girl in the Hawks–Bogart film merely seems to indicate the girl's sudden physical appearance and an unanticipated awareness of her on screen. At the same time, referring to her as mysterious also hints at certain connotations of presence as suggesting a distinct bearing, even charisma or uniqueness.

On another level, however, presence in this scene at this moment also literally means and dramatizes existential presence in the sense of bringing to life, coming to being, a birth to presence. As Mulvey makes clear, without the slowness of the movement of the film, the girl would remain unseen, unknown, virtually pre-nascent and unborn.

At the same time, Mulvey's understanding and use of "ghostly presence" for the indexical image proves interesting in her discussion of the technological world of digital production and computer-generated images as opposed to celluloid-era film. She notes the crucial difference between an iconic and indexical photographic image of reality and a digital image but suggests a pragmatic approach to this difference, one based in part on time and the presence of the image. Mulvey writes, "Digital technology enables a spectator to still a film in a way that evokes the ghostly presence of the individual celluloid frame. Technically this is an anachronism" (*D24*: 26). She observes how "an imaginative association with film's archaic structure . . . can lead to intellectual and aesthetic reverie" so that "multiple possible channels" become available for discussion "from personal memory to textual analysis to historical research," thereby "opening up the past for a specifically cinematic excavation" (*D24*: 26).

Asserting the relevance of the indexical image even as a "ghostly presence," Mulvey repeats that "technology has rendered the presence of the index anachronistic," but then she says that precisely this "ghostly presence can enhance reflection on the actual filmic image under consideration, its presence as an inscription of a moment in time" (*D24*: 26). Mulvey suggests that the temporality of the image can sustain textual study, critical analysis, and maybe even some pleasure. She writes, "The dialectic between old and new produces innovative ways of thinking about the complex temporality of cinema and its significance for the present moment in history." She claims that "rather than killing the cinema," the new "digital technology" of delayed cinema assures "that old films can be seen with new eyes," a viewing that can interrupt and reorganize "the flow of cinema" (*D24*: 26). For Mulvey, the promise of digital technology for "interactive spectatorship brings with it pleasures reminiscent of the processes of textual analysis that open up understanding and unexpected emotion while also attacking the text's original cohesion" (*D24*: 28). Understood in this compelling way by Mulvey, digital technology serves in initiating the emergence to existential presence in cinema.

Mulvey's delayed cinema especially helps to exhibit the power of performance to animate abstract and complex issues. The shifting temporalities of delayed cinema expose and highlight details of performance and direction, often suggesting multiple spheres of experience and meaning. Also, the timing of delayed cinema enables concentration on factors that Nancy employs to discuss the body, such as determining and articulating "tension" and "tone" for "possibilities for ethical development" (*C*: 134). Thus, for both Mulvey and Nancy, the body on screen carries the weight in performance of working in a zone of spatialized time that interacts with a film's multiple temporalities.

Performance in delayed cinema of stillness and the moving image regularly exhibits emerging existential presence. Going back to one of America's earliest film classics, Al Jolson in *The Jazz Singer* (1927) looks at himself in blackface in a mirror and sees overlapping images of his father singing as a cantor at their synagogue on the High Holy Days. Delayed cinema of the moving image in this sequence accentuates the visual drama of the psychological internalization of religious, racial, and cultural conflicts. The mirror reflects Jolson's projection of divided identity and consciousness. In the same film, delayed cinema can linger over a quick shot of the backstage exchange of looks between a religious Jewish man who glimpses with curiosity at a chorus girl with bare legs. Slower viewing of this shot encapsulates the challenge to traditional piety and orthodoxy from the temptations and values of the jazz age.

Other examples of delayed cinema's revelatory power regarding emerging existential presence and the ethical imperative include: in *The Misfits* (1961), Marilyn Monroe's flash of self-recognition of her sexualized identity when looking at calendar photos followed later by her discreet glance of awareness of a special connection to Montgomery Clift; in *L'avventura* (1961) Monica Vitti's hesitation while gesturing forgiveness toward her unfaithful lover at the end of the film; and in *The Unbearable Lightness of Being* (1988), Lena Olin's look of vulnerability in an early sequence with her lover Daniel Day-Lewis that contradicts her usual self-confidence.

Also, director Tommy Lee Jones' quick cutting in *The Three Burials of Melquiades Estrada* (2005) punctuates the shocking sense of epiphanic revelation for Barry Pepper and Vanessa Bauche when the similarity of their bandaged noses resulting from the blows they inflicted on each other demonstrates their common humanity. Stillness and delayed cinema clarify the existential and ethical imperatives of the moment of recognition in Jones' film. More recently, in *The Girlfriend Experience* (Starz 2016), Riley Keough's pleasure, empowerment, and excitement as a prostitute during sex with particular customers contrasts with her ambivalence about herself as suggested by delayed cinema when she uses a kind of delayed cinema of her own to study herself on a surveillance video having sex by and with herself.

As evidenced by Vertov's film, directors also employ delayed cinema. In a kind of delayed cinema, John Ford in *The Searchers* (1956) famously holds a close-up of John Wayne looking from behind his horse into a psychological and ethical abyss with the realization of the impending massacre of his family that he left unprotected. Fooled by renegade Indians into leaving the family, Wayne stands as a helpless figure of bodily finitude and death. The image itself conveys temporal finality. The stillness of both the image and of Wayne intensifies his entrapment in a lost present between an unredeemable past and a future of guilt, lack, and ontological despair.[19]

Wayne's being and performance in this scene exemplify Mulvey's argument regarding the importance of the latent power of stillness and the pose in star performance (*D24*: 162). Standing still in desperate loss and finality, he epitomizes star-power significance. Wayne demonstrates how performers, as Mulvey argues, enact in their bodies, being, and work the tension between stillness and movement. In the scene, Wayne mounts and rides what Jean-François Lyotard calls "the great temporal hinge between too early/too late."[20] Such performers live and work in multiple temporalities emphasizing the urgency of a lost presence.

JEAN-LUC NANCY, PRESENCE, AND SPACING TIME

While one track of this study focuses on the inherent temporal and spatial complexities involved in the stillness, slowness, and movement of the cinematic image, another track concentrates on the philosophy of coming to presence. This second track focuses on the existential encounter in a culture that often discusses meaning to the depreciation of presence, as proposed in the work of Gumbrecht, Steiner, and Nancy, among others.[21] In this group of prominent thinkers, the work and thought of Nancy constitute a major influence in the turn toward presence in contemporary philosophy and thought. He has articulated and advanced what could be dubbed his own unique brand of existentialism as part of his overall philosophy. Gumbrecht, in his carefully constructed project for giving greater attention to presence in relation to meaning, finds enlightenment and inspiration in Nancy. Gumbrecht clearly sees himself and Nancy as cohorts in the movement in modern thought to advance and study presence. Indeed, Gumbrecht claims to "feel such a strong affinity with the point of departure of Jean-Luc Nancy's book *The Birth to Presence*" (*PP*: 57). *Birth to Presence,* along with Nancy's many other related works, proffers a theory of presence that could fulfill the aspirations of, as Gumbrecht notes, "a number of philosophers interested in phenomena of presence" (*PP*: 58).

Nancy propounds an intense existentialism that resonates at times with Jean-Paul Sartre's famous dictum of existence before essence. Frédéric Neyrat defines "Nancy's philosophy as a radicalized existentialism."[22] Nancy writes, "Essence is of the order of having: an assembly of qualities. By contrast, existence is itself its own essence, which is to say it is without essence" (*FT*: 12). Nancy's thinking on existence and essence intimates his answer to his "question of what *coming* or *birth to presence* means" (*FT*: 23; emphasis in the original). He writes, "This presence is not essence, but . . . birth to presence: birth and death to the infinite presentation of the fact there is no ultimate sense, only a finite sense, finite senses, a multiplication of singular bursts of sense resting on no unity or substance" (*FT*: 27). In other words, existence as its own essence.

At one point, Nancy pivots with his language, resorting to something close to an apocalyptic tone to dramatize the urgency he feels about the need for humanity to take responsibility for itself, for its own existence and being. To achieve this existential struggle for emerging being, he proposes an alternative between thinking what "is most necessary" for "access to who we are" as opposed to "never" gaining such access through a failure of thinking (*BSP*: 17). He maintains that such thinking for being requires thinking about time itself to find access to a spatio-temporality to cultivate the conditions for birth to presence.

Accordingly, the existential struggle for the birth and emergence to presence compels the creation of a time that discards a conventionally structured and lived temporal regime and replaces it with another temporal order of existence. For Nancy, the "happening" of existential presence requires a temporal domain of "*our* creation" outside of a logic and order of time that predetermines and rigidifies meaning (*BP*: 151; *BSP*: 17; emphasis in the original). Existential presence must preclude the time of essence with its structured, organized linearity.

Nancy, therefore, endeavors to conceptualize a new temporal logic for presence to counter the logic of linear time. He challenges "the reign of process and the linking of *time* to the logic of process and procedure: that is, a linear, continuous time, without *space* (of time), and always *pressed up* against its own 'after'" (*FT*: 21; emphasis in the original). Nancy notes of his temporal project that "it is, of course, not a matter of chronological time," thereby developing the possibility of a new time for emerging existential presence (*BP*: 151).

Nancy's concepts of "spacing" and "happening" become key elements in his temporal regime for being and presence. He says "time presents itself to us as this spatiality or 'spacing' [*espacement*] of a certain suspension" (*BP*: 150). Spacing functions as a kind of ambience for time and happening. Nancy says, "Happening consists in bringing forth a certain spacing of time, where something takes place in *inaugurating* time itself" (*BP*: 151; emphasis in the original).

Describing time in terms of spacing and happening enables Nancy to make what amounts to an ethical as well as an aesthetic and existential leap to rethinking time as an environment for "otherness" and "togetherness." Time becomes a universal, open space. Nancy maintains that "time gives us, by its spacing, the possibility of being *we*, or at least the possibility of saying 'we' and 'our.'" He writes, "In order to say 'we,' we have to be in a certain common space of time—even if by our 'we,' 'we' mean to include all mankind" (*BP*: 151; emphasis in the original). Spacing and happening facilitate the sharing of time with others, cultivating a sense of "we" in temporal structures for including others. Spacing and happening create community.

Given Nancy's understanding of time as shared space, the emergence to presence transforms into the relationship to "otherness" (*BP*: 154–155). Nancy insists, "A single being is a contradiction in terms. Such a being, which would be its own foundation, origin, and intimacy, would be incapable of *Being*, in every sense that this expression can have here" (*BSP*: 12; emphasis in the original). Nancy's insight means that "all appearance" becomes "co-appearance." Nancy contrives an existential view of co-appearance and co-presence that turns things inside out. As Nancy says, "the outside is inside" (*BSP*: 12, 13). If co-appearance becomes a condition for presence, then inner being invariably alternates with exterior relations.

Nancy's otherness of existential presence—a kind of dual existentialism and a possible contradiction in terms—becomes a rather remarkable gesture for inclusion, openness, and a generosity of spirit. Spacing, happening, co-appearance, and co-presence create a common ground for being and existential presence in a shared temporality. Birth to being becomes existential presence with and in relation to others. Existential isolation turns into isolation "with."

At the same time, nothingness and lack remain close at hand. In Nancy's existential view, lacking essence except for existence as its own essence puts "lack and need" and nothingness at the core of being. Following Heidegger, Nancy's concept of nothingness suggests what George Steiner terms the "generative nothingness at the heart of being."[23] Thus, implying a complex meaning for nothing, Nancy writes, "To lack nothing, despite everything that's lacking: this is what it means to exist." The "nothing" that Nancy proclaims relates for Nancy, as Steiner similarly maintains, to "the rupture of the century, measuring up to the 'death of God' because they show, or at least suspect, that what is at stake here is sense, all sense" (*FT*: 12, 13).

Concepts and terms such as spacing and happening in Nancy's philosophy of time and birth to presence also could inform the study of time and presence in film. Nancy's work on film, however, also tends toward a different direction with his proclivity toward movement.

NANCY AND MULVEY ON FILM

Nancy places considerable importance on film in his search for presence, being, and meaning as evidenced in his book on Iranian director Abbas Kiarostami, *The Evidence of Film* (2001), as well as his other work in film such as his study of Claire Denis. Studying Kiarostami, Nancy sees and analyzes film in classic critical and technical terms of the real, gaze, look, and image. Although somewhat uneven and unsystematic, Nancy in this book gives careful attention to the basic elements of cinema for their importance to the "process" of creating presence. He writes, "The framing, the light, the length of a take, the camera's movement contribute to free a motion, which is that of a presence in the process of making itself present."[24] He articulates contrasting differences in film between close-ups and distant shots, mobile and immobile images, tracking and still shots for the development of meaning and aesthetic effect (*E*: 72). Using such elements of film art as a basis for criticism and analysis, Nancy suggests that putting presence on the screen as a moment of the "real" constitutes a vital cinematic achievement. So he says of "the steadfastness of landscapes" that when "these wide presences meet our gaze" such scenes become "an instant when the real has come to presence" (*E*: 54, 56).

To a considerable degree, Nancy reinforces Mulvey on the significance of stillness and the moving image in realizing presence on film. Nancy's work similarly suggests that the tension between stillness and the moving image engenders the temporal and spatial dimension for the emergence to existential presence and being. He writes, "Motion is the opening of the motionless, it is presence insofar as it is truly *present*, that is to say coming forward, introducing itself, offered, available, a site for waiting and thinking, presence itself becoming a passage toward or inside presence" (*E*: 30; emphasis in the original). Thus, Nancy's use of "motionless" compares to Mulvey's "stillness."

In contrast with Mulvey, however, Nancy breaks from emphasizing the tension between motionlessness and motion to concentrate on movement. He says that "*cinema* means: continuous movement, not representation animated with mobility, but mobility as essence of presence and presence as a coming, coming and passage" (*E*: 66; emphasis in the original). He deems movement a defining quality for film, including in film's connection to presence.

Thus, what Nancy terms "cinematic metaphysics, cinema as the place of meditation" (*E*: 44) becomes a case for a cinema of continuous movement. He writes, "Cinema is marked by the heaviest and the most ambiguous of signs—myth, mass, power, money, vulgarity, circus games, exhibitionism and voyeurism. But all that is carried off in an endless movement (*defilement*) to such an extent that evidence becomes that of passage rather than some epiphany of meaning or presence" (*E*: 78). He adds that cinema "carries off all epiphanies of meaning and of immobile presence into the evidence of movement" (*E*: 78).

In spite of their differences about movement and stillness, Mulvey and Nancy cohere on the need for rethinking cinematic time. They do so in ways that propel emerging birth to presence. Nancy's work and thought support Mulvey's project. Thus, in light of her film theory, Mulvey's relationship to presence suggests an insight that Steiner draws from Heidegger. Discussing Heidegger's concentration on "the things and presences that furnish our world," Steiner says that for Heidegger "the presence of all that is present" becomes "possible by virtue of an illumination, a 'being lit.'"[25] So while the presence thinkers can enlighten film, the cinema, as described by Mulvey in her theory of delayed cinema, can provide its own form of artistic "illumination" or even epiphany for existential presence. The interweaving of existential presence and delayed cinema can initiate new ways of viewing and understanding cinema while infusing fresh energy into achieving presence and being, of getting and being in touch.[26] A new ontology of cinema can lead in encouraging new thinking about being, otherness, and ethics.

The thought and practice of Mulvey and Nancy enlighten a crucial scene in Frank Capra's *Mr. Smith Goes to Washington* (1939) that I have discussed in previous work.[27] It occurs when James Stewart as Senator Jefferson Smith returns to the Lincoln Memorial after being debased and humiliated by entrenched lying and corrupt political and economic forces. Originally filmed as a kind of cathedral of democracy when Smith first visits the capital, the Lincoln Memorial upon his return becomes a tomb. Filmed the second time primarily in shadow and darkness as opposed to the solemn grayish tones of the first visit, the Lincoln Memorial in the second scene conveys a sense of mourning not just for the death of Smith's hopes and ambitions but also for what his failure implies about Lincoln's irrelevance to modern America.

The scene opens with key lighting on the concluding words of Lincoln's Gettysburg Address: "and that government of the people by the people for the people shall not perish from the earth." A sharp cut to the well-lit close-up of Smith's face indicates his awareness of the irony of the hollowness of Lincoln's words in the film's corrupt, anti-democratic political culture that mocks them. Looking up to the Lincoln statue, Smith's face conveys disappointment and then confusion about where to turn right or to the left for help. Then, picking up the briefcase and luggage he brought with him for his departure—more likely his escape—from Washington, D.C., Smith lurches into the Memorial, finding a place to stop in the shadow of an impressive pillar.

A medium shot of Smith sitting on his luggage in the darkness of the shadow diminishes his size and significance. He hunches over, recoiling within himself as an expression of utter despair and failure. Sounds of his weeping softly punctuate director Frank Capra's sentimental non-diegetic soundtrack of the classic "I Dream of Jeannie with the Light Brown Hair." On the margin of the scene, Saunders (Jean Arthur), the senator's assistant and eventual love interest, emerges from nowhere out of the darkness without any suggestion of cinematic temporal continuity other than to say she thought she would find him there. Working from this different temporal dimension, in this scene she transforms the darkness of the tomb into the maternal darkness of the passage to new life for both the senator and for the film's veneration of Lincoln. Moving out of her own spot of darkness, she looks down at the distraught senator.

The cut to Smith shows his face buried in the palms of his two hands that form a V for support and coverage. Stilling this frame enables better study of the image's meaning and significance. With his face secured in this position of his hands, Smith demonstrates a desire to lose himself in a deeper escape from his condition of loss and despair. Psychologically and existentially, Smith at this moment seeks death and a return to the womb.

Continued study of this still image, however, can render greater meaning to Smith's hands as a structure that signifies the ultimate impossibility of grounding and sustaining his isolated self. In the shadow, Smith sits alone as the alienated man without beliefs or allies. He disavows as phony and dishonest the words, monuments, and rituals that have supported him and inspired his beliefs and behavior. Like Gatsby, he now rests on "nothing" except himself. He must face the freedom of his existence. The image begins his existential emergence to freedom.

The insertion of Saunders turns the scene into what Nancy calls "the free space of time" (*EF*: 147). As the stilled image stretches out into movement, Saunders becomes the agent for transforming space into temporal relationships for rebirth. She initiates Smith's passage to existential and ethical presence by creating a temporal space of otherness for the two of them. Breaking Smith's mood of solitary nihilism, she proffers what Nancy would call a form of existential freedom of "plural singularity" (*EF*: 147). The scene enacts on the space of the screen Nancy's "spacious temporality" that opens space for free time (*EF*: 18). The construction of such a free space of time requires "a new space for meaning" (*EF*: 18) that promulgates seeing, thinking, and imagining shared space and time with others as opposed to conventional linear time. Significantly, the words Smith and Saunders exchange suggest within them a latent appreciation for basic sources in serious thought and belief for the political freedom the film espouses. In a form of mistaken idolatry, Smith once naively "worshipped" a political figure who comes to embody lies and dishonesty, while Saunders evokes biblical and philosophical concepts when she compares Smith to "fools with faith" who had the courage to act in the face of uncertainty. Interestingly, the Capracorny rhetoric and tone of Saunders's words to Smith manage to convey a deeper meaning of existential freedom.

The film art and style of the long take of Saunders's speech to Smith helps to establish the temporal spacing of the scene as a free time for emerging existential presence. In effect, the scene extends linear time to another temporal dimension of renewal and ethical responsibility. At first, the camera cuts back and forth between Smith and Saunders as each speaks. The camera then focuses on her profile, maintaining a two-shot for her speech of faith that she directs toward Smith. The long take establishes the two together in spatial continuity rather than dividing them in separate speaking and reacting fragments. Without the sharp cuts and dramatic gazes that often imply privilege or dominance for a particular character, the speech scene suggests free temporal space rather than manipulation. During the climactic part of her speech, the artistic design of the scene and the positioning of their bodies indicate a new equality between Smith and Saunders. As she speaks, Saunders leans into Smith's space. When she completes her talk, Smith tilts ever so slightly toward her. They form a kind of open visual parallelism that replaces the false security of Smith's hands at the beginning of the scene. Filmed in a silhouette style with a lit background that marks the tension between light and dark, being and nothingness, Smith and Saunders stand out in their own special temporal and spatial relationship to each other and to the Lincoln Memorial setting. For both characters, the interior space of singular inner identity and being opens onto a common external space of shared being and time.

The power and authority of Stewart and Arthur as actors to garner and maintain attention grow stronger through their shared energies and efforts. Their individual performances become co-performance and co-appearance in their relationship to each other. Stewart and Arthur enact a happening of togetherness between Smith and Saunders in the framed Lincoln Memorial setting. They create new being individually and together. She speaks softly with a restrained urgency that suggests an inner tension of anticipated expression and release. Listening to Saunders' inspired words, Smith advances his emergence to existential presence, moving toward a new time and way of being with others.

In the long take of Saunders' speech, the combination of elements of lighting, body positioning, performance, and subdued emotion imbues the scene with a muted tension and anticipation. The expectation can be described as spiritual. They await an awakening or revelation of redemption. Their words and their bodies demand fulfillment. The scene intimates the continuity of body space with the spiritual calling of the soul to open body and soul to meaning. The scene suggests Nancy's notion of "entelechy" (*C*: 128) or the inherent relationship of mutual dependence between body and soul. Saunders endeavors to turn Lincoln's words into flesh. Smith freely sacrifices his flesh during his famous filibuster to revivify Lincoln's words.

Smith journeys in the film through an emotional and existential valley of

Figure I.1 *Mr Smith Goes to Washington*: Jimmy Stewart as Mr. Smith carries time and infinite responsibility on his shoulders

death to emerge reborn on the Senate floor with the burden of oppressive chronological time symbolically over his shoulders in the form of the Senate clock above him. As an even greater test, the clock over his shoulder also suggests doubling Smith's burden with the challenge to open a new time based on the other and the love for one's neighbor. In the Senate setting, the extended time of the graphic image of Smith's iconic appeal to heaven exemplifies the power of the tension between stillness and the moving image to suggest the drama of emerging existential presence.

Accordingly, the second Lincoln Memorial scene in *Mr. Smith Goes to Washington* can be seen to enact Nancy's words when he speaks of "this freedom which gives birth to me." He writes, "It is in this way that being-in-common takes place: through this free space where we come into mutual presence where we com-pear. The opening of this space—spacing of time, exposure, event, surprise—is all there is of being, inasmuch as it 'is' free" (*EF*: 169).

Following the stilled image of Smith's despair and dejection and the long take of Saunders's speech, the scene breaks into the momentum of the moving image as the two of them, the new couple Saunders and Smith, happily race out to satisfy Smith's sudden urge for a drink, a desire supposedly validating his emergence into manhood. A pause for the stilled image of the two crossing the long shadow line of a mysterious figure, apparently a security officer and symbol of authority, deserves mention. The shadow line of the figure diagonally divides the scene between upper and lower spheres.

Studying the stilled image suggests the shadow line as opening rather than closing and dividing space. Like the clothesline in the toll booth scene in *It's a Wonderful Life* (1946), the shadow line insinuates a connection to a different temporal dimension and space of meaning; it intimates a transcendent temporality. Stilling the image of this instant in the scene suspends the passage of time, raising the idea of a future of infinite possibility. As Nancy writes in a very different context, "the suspension of presence" includes "uncanny" and "infinite estrangement."[28] Thus, a stilled image at the end of the scene bookends the earlier stilled image of Smith weeping, suggesting not the end of time, meaning, and the narrative segment but the potential for new and greater meaning.

THE ETHICAL IMPERATIVE: TILLICH, LEVINAS, AND KRISTEVA

Nancy's existentialism of otherness and togetherness rests on his call for new thinking about time in terms of spacing. He promotes a non-linear, non-chronological temporal regime. Other modern philosophers also discuss time in ways that clarify how time in the relationship between delayed cinema and existential presence can become a time for film art and the ethical encounter in film. In different ways, such thinkers as Paul Tillich, Emmanuel Levinas, and Julia Kristeva envision an alternative temporal dimension beyond ordinary linear time as crucial for realizing the ethical imperative in contemporary life and culture. The shifting temporalities of delayed cinema in relationship to emerging presence also can work toward expressing such a temporal dimension that these thinkers articulate in a variety of forms.

Thus, in the mid-twentieth century, Paul Tillich, the celebrated Christian existentialist, considered the perplexities of presence as an opening for new thinking about time and ethics. He writes, "The riddle of the present is the deepest of all the riddles of time."[29] Expatiating upon these thoughts on presence, Tillich writes, "We go towards something that is not yet, and we come from something that is no more. We are what we are by what we came from. We have a beginning as we have an end. There was a time that was not *our* time" (*T*: 126; emphasis in the original).

Tillich believes that recognizing the eternal opens access to existential presence. The eternal makes the moment of now possible. He says, "It is the eternal that stops the flux of time for us. It is the eternal 'now' which provides for us a temporal 'now'" (*T*: 131). He argues for finding the courage to face both presence and the eternal. Tillich writes, "Perhaps this is the most conspicuous characteristic of our period, especially in the western world and particularly in this country. It lacks the courage to accept 'presence' because it has lost the dimension of the eternal" (*T*: 131). Using Greek and biblical sources, Tillich famously and dramatically described his theory of eternity and time as the moment of *kairos* when eternity touches time, interpreting *kairos*, as Mark Lilla says, as the "'right time'" or the "'fullness of time.'"[30]

Placing the emerging ethical subject in a diachronic temporal regime of absolute responsibility to the other, Emmanuel Levinas changes the terms and language of the discussion of existential presence. He discusses the sameness of presence in the context of his overall ethical philosophy. Levinas proffers ethics as opposed to being or ontology as a first philosophy. Ethical subjectivity for him involves the relationship and time of the other. The ethical subject becomes hostage to his or her responsibility to the other. Such commitment, for Levinas, compels adherence to a diachronic temporality of the intervention of the other that counters the subject's time of synchronic sameness. Diachronic time imposes the meaning of the other onto the sameness of the enclosed autonomous subject. Elsewhere I have discussed my understanding of Levinas's conception of the difference between ordinary synchronic linear time that regulates daily events and life as opposed to a diachronic temporality that strives for the infinite and transcendence.[31] The diachronic time of the relationship to the other interrupts regular order to create a condition of transformative ethical responsibility.

As part of his ethics, for Levinas the time of stalled presence suggests synchronic sameness. Presence as stilled sameness compares and equates to self-contained thinking. He writes, "Presence applies to consciousness [*connaissance*] and to intentionality, which are always consciousness in proportion to its own powers, a correlation and equality between what is thought and thinking itself."[32] Levinas oppugns "the basis of presence which qualifies the time of the Same" and results in "a restriction of meaning" and "again a shadow meaning" (*GDT*: 205). Presence as sameness, for Levinas, constitutes a self-enclosed consciousness that equates truth with itself. Such presence enervates ethical potency.

From a temporally static position, presence as a frozen moment in time initiates action or acts, but it does so, according to Levinas, as an extension of itself with a predictable teleology based on the sameness of its origin. Levinas writes, "The present is the site of initiative and of choice" (*GDT*: 177). For Levinas, presence as contained consciousness proves unable to think beyond its borders to consider an opening toward the transcendence of genuine ethical responsibility. He asks, "How is the beyond being thinkable in its transcendence?" (*GDT*: 205) He concludes that the inability of a stilled presence to gain transcendence means "Responsibility cannot be stated in terms of presence" (*GDT*: 195).

Accordingly, Levinas rethinks and reimagines presence to suggest the fresh possibility of an opening to transcendence. He envisions presence in terms of a move toward "excess" for fulfilling the demand for infinite ethical responsibility. He says, "The excess over the present is the life of the Infinite" (*GDT*: 195). Instead of thinking of a starting point for time and thought as a synchronic, linear present, Levinas argues for a new origination based on the ethical and the diachronic time of the infinite and transcendence. He calls for an infinite time of "awakening" and proposes to start thinking and working from a temporality based on the responsibility to the other. To be ethical, he insists, "it is necessary to think in an ethical manner." He says, "It is ethical from the first" (*GDT*: 111). Thus, Levinas transforms existential presence by putting it in the context of his ethics of infinity, transcendence, and responsibility to the other.

This ethical thinking in a new time can prove painful, Levinas says, for it involves "this tearing of the Same by the Other" (*GDT*: 111). In another lecture, Levinas again alludes to the pain of such ethical new thinking as a tearing off from secure sameness. He says, "Here we are speaking of a bursting of the Same, whom the Other disturbs or tears out of his repose" (*GDT*: 195).

So, for Levinas the meaning of presence in achieving "ethical subjectivity" involves a tearing or breaking from a regular temporal regime. The subsequent present of Levinasian ethical subjectivity has "no beginning" in linear synchronic time but opens to a dimension of transcendence and the infinite beyond consciousness and language. This transcendent present entails finding an ethical position and time on "the in-side of every present time" that relates "to a past that was never present, to an immemorial past" (*GDT*: 162). Levinas's "paradoxical approach" to the present of the "'intersubjective'" relationship "inscribes the glory of the Infinite" upon time and presence. He says, "From this relationship, the Infinite rises up gloriously" (*GDT*: 162). Consistent in his world view of ethical subjectivity, Levinas melds the time of the immemorial past and the infinity of the present relationship with the other, thereby adhering to his mission, as Martin Kavka says, "to defend and re-energize the modern moral project, by understanding that project in terms of an ethical subject grounded in infinity."[33]

Imagining the world paradoxically in terms of the glorious rising of the infinite directs vision and opens the eyes to the possibility of the sacred. Levinas claims that "the sky calls for a gaze other than that of a vision that is already an aiming." He says, "It calls for eyes purified of covetousness, a gaze other than that of the hunter with all his ruse, awaiting the capture." He continues, "Raising itself toward the sky, the gaze thus encounters the untouchable: the sacred" (*GDT*: 163). He argues that understanding ethics "as a modality of transcendence" makes it "concretely possible" to realize ethics "on the basis of the secularization of the sacred" (*GDT*: 163).

In contrast, Julia Kristeva looks inward to the Freudian unconscious in her search for the time of the secularized sacred. She makes Freud's theory of "lost time" or *zeitlos* an indispensable element in the linkage she proposes of the sexualized unconscious to the sacred. Kristeva writes, "The term *timeless*, which I analyzed in *Intimate Revolt*, is a Freudian notion that applies to the time of the unconscious: the unconscious is not aware of time; it is *zeitlos*, timeless, outside time."[34] She says that for Freud "the unconscious as well as the id enjoy a temporality called *Zeitlos*."[35] Kristeva sees Freudian *zeitlos* as a creative force for change and renewal. *Zeitlos*, she believes, turns libidinal energy into sacred belief. This lost time becomes a means for existential awakening and revelation as well as psychoanalytical insight. Thus, Kristeva calls the lost time of *zeitlos* "the expression of a new relationship to time" and "another conception of time" that opens access to "intimate depths" of the psyche. She says that "the analytical experience" that employs this new conception of time "leads us to the borders of thought" for both the "philosopher" and the "moralist" (*IR*: 28, 12). For her, Freud evidences unique genius, "an incomparable originality in the Freudian *Zeitlos*," in connecting the pre-linguistic, presymbolic timelessness of the unconscious to the body and the body's relations to the mind (*IR*: 30–31).

Significantly, Kristeva also notes that Freud's lost or "detained temporality" (*IR*: 31) inevitably suggests a binary opposition to an ordinary, conventional linear time. The subversive and regenerative powers of lost time challenge and disrupt regular time. Kristeva writes, "Freudian temporality relies on the linear time of consciousness in order to inscribe a rift there, a breach, a frustration: this is the scandal of the timeless (*Zeitlos*)" (*IR*: 30). Interestingly, this puts Freud in line with a long history of other thinkers who also propose an engagement with linearity to mark and define the contrast with non-linear temporal regimes.

Having proposed this tension in Freudian temporality between linear and lost time, Kristeva takes what seems like a shocking step considering Freud's well-known atheism as well as her own atheism by extending the meaning of the concept of *zeitlos* to another category of thought that resonates with religious language and sensibility. She uses the word "grace" to describe the significance of the connection between the two temporalities of *zeitlos* and the finite. She calls "this intersection of time and timeless" as "nothing more or less than the moment of grace that signals what has been called the analysand's rebirth" (*IR*: 38, 36). She develops this argument of temporal intersection in the Freudian context of the relationship of the unconscious to the body and language that becomes manifest in dream analysis. She claims, "This state of grace, this conjunction of the linear and the indestructible, is an inflection of the timeless specific to the analytical process. It passes through the image of dreams and through the hallucinatory image before attaining speech" (*IR*:

38). The interaction between the two temporal regimes occurs in the tension between the mind and the body. The different temporalities of infinite, unstructured lost time and organized linear time work to inspire, for Kristeva, the call in the body and the soul for infinite grace.

Moreover, Kristeva suggests motherhood houses and initiates the desire for a form of grace by conjoining the infinite boundlessness of the motherly bond with the infinity of the *zeitlos*. She intimates that the multiple diverse temporalities involved in mothering instill an awareness of the possibility of a time of at least a "double infinity." She proposes that the time of grace, "this experience at the crossroads of time and the timeless," becomes a "temporality of a double infinity" marking the tension between the "timelessness of the mother-daughter symbiosis" and "linear time" (*IR*: 40, 38).

Thus, in her case for "a double infinity" and multiple temporalities, Kristeva provides psychoanalytical and philosophical insights into the promise of spiritual grace in the form of "the sense of continual rebirth" (*IR*: 42). For Kristeva the possibility of experiencing continual renewal through grace makes "the psychical and existential risks that it entails" worthwhile (*IR*: 42). The project for grace, therefore, becomes for Kristeva an existential and ethical imperative. Speaking and thinking both existentially and psycho-analytically, Kristeva resonates somewhat with Tillich by evoking *kairos* as a "divine" intervention "in a specific temporality" that "cuts through the homogeneous flow of time" and that "breaks up the usual chronological experience." She says this force of "*kairos* that cuts, incises, and inscribes in the cosmic and vital flux" ultimately proclaims "the Parousia, of the *presence* of the Messiah following the *resurrection*, the bond with the divine."[36]

Throughout her extensive body of work, Kristeva has focused on the transformation of what she dubs the "semiotic" impulses and rhythms of the body and the unconscious into symbolization and language.[37] Invariably emphasizing motherhood, she insists on the maternal as the basis for this transformation of unconscious, psychological, and biological forces into the sacred. Relying on an inevitable bond between the sacred and the maternal, she oppugns traditional, institutional, and orthodox religion and belief. Thus, she speaks of "atheism as the resorption of the sacred into the tenderness of the connection to the other. And that sober and modest atheism relies on the maternal."[38] Continuing her interest in the porosity of borderlines, she asks, "What if the sacred were the unconscious perception the human being has of its untenable eroticism: always on the borderline between nature and culture, the animalistic and the verbal, the sensible and the nameable?" (*FS*: 26-27) Kristeva thereby takes the ethical concept of the commitment to the other and embeds it in the energy and vitality of the body. She writes, "It is truly at the dawn of the mother's connection to the child that a miraculous alchemy occurs: the 'object' of erotic satisfaction, the father (or some relationship, profession, or gratification) is slowly resorbed into a loved, and only loved, 'other.' Love-tenderness takes the place of erotic love: the 'object' of satisfaction is transformed into an 'other'—to care for, to nourish. Care, culture civilization." Kristeva insists, "Outside motherhood, no situations exist in human experience that so radically and so simply bring us face to face with that emergence of the other" (*FS*: 56–57).

Accordingly, Kristeva melds in her philosophical and psychoanalytical examinations a new thinking of time and the body for an original construction of the ethical relationship to the other in terms of the sacred. *Kairos*, the time of grace when the eternal and infinite touch the moment, intensifies existential presence for the maternal and embodied sacred. Kristeva's theoretical intersection of temporalities projects a time of emerging presence in the formation of ethical subjectivity.

A NEW TIME FOR FILM: EXISTENTIAL PRESENCE AND THE ETHICAL IMPERATIVE

The movement to rethink time and presence by modern presence philosophers finds an important ally in Laura Mulvey and her project on the delayed cinema of stillness and the moving image. This alliance of intellectual and artistic forces engenders a new thinking about time for film with important implications for the broader culture and society.

For Mulvey, as we have seen, digital and computer technologies produce a new ontology of cinema with the delayed cinema of stillness and the moving image. As Mulvey says, this new ontology of cinema involves temporal and spatial shifting that stretches the cinematic image. Temporalities of delayed cinema include contrasting forces of stillness and movement; the filmic time of the image versus the cinematic time of narrative; narrative finality versus repetition; and exploratory temporal strategies, such as freezing the frame versus narrative linearity.

In effect, time simply works differently in film now. The stillness, slowness, and movement of delayed cinema create the possibility of working in virtually an endless variety of ways with time and film that previously had not been available or accessible for most people involved in the viewing, study, and even in the making of film.

At the same time, a new temporal and digital aesthetic for film has implications that go beyond the art form. Mulvey clearly notes how rethinking time in delayed cinema has important implications for understanding and appreciating time outside of cinema. Thus, she says of the new "aesthetic of delay" and "the new stillness" that "its significance goes beyond the image itself towards the problem of time, its passing, and how it is represented or preserved" (*D24*: 22).

The impact outside of cinema of the "aesthetic of delay" becomes especially interesting in the relationship of delayed cinema's non-linear, non-chronological temporal regime to the effort of modern thinkers to articulate a case for existential presence and the transcendence of the ethical imperative. The aesthetic of delayed cinema's dynamic and changing temporalities can help in the expression of a time of epiphany and revelation. In the context of the relationship between emerging existential presence and the ethical imperative, the digital revolution of delayed cinema can provide access and structure in film to a temporal regime for articulating ethical renewal and awakening. Emerging existential presence and the ethical imperative form a matrix in digital cinema for structuring the search for a regenerative temporality as envisioned by a diversity of presence and ethical thinkers. With the new aesthetic of delayed cinema, film can animate and illuminate the argument by modern thinkers for a temporal realm of ethical subjectivity and responsibility that exceeds the bounds of the linear and chronological. New thinking about a new time in film can instigate and motivate a time for change and renewal outside of cinema.

Thus, the new time of digital cinema suggests not only another way of seeing film; it also insinuates the possibility for expressing and visualizing a transcendent temporal regime of the ethical. Delayed cinema can work to transform the intellectual abstraction of such a time into felt experience. Starry visions of a temporal dimension of *kairos, zeitlos*, ethical subjectivity in relation to infinity, and the happening of the otherness of existence potentially can become manifest in the aesthetics of the temporal fluidities of delayed cinema. In *The Searchers, Mr. Smith Goes to Washington, The Three Burials for Melquiades Estada*, and *The Misfits*, for example, temporal shifting of delayed cinema, as previously noted, suggests a transcendent temporal dimension of emerging presence and the ethical imperative as expressed in the spacing of time, happening, revelation or epiphany. John Wayne's anxious awareness of his finitude in the face of infinite responsibility, Jimmy Stewart's surrender to faith in a force greater than himself, Barry Pepper's revelation of existential responsibility to the other, and Marilyn Monroe's recognition of her sexual objectification as well as her responsibility and love for Montgomery Clift as a lost soul all demonstrate delayed cinema's projection of temporal transcendence. In these scenes, delayed cinema helps to show how directors match, in Sarah Cooper's terms, "spiritual optics" with the "visible world."[39]

In film the multiple temporalities of emerging presence resonate to the rhythm, beat, and measure of the spatio-temporal fluidities of the slowness and movement of delayed cinema. This shifting, non-linear time of delayed cinema commingles with the challenge in modern thought to conceptualize and achieve an accessible transcendent-temporal dimension for presence, lived experience, and ethics. Recognition of the ethical and social implications of this new cinematic time for influencing belief, values, and attitudes can position film at the forefront of the project to engender, as Nancy proposes, a new time and thinking about existence and ethics. Cinema could then place a wager on humanity by playing its part in examining what Steiner deems the ruptures in the modern mind and experience. Steiner, as we recall, bets on transcendence for achieving aesthetic, existential, and ethical presence. Thus, the new time for film becomes a time for emerging existential presence and the formation of ethical subjectivity.

The new time of film also could mark a new beginning for film itself in the digital age. As part of new thinking about ethics and the other, delayed cinema can propose a form of rebirth of film with new authority and responsibility as art, documentary, and product in our time.

NOTES

1. See Ira Jaffe, *Slow Movies: Countering the Cinema of Action* (New York: Wallflower/ Columbia University Press, 2014); Tiago de Luca and Nuno Barrados Jorge, eds., *Slow Cinema* (Edinburgh: Edinburgh University Press, 2015); and Lutz Koepnick, *On Slowness: Toward an Aesthetic of the Contemporary* (New York: Columbia University Press, 2014).

2. See Laura Mulvey, *Death 24x a Second: Stillness and the Moving Image* (London: Reaktion Books, 2006), pp. 37, 39, 60, 96–98. All future references to this work will be to this edition and will be cited parenthetically in the text as *D24*.

3. See Jean-Luc Nancy, *Corpus*, trans. Richard A. Rand (New York: Fordham University Press, 2008), p. 63; emphasis in the original. All future references to this work will be to this edition and will be included parenthetically in the text as *C*.

4. Jean-Luc Nancy, *The Experience of Freedom*, trans. Bridget McDonald, foreword Peter Fenves (Stanford: Stanford University Press, 1988), p. 58. All future references to this book will be to this edition and will be included parenthetically in the text as *EF*.

5. Hans Ulrich Gumbrecht, *Our Broad Present: Time and Contemporary Culture* (New York: Columbia University Press, 2014), p. 32. All future references to this work will be to this edition and will be included parenthetically in the text as *OBP*.

6. See Asbjørn Grønstad, "Slow Cinema and the Ethics of Duration," in *Slow Cinema*, eds. de Luca and Jorge, pp. 276–279.

7. George Steiner, *Real Presences* (Chicago: University of Chicago Press, 1989), pp. 90, 93; emphasis in the original.

8. Ibid., pp. 154, 214, 24–50.

9. See Jean-Luc Nancy, *Birth to Presence*, trans. Brian Holmes *et al.* (Stanford: Stanford University Press, 1993); emphasis in the original. All future references to this work will be to this edition and will be included parenthetically in the text as *BP*. See also Jean-Luc Nancy, *Listening*, trans. Charlotte Mandell (New York: Fordham University Press, 2007), pp. 13, 16. All future references to this work will be to this edition and will be included parenthetically in the text as *L*.

10. See Hans Ulrich Gumbrecht, *Production of Presence: What Meaning Cannot Convey* (Stanford: Stanford University Press, 2004), pp. 113, 112, 118. All future references to this work will be to this edition and will be included parenthetically in the text as *PP*.

11. Nancy, *Listening*, p. 66. See also Steiner, *Real Presences*, pp. 217–218. Thanks to Zoë Shacklock of the University of Warwick (United Kingdom) Film and Television Graduate Research Seminar who suggested the relevance of Nancy's work on music to me.

12. Jean-Luc Nancy, *Being Singular Plural*, trans. Robert D. Richardson and Anne E. O'Byrne (Stanford: Stanford University Press, 2000), pp. 61, 62; emphasis in the original. All future references to this work will be to this edition and will be included parenthetically in the text as *BSP*.

13. Jean-Luc Nancy, *A Finite Thinking*, ed. Simon Sparks (Stanford: Stanford University Press, 2003), pp. 187, 188. All future references to this work will be to this edition and will be included parenthetically in the text as *FT*.

14. Steiner, *Real Presences*, p. 214.

15. See Mary Ann Doane, *The Emergence of Cinematic Time: Modernity, Contingency, the Archive* (Cambridge, MA: Harvard University Press, 2002), pp. 22, 23. She writes, "Film was perceived as the imprint of time itself . . . a time unharnessed from rationalization, a nonteleological time in which each moment can produce the unexpected, the unpredictable, and temporality ratifies indeterminacy." She adds, "The indexicality of the cinematic sign appears as the guarantee of its status as a record of a temporality outside itself—a pure time or duration which would not be that of its own functioning."

16. Andrei Tarkovsky, *Sculpting in Time: Reflections on the Cinema* (Austin: University of Texas Press, 1986), p. 63.

17. Quoted in Gilberto Perez, *The Material Ghost: Films and Their Medium* (Baltimore: Johns Hopkins University Press, 1998), p. 345.

18. See André Bazin, "The Ontology of the Photographic Image," in *What is Cinema?* ed. and trans. Hugh Gray, 2 vols (Berkeley: University of California Press, 1967), vol. I, p. 14.

19. For further discussion of some of these scenes see Sam B. Girgus, *Hollywood Renaissance: The Cinema of Democracy in the Age of Ford, Capra, and Stevens* (Cambridge: Cambridge University Press, 1998) and Sam B. Girgus, *Levinas and the Cinema of Redemption: Time, Ethics, and the Feminine* (New York: Columbia University Press, 2010).

20. Jean-François Lyotard, *The Inhuman: Reflections on Time*, trans. Geoffrey Bennington and Rachel Bowlby (Stanford: Stanford University Press, 1991), p. 80.

21. If Mulvey can be read as a guide for appreciating the significance of the breakthrough for film studies of stillness and the moving image, then Gumbrecht can be taken at his word as working to establish something of "a specific framework" for strengthening presence in art, thought, and experience (*PP*: 107). A rebalancing of the tension between presence and meaning in the academy would be consistent for Gumbrecht with a historic transformation he perceives to be underway now about time and presence in the overall culture. He believes that while many continue an endlessly repetitive and regressive cycle of meaning searches, the culture at large currently embraces a growing change of attitude with a sense of broadened and expanded presence that reflects an underlying uncertainty about the future and the pervasive influence of the past.

Following such figures as Mikhail Bakhtin, Edmund Husserl, Michel Foucault, and Reinhart Koselleck, Gumbrecht maintains the occurrence of a shift in the *chronotope* or "time-form" that describes our era's "construction of time" (*OBP*: 50). The chronotope structures how people and cultures see and organize themselves in terms of a generally accepted understanding of time and its operations. Gumbrecht says a new "configuration of time" that concerns "our own time" can be found throughout popular and elite culture in the West. Signaling the end of "the present of the Cartesian subject," the new chronotope for Gumbrecht helps to explain "our renewed concern with the physical aspects of human existence and with space as the dimension in which they emerge against the grain of the Cartesian tradition." He believes "the new, posthistoricist construction of time too is a reaction to phenomena and effects of globalization" (*OBP*: 21). Gumbrecht points to obsessions today with sports, exercise, and body alterations as telling examples of widely held manifestations of the desire for grounded presence (*OBP*: 21).

22. Frédéric Neyrat, "No/Us: The Nietzschean Democracy of Jean-Luc Nancy," *Diacrticis*, vol. 43, no. 4 (2015): 68.

23. George Steiner, *Martin Heidegger* (Chicago: University of Chicago Press, 1989), p. 115.

24. See Jean-Luc Nancy, *The Evidence of Film: Abbas Kiarostami*, trans. Christine Irizarry and Verena Andermatt Conley (Brussels: Yves Gevaert, 2001), p. 38. All future references to this book will be to this edition and will be included parenthetically in the text as *E*. See also Jean-Luc Nancy, "Claire Denis: Icon of Ferocity," in *Cinematic Thinking: Philosophical Approaches to the New Cinema*, ed. James Phillips (Stanford: Stanford University Press, 2008), pp. 160–168. See also Laura McMahon, *Cinema and Contact: The Withdrawal of Touch in Nancy, Bresson, Duras and Denis* (London: Legenda, 2012); Josef Früchtl, "The Evidence of Film and the Presence of the World: Jean-Luc Nancy's Cinematic Ontology," in *Critical Studies*, ed. Leslie Kavanaugh (Amsterdam: Rodopi, 2010), pp. 193–201; Laurent Kretzschmar, "Is Cinema Renewing Itself?" *Film-Philosophy*, online, vol. 6, no. 15 (July 2002); Kristin Lené Hole, *Towards a Feminist Cinematic Ethics: Claire Denis, Emmanuel Levinas and Jean-Luc Nancy* (Edinburgh: Edinburgh University Press, 2016).

25. Steiner, *Martin Heidegger*, p. 65.

26. See Jacques Derrida, *On Touching–Jean-Luc Nancy*, trans. Christine Irizarry (Stanford: Stanford University Press, 2005).

27. See Girgus, *Hollywood Renaissance*, pp. 56–107 and Girgus, *Levinas and the Cinema of Redemption*, pp. 49–76.

28. Jean-Luc Nancy, *The Ground of the Image*, trans. Jeff Fort (New York: Fordham University Press, 2005), p. 61. All future references to this work will be to this text and will be included parenthetically in the text as *GI*.

29. Paul Tillich, *The Eternal Now* (New York: Charles Scribner's Sons, 1963), p. 130. All references to this work will be to this edition and will be included parenthetically in the text as *T*.

30. See Mark Lilla, *The Stillborn God: Religion, Politics, and the Modern West* (New York: Vintage, 2008), p. 281.

31. For more explanation of these Levinasian terms and themes, see my introduction and discussion of Levinas's ethical philosophy and its relationship to film in *Levinas and the Cinema of Redemption: Time, Ethics, and the Feminine* (New York: Columbia University Press, 2010).

32. Emmanuel Levinas, *God, Death, and Time*, trans. Bettino Bergo (Stanford: Stanford University Press, 2000), p. 195. Future references to this work will be to this edition and will be included parenthetically in the text as *GDT*.

33. See David Kangas and Martin Kavka, "Hearing Patiently: Time and Salvation in Kierkegaard and Levinas," in *Kierkegaard and Levinas: Ethics, Politics, and Religion*, eds. J. Aaron Simmons and David Wood (Bloomington: Indiana University Press, 2008), p. 139. In this statement, Kavka refers specifically to Levinas's intention in his crucial work, *Totality and Infinity: An Essay on Exteriority*, trans. Alphonso Lingis (Pittsburgh: Duquesne University Press, 1969).

34. Julia Kristeva, *Hatred and Forgiveness*, trans. Jeanine Herman (New York: Columbia University Press, 2010), pp. 285; emphasis in the original.

35. Julia Kristeva, *Intimate Revolt: The Powers and Limits of Psychoanalysis*, trans. Jeanine

Herman (New York: Columbia University Press, 2002), p. 30. All future references to this work will be to this edition and will be included parenthetically in the text as *IR*.

36. See Julia Kristeva, *The Incredible Need to Believe*, trans. Beverley Bie Brahic (New York: Columbia University Press, 2009), pp. 30–31; emphasis in the original.

37. For my extensive and detailed discussion of Kristeva see *Clint Eastwood's America* (Cambridge: Polity, 2013).

38. See Catherine Clément and Julia Kristeva, *The Feminine and the Sacred*, trans. Jane Marie Todd (New York: Columbia University Press, 2001), p. 60. All subsequent references to this book will be to this work and will be included parenthetically in the text as *FS*.

39. See Sarah Cooper, "Mortal Ethics: Reading Levinas with the Dardenne Brothers," *Film-Philosophy*, vol. 11 (August 2007): 69.

The Otherness of Existence and "Spacious Temporality": Delayed Cinema and Freedom

Delayed Cinema and "This Space-Time of Freedom": De Sica's *Bicycle Thieves* (1948)

The theory of "spacious temporality" figures significantly in the fulfillment of the radical existentialism of French philosopher Jean-Luc Nancy. Spacious temporality or "this space-time of freedom" develops Nancy's argument for emerging existential presence or the coming and birth to presence.[1] Existential presence occurs as a happening and experience in time, including the intervention of a nonchronological temporal regime that can transform the way of being in the world with the suddenness of a revelation or epiphany. The temporality of emerging presence ineluctably gravitates toward spacious temporality or space-time. Indeed, for Nancy the happening of the birth to existential presence requires spacious temporality. An original thinker and writer, Nancy's existentialism of existence as its own essence must happen in relation to otherness. Nancy writes, "The otherness of existence happens only as 'togetherness.'"[2] Thus, the otherness of existence for Nancy compels spacious temporality as a dimension of thought and being in a space-time for togetherness.

For Nancy, spacious temporality and space-time mean "the opening of time." The spacing of time engenders a fresh fluidity and malleability of time. Spacious temporality, as Nancy sees it, opens free space-time for existential freedom to reexamine time itself in the face of groundless being. Nancy writes that free space-time "is opened onto a new spatiality, onto a *free space* at the heart of which freedom can exist, at the heart of which freedom can be freed or renounced" (*EF*: 18, 19, 184; emphasis in the original).

Such opening of "free space of time" fosters the singularity of existential presence in its engagement with otherness and the ethical imperative. The freedom of spacious temporality relates the singular to the plural. Spacious temporality invokes "the generosity" of "the plural singularity of 'us'" (*EF*: 147). Nancy asserts "freedom is that which spaces and singularizes" (*EF*: 68).

Spacious temporality can render fresh meaning to Laura Mulvey's paradigm of the dynamic of "delayed cinema" and "stillness and the moving image." The tension between stillness and the moving image, as described by Mulvey, creates a scenario for dramatizing the existential coming of being and presence. Nancy's spacious temporality insinuates a correlation with the fluidities of shifting time in delayed cinema for the enactment of emerging existential presence.[3]

Working in conjunction with the operations of delayed cinema, the aesthetic and ethical potential of spacious temporality in film achieves special acuity and brilliance with the staging of a creative and dynamic mise en scène. The design and resonances of a vital and compelling mise en scène can vivify spacious temporality. Such a mise en scène enables the happening of emerging existential presence and the ethical imperative to occupy and pervade cinematic space. A mise en scène style and art in film, as exemplified in the case of Italian neo-realism, can be sensitive and receptive to the energy and creativity of delayed cinema and spacious temporality for establishing an aesthetic for cinema art and criticism.

For Nancy, the sharing of time and space becomes an ethical and existential imperative of understanding existence in terms of the relationship to otherness. Free and open spacious temporality intimates the ethical encounter with the other. Shared time and space make the otherness of "we" possible. The happening of existential presence sustains the possibility of the ethical imperative in the relationship to the other. Nancy's "otherness of existence" and "'togetherness'" become "the community of *others*" (*BP*: 155; emphasis in the original). He believes that "Being is being-with." He writes, "The *with* is the most basic feature of Being, the mark [*trait*] of the singular plurality of the origin or origins in it." Nancy maintains "Presence is impossible except as copresence."[4]

Also, emerging existential presence as a happening in time engages the paradoxical relationship of representation to the absence of presence. The tension between presence and representation insinuates an inexorable incompleteness and incoherence in film as in experience in general, a break or gap in knowledge and being that compels the existential encounter with nothingness. Discussing the work of Iranian director Abbas Kiarostami, Mulvey describes this paradox of presence and representation as "the distance between a reality and its representation" (*D24*: 128).

For Nancy, spacious temporality encounters the void or chasm of nothingness at the core of existence. In the absence, he believes, of a permanent grounding in reality or a solid foundation or consensus regarding universal meaning, spacious temporality endeavors to open and broaden experience. Sense as real-felt experience and spacious temporality shape experience from the freedom of nothingness. Nancy says that "the sense of the world opens up as a spacing" in the world. He believes "the world opens onto nothing but its own chasm." He argues "there is neither world nor afterworld, but an opening of sense that produces the spacing of the world and its relation to itself." Nothingness, spacing, and, existence remain tightly entwined. He writes, "*Nil* would thus be spacing itself, the tension of the gap, the beating [*pulsation*] or drive [*pulsion*] that causes it to open up."[5] Emerging existential presence insinuates spacious temporality.

In conjunction with the theory and apparatus of delayed cinema, spacious temporality opens new ethical and artistic space on the screen. The temporal fluidity of delayed cinema can uncover and explore on-screen free space to propose a fresh ethical and aesthetic context for cinematic images. Spacious temporality of relationships and representations through the auspices of delayed cinema can invigorate and revivify the cinematic experience. Delayed cinema and spacious temporality make possible the intimacy of a deeper and tighter on-screen look at images. Contrastingly, delayed cinema's spacious temporality of relationships and representations can transform the still and the moving frame into a horizon of ethical and existential encounter and possibility. The space-time of freedom can open "a new space for meaning" (*EF*: 18) in cinema for the drama and realization of the infinite ethical and moral responsibility to the other.

The paradigm of delayed cinema and spacious temporality helps define and structure the existential and ethical encounter in film. The paradigm examines the possibility of shared time and space on screen, what Nancy terms the otherness of existence. Spacious temporality and delayed cinema uncover the shared time and space of co-presence and co-appearance for the otherness of existence on film.

Thus, delayed cinema and space-time proffer a critical construct and method for studying the existential encounter on the screen. While spacious temporality and delayed cinema can facilitate and dramatize birth to presence as freedom and relation, the paradigm also has the potential for demonstrating and highlighting failure of all sorts—aesthetic, ethical, political, and cultural. The aesthetic, critical, ethical, or ideological constriction of freedom and shared space and time can infringe upon co-presence and spacing for presence. Obviously, conditions of existence, whether social, psychological, or economic, can inhibit, impede, or obstruct emerging presence and the otherness of existence. For Nancy, the attenuation of the impulse for emerging existential presence and co-presence can cultivate and advance a kind of metaphysical fascism of totalized thought and conformist behavior that enervate creativity and originality, free thinking, and existential spontaneity.

Three historically and culturally different films of modern neo-realism come together in their shared search for a mise en scène aesthetic of freedom, emerging presence, and shared space. Vittorio De Sica's *Bicycle Thieves*

(1948), Rodrigo Plá's *La Demora* (2012), and Jean-Pierre and Luc Dardenne's *Two Days, One Night* (2014) progress from looking for presence as co-presence in *Bicycle Thieves* to the otherness of existence as a kind of ethical revelation in *La Demora* and *Two Days, One Night*. A neo-realistic mise en scène of spacious temporality and freedom in these films incubates the potential for aesthetic and ethical freedom in environments of ethical oppression and conformity.

MISE EN SCÈNE AND SPACIOUS TEMPORALITY

Opening free space-time in cinema inevitably involves proposing an aesthetic for such a cinema of spacious temporality. A mise en scène aesthetic of filming, designing, and editing can serve convincingly and compellingly as an aesthetic of free space-time. Mise en scène offers the cinematic spacing for aesthetic development and ethical engagement, thereby providing the possibility of spacious temporality for freedom and art. Moreover, mise en scène opens spacious temporality from within on-screen space itself, not unlike Nancy's description of a world of spacious temporality.

The school and movement of Italian neo-realism provides a history and model for, in Peter Bondanella's words, "the aesthetic possibilities of *mise en scène* editing" that can be directed toward expressing and dramatizing a cinema of spacious temporality. The elements of mise en scène that constitute and define the art of Italian neo-realism are rooted in the cinema of Orson Welles and, as Bondanella says, the "French masters of a preceding generation" such as Jean Renoir. "Mise en scène techniques" for shots and photography emphasize deep focus, depth of field, multiple "visual planes" of action, long takes, visual "complexity," and density. The mise en scène techniques of classic Italian realism also tend toward the use of nonprofessional actors, documentary-style filming, and "on-location shooting."[6]

Thus, the mise en scène style and method of shooting, filming, directing, editing, and analysis can be used to open spacious temporality for free space-time in cinema. As evidenced in the example of Italian neo-realism, mise en scène techniques and possibilities in concurrence with the temporal fluidities of delayed cinema provide the creative resource and visual context for making and studying a cinema of spacious temporality.

In light of Nancy's philosophy of the interrelatedness of freedom, spacious temporality, and otherness, a cinema of spacious temporality can become a cinema of freedom for the creation of relations of otherness. Nancy asserts that "freedom is relation" and that "relation is freedom" (*EF*: 69). Before being socialized, collectivized, legislated, or institutionalized, freedom entails "existence in accordance with relation" (*EF*: 74). Existence and relation prove crucial in Nancy's commitment to the idea of freedom. Nancy's ethical theory of the otherness of existence and his emphasis on the free relation to "we" in shared time and space potentially infuse a cinema of spacious temporality with existential and ethical meaning.

Nancy's word "relation" fittingly works as a term for the adaption of the mise en scène aesthetic of Italian neo-realism to a contemporary existential context of spacious temporality, broadened presence, and the ethical imperative. While retaining Italian neo-realism's commitment to viewing and exposing the world as it is, a mise en scène cinema of relation complicates the perspective on conditions to focus on existential and ethical relations. A cinema of relation extends the visual and cinematic landscape beyond neo-realism to highlight the existential freedom and openness of spacious temporality. Relation insinuates positioning such realism on a heightened philosophical stage that engages the existential and ethical crises of our time of doubt, skepticism, and disbelief regarding diminished expectations of progress in the future and the sense of the irrelevance of the past.

The style, art, and context of a mise en scène aesthetic of existential relation resonate in the dynamic mise en scène of three aesthetically, ethically, and intellectually impressive films from different countries, cultures, and times. De Sica's *Bicycle Thieves*, Plá's *La Demora*, and the Dardenne brothers' *Two Days, One Night* use the time and space of mise en scène filming and editing to suggest compatibility with the theory of the free space–time of spacious temporality.

Taken together, the three films can constitute a basis for developing a discussion of spacious temporality and existential relation as an emerging contemporary mise en scène of post neo-realism. Coming from different origins, environments, places, and periods, the three films indicate that the theory of relation and spacious temporality possesses the potential for enlightening a broad and diverse range of films. The films would suggest the considerable relevance and significance of spacious temporality and relation to current cinematic and critical sensibilities. Interestingly, Philip Mosley uses the phrase "responsible realism" in the sub-title of his study of the Dardenne brothers, thereby suggesting a similar effort to rethink the relevance and significance of cinematic realism for our times.[7]

Bicycle Thieves, *La Demora*, and *Two Days, One Night* follow the example of Italian neo-realism in their emphasis on a mise en scène aesthetic for narrative, visual expression, and meaning. The three films explore meaning in the art of the cinematic space itself as opposed to using external or so-called "extra-literary" sources from outside the "cinetext" or film and cinematic text for the imposition of meaning. In the films, the mise en scène of free spacious temporality supersedes another style and art of filming that emphasizes the manipulation of the emotional and intellectual impact of the tempo, rhythms, and sensationalism of shots and moving images.

While aesthetically and philosophically complicating their perspective on reality, the directors of *Bicycle Thieves*, *La Demora*, and *Two Days, One Night* also build on the art and history of neo-realism, closely examining in intimate and specific detail the social and economic conditions that engulf the people, cultures, and historic periods of their films. They look at these conditions as original auteurs with a vision informed by an artist's documentary sensibility. They emphasize the plight of the poor, the powerless, the impotent, the insecure, the displaced, and the alienated. They imbue their mise en scène with sensitivity toward the underprivileged. They all give exposure to the unseen and give voice to the voiceless.

At the same time, reflecting the proclivities of the modernism and postmodernism of their times, in *Bicycle Thieves*, *La Demora*, and *Two Days, One Night*, De Sica, Plá, and the Dardenne brothers, respectively, also see beyond the social and economic horizon to search for meaning in an existential and ethical temporal dimension. Spacious temporality presents the possibility of opening to a new free space-time of awakening and revelation in their films. In these three films, delayed cinema and spacious temporality work to discover within the mise en scène of specific shots, scenes, and segments the moral imperative of a domain of ethical responsibility to the other that can change time from the ordinary, daily chronological temporal regime to a time that proposes the possibility of a relationship to infinity.

Thus, *Bicycle Thieves*, *La Demora*, and *Two Days, One Night* eschew editorializing and or intruding on the realism of carefully constructed mise en scène with judgments or commentary from positions of privileged ethical and moral authority. Instead, in all three films, a mise en scène of harsh, pungent, and striking realism opens from within its economic, social, and cultural temporal spaces for the emergence of another dimension of the reality of human relations. In each of the films, a mise en scène aesthetic creates the means for in-depth exploration of ethical relations and boundaries.

Of utmost importance, spacious temporality as art form and style and as critical construct and apparatus opens free space-time for emerging existential presence and the ethical imperative. Spacious temporality serves to insist on the transforming power of the otherness of existence.

Bicycle Thieves has a unique role to play in this group of three films in marking the transition from neo-realism to existential relation. The film overlaps between Italian neo-realism and the emergence of an aesthetic of free space-time and relation that becomes apparent through the new perspectives of delayed cinema and spacious temporality. A foundational classic of neo-realism, *Bicycle Thieves* can suggest how spacious temporality and delayed cinema can transform cinematic realism into a different kind of space for seeing and understanding the dimension of ethical relationships to the other. In doing so, *Bicycle Thieves* becomes a model for moving, in Pasquale Iannone's phrase, "beyond neorealism" to a post-neo-realism with films of transcendent ethical and existential engagement.[8]

SPACIOUS TEMPORALITY AND EXISTENTIAL RELATION IN *BICYCLE THIEVES*

As part of his overall philosophy of existential freedom and relation, spacious temporality, and the otherness of existence, Nancy's discussion of the freedom of public spaces provides a valuable opening for studying De Sica's *Bicycle Thieves*. *Bicycle Thieves*, as Robert S. C. Gordon says, "is one of the great city films." A film, as Gordon notes, of "modern urban space, both real and imaginary," *Bicycle Thieves* initially can be examined in the context of placing and adapting Nancy's paradigm of spacious temporality to urban space and the public sphere.[9] The life of the city of Rome, the natural and cultural geography of Rome, and landscapes of the city become integral to the story and meaning of *Bicycle Thieves*.

Nancy's theory of spacious temporality moves to the public sphere in part with his brief discussion of famed political philosopher and social historian Hannah Arendt. Nancy explains Arendt's notion that the idea of freedom originated in what Nancy terms "a spontaneous sense of free public space."[10] For Arendt, according to Nancy, "the very idea of freedom" originated in the committed investment of "an ancient city" to open public space. Nancy finds it not only "possible" but even "necessary" to "represent the originary form of freedom as a free space of movements and meetings: freedom as the external composition of trajectories and outward aspects" (*EF*: 74).

Thus, Nancy transfers the freedom of open spacious temporality to urban spacing that becomes "the political space or the political as spacing" (*EF*: 75). The urban dynamics of, to repeat Nancy, the "movements and meetings" of free public space expand the openings and fluidities of spacious temporality. Spacious temporality moves to an expanded space-time on the larger geographic scale of free public space. For Arendt, as Nancy understands her, free public urban space serves as a kind of *chora* or creative core for political and existential freedom. Free public space generates the movements, associations, thoughts, and experiences that create a vital democracy. Such space becomes the sanctuary for engendering a true community of otherness and care.

Accordingly, Nancy's discussion of urban spacing as "political space" and "the political as spacing" continues his expatiation upon existential freedom, presence, and spacious temporality. The elements of Nancy's philosophy cohere around creating "community" and freedom. Community and freedom realize the otherness of existence through spacious temporality. The sharing of being in freedom and community anticipates, for Nancy, the internalization of the values, ideals, and behaviors that ultimately constitute a community and strengthen the commitment to existential freedom. Nancy writes, "Freedom does not appear here as an internal rule of community, nor as an external condition imposed on the community, but it appears as precisely the internal exteriority of the community: existence as the sharing of being" (*EF*: 75).

In contrast to this ideal of community, strong and established boundaries between interior and exterior spaces persist in *Bicycle Thieves*. Overcoming such boundaries to create a shared sense of being becomes a major challenge and inevitable failure in much of *Bicycle Thieves*. Boundaries throughout the film remain entrenched between inner being and exterior public life and between existential freedom and relationships to others. The lack of freedom of urban spaces infects inner being and relationships. The oppressive urban environment poisons existential experience and engagement.

Discussing Nancy's idea of community, Lorna Collins says that Nancy indicates "how we exist as being-in-common, how we come together in the world." She says Nancy has "a sense of the community of existence" with an "ontology in terms of sharing."[11] A model of Italian neo-realism, *Bicycle Thieves* from the very beginning of the film painstakingly documents the conditions of life in Rome and wider Italy in the wake of the Second World War as the very opposite of this idea of community and shared existence and space. The film dramatizes the legacy of fascism and the difficulty of postwar reconstruction. Gordon neatly and efficiently summarizes the details of the postwar conditions. He reports that "housing shortages and unemployment, especially among the millions of conscripts returning from fighting or from imprisonment, ran higher and higher into the late 1940s." Gordon further notes, "Official figures indicate 1,700,000 unemployed (8.9 per cent) in 1948 and the real figure was certainly considerably higher than that, possibly more than double."[12]

De Sica conveys this environment with brilliant accuracy and acuity. De Sica's realism, however, also included what he called the "poetry" of filmmaking that conveyed the flavor and feeling of human existence under the oppressive conditions of the times. De Sica sought, as Christopher Wagstaff notes, "the pathway to *poetry* enabling his camera to assemble imagery expressing feeling and experience." Wagstaff quotes De Sica as saying, "Neorealism is a certain cinema, it is a way of feeling." De Sica went on to say, "It is a transfigured reality. It is a transposition on the lyrical plane, onto the poetic plane, onto an elevated plane. Woe betide it if it were reality! If it is a reality, then it is chronicle, it is a banal truth."[13]

De Sica, it can be said, filmed the depression and pain of Italian conditions through a projection of feelings and emotions of the bitterness, hostility, despair, and violence that the people of the film feel toward their surroundings and to a considerable extent toward one another and themselves. With a few notable exceptions that prove crucial to the film's narrative and meaning, De Sica depicts urban life, space, and people through images of despair and alienation. He does so by developing a mise en scène art and style that became a seminal force in creating and advancing Italian neo-realism.

FREE ART AND CONSTRICTING PLACES: EXTERIOR AND INTERIOR SPACES

Thus, De Sica creates a mise en scène art of free and open space to dramatize and record the loss of freedom through poverty and social deprivation. From the beginning of *Bicycle Thieves*, De Sica's temporally free and open mise en scène exposes urban spaces that stultify freedom, happiness, and opportunity rather than cultivating them. Scenes and segments of the film that have been viewed and studiously examined over several decades illustrate and dramatize the impoverished quality of life of the film's characters. Delayed cinema that opens the space and time of the cinematic image can offer new insight into these scenes and segments for expressions not only of the art and social significance of Italian neo-realism but also for dramatizing existence as space. Such a reexamination could enable deeper and longer study of images and scenes depicting the urban space of alienation and danger.

New study of *Bicycle Thieves* also could note with increased interest and emphasis how at least two scenes of interior spaces contrast considerably in terms of the space-time of freedom and relation with the exterior urban landscape of deprivation and limitation. The association of both scenes with different bicycle thieves accentuates their significance for emphasizing the importance of cultivating free space-time and the ethical imperative in the face of conditions that challenge and weaken freedom and ethical engagement. Reviewing and studying De Sica's scenes and segments of such repression and corruption of freedom prove worthwhile for an elaboration upon his neo-realistic mise-en-scène of spacious temporality, a film art for freedom and relation.

Accordingly, delayed cinema and spacious temporality stretch and deepen De Sica's urban mise en scène of trauma and turmoil. The pattern throughout the film of images and scenes of a hostile public space and urban environment begins at the beginning. The hostility and tension of the urban environment becomes apparent in the opening scene at a housing development or *borgate* called Val Melaina in the undeveloped outer fringes of Rome, when men angrily bicker and squabble with one another as a city employee calls out names for a few available jobs. De Sica immediately establishes his signature neo-realistic mise en scène style of projecting multiple layers of action and meaning. The men gather on an outer stairway of a large government building. The city employee calls out the name of Antonio Ricci, who is played by Lamberto

Maggiorani, a worker from the Brenda arms factory famously chosen by De Sica to star in the film. In the scene, Ricci has separated himself at a distance from the crowd of men to sit dejectedly by a water pipe as a woman gets water. Shot with Ricci sitting on the ground in the foreground of the scene, the background shows the open unused space of the area. The empty background space dominates the mise en scène. The empty public space clearly suggests the void of existence for both the city and its people as represented by Ricci. Ricci appears frozen in the mise en scène of this shot. The shot indicates the absurdity of an excessively large civic building ruling over a barren, undeveloped landscape. Responding to the city official's call to him with the offer, Ricci takes the job of gluing posters on walls around the city even though it requires the use of a bicycle that he has pawned to feed his family.

The mise en scène of the following shot also emphasizes the area's bleakness as Ricci walks past the lifeless architecture and design of the public housing on his left side and the undeveloped barren landscape on his right. He finds his wife Maria, played by Lianella Carell, who had been a reporter wishing to write about the film until De Sica hired her as the female lead. Antonio sees her behind an iron fence with several other women fighting over access to a water pipe and the use of a bucket. The women in the background of the shot and scene function as a kind of counterpart to the men who were arguing in the preceding scene. So caught up in his frustration over not having the bicycle that he needs for the job, Antonio walks ahead of Maria letting her carry two heavy buckets of water by herself, at one point stopping to turn and gesture angrily toward her with his extended hand, "And a good city job too."

On the street until reaching their apartment building, Maria clearly plays a secondary role to Antonio. His mood and attitude of complaint dominate the scene even as he and Maria bicker like the unemployed men and the women at the water pump, trading accusations and charges over where to place the blame for the fact that Antonio pawned his bicycle that he needs for this new job. He complains they needed the money for food. The tensions and anxieties of the street stay with Maria and Antonio as they walk into the building of their small but neat and well-kept apartment.

Mise en scène in this opening segment emphasizes the emptiness of urban spaces that dissipate freedom and diminish the otherness of existence. Human interaction, including the relationship between Antonio and Maria, echoes the absence of such existential connection and meaning.

At Maria's instigation, the couple pawn their bedsheets to recover their pawned bicycle, discovering in the process that the pawned sheets of other desperate Romans reach, as shown in a famous tilt shot, to the high ceilings of the pawning establishment. Starting work on the following day, Antonio happily and enthusiastically posts and glues posters of Rita Hayworth at the Florida movie theatre on the Via Francesca Crispi until Alfredo Catelli

(Vittorio Antonucci) steals and rides off with Antonio's bicycle getting the help of two accomplices. Antonio races after the thief but gets misdirected by one of the accomplices to chase after the wrong person riding another bicycle through a dark tunnel identified by Gordon as the "'Traforo.'" Gordon effectively describes the elements that work in the film to create a shift of mood and feeling that occurs when Antonio emerges from the tunnel. He writes, "The play of light and dark, sun and shadow (as in the tunnel sequence) is similar if not more elaborate than the use of music in *Bicycle Thieves,* marking shifts of mood and emotion but also more keenly opening up the moral dimensions of the drama as well."[14]

The theft of Antonio's bicycle leads to a pivotal scene for showing the way that space-time and delayed cinema can offer fresh insight into the film. In the scene, Antonio experiences an acute sense of the groundlessness of his existential being. Antonio undergoes a level of existential despair and challenge that Wagstaff describes in terms of "existential space" and "a vision of an existential experience of lack."[15] The scene effectively dramatizes the violence, alienation, and hostility of the urban landscape.

Delayed cinema allows for concentration on details and specifics for insight into the spacious temporality of the scene. In a long shot, Antonio emerges from the darkness of the tunnel into an immediate transition to a new existential reality and imperative. Antonio runs to the camera that closes on his horrified face as he searches the street for the thief. As Antonio moves forward, the camera backtracks staying on his face. It then cuts and shoots from his perspective, showing the street occupied by unfamiliar people and action totally disconnected from him. Losing his bicycle to the thief, he has lost his means of livelihood, of living, but the scene before him after his emergence from the tunnel emphasizes a world full of life without him. All the activity of the street insists on his lack of existence. He confronts life and the living without his participation.

Suddenly, two anonymous, unidentified women walk right before the camera and Antonio's vision, the elbow of one of them so close as to seem to touch the camera. Delayed cinema emphasizes how they completely disregard and fail to notice Antonio. They walk, talk, and gesture with animation. They enact suddenness, the passing of time with the instantaneousness of the passing from life into death. Antonio does not exist for the women. He never appears to them. He has neither presence nor co-presence. The women disappear into a kind of oblivion without noticing him. They walk off, in a sense leaving Antonio's lost identity and lifelessness behind. They finish him off, completing his experience of existential lack and demise after his emergence from the tunnel. The women in passing confirm his living death, his ghostliness.

Interestingly, delayed cinema shows specific details of the woman closest to the camera, such as the pattern of her dress and the well-lit skin of her arm, but reveals nothing of her face. Delayed cinema also just barely captures the profile of the second woman, whose dark glasses further obscure her identity, just before the woman gets blocked by her companion closest to the camera. Such small details highlight and accentuate the passing of humanity before Antonio's absent presence. He has nothing to hold or hang onto, not even graspable pieces of experience. The women deny his humanity and existential reality.

The camera cuts to other urban shots and scenes both from Antonio's perspective and of Antonio himself on the street at a distance that diminishes his size and signals his disappearance into the city and crowd. Antonio's anonymity amidst all the activity on the street dramatizes his insignificance. During a visit to the police station to report his stolen bicycle, an officer trivializes Antonio's loss. In another scene of dejection, Antonio struggles with people on a sardine-packed bus line in order to reach his son Bruno (Enzio Staiola) to take him home from the boy's own daily job. Bruno's expression upon seeing his father without the bicycle encapsulates Antonio's failure and desperate situation.

Antonio's loss becomes a journey into darkness in a brilliant nighttime scene that De Sica creates. The scene demonstrates the significance for De Sica of a mise en scène of spacious temporality for animating and enacting a condition of absence and lost being. Antonio goes off by himself to seek out friends for help in finding the stolen bicycle. It has grown dark and the camera cuts to a shot of the street of the *borgate* or housing development in their area of the Val Melaina. The camera holds on the deep focus and depth of field of the shot of rectangular blocks of apartment buildings on different planes of the mise en scène. The buildings seem generally vacant except for lighting from a few apartments that only suggest but do not confirm or reveal life. They punctuate the darkness with absence and loss. Lights on the buildings fail to penetrate the shadows. The combination of darkness, shadow, and emptiness emphasizes the situation of uncertainty for Antonio in this public space. Antonio plunges into an ever-deepening darkness of existential loss that the buildings mark off from their spaced positions in the dark nighttime scene. The rectangular spacing of the buildings in the scene measures his immersion into the darkness of the street. The scene suggests a hidden temporality, a lost and irregular time under the cover of night.

Antonio's walk into darkness on urban streets leads him to the *casa del popolo* and the *dopolavoro* to seek help. At first, inside this building of the people and the working men's club, Antonio actually only finds further estrangement rather than community. As on the streets of Rome, life goes on without him. At one end of the interior space of this community center without a true sense of community, workers hear a lecture on employment and sociology while at the other end Antonio's friend Baiocco (Gino Saltamerenda), a local official of sorts who will try to help, leads a little amateur musical rehearsal obviously for some kind of entertainment for the workers. Antonio clearly feels alienated from everything around him, as evidenced by his exchange of looks with a man putting up a poster. Key lighting on the man's face gives him a degree of significance for his indifference to Antonio's existence, plight, and pain as Antonio observes life without him, including the work of another man putting posters on walls.

Having learned about the stolen bicycle from Bruno, Maria enters the workers' center to confront Antonio about the matter. The two put on a brave front together as chaos erupts around them from the rehearsing musical players and the workers. A tracking shot then follows Antonio and Maria leaving together. This brief shot punctuates the emptiness and loss facing the couple at the end of their day. Isolation and loss bring the couple together in the scene and shot. The two do not look at each other but look down and straight ahead instead. Nevertheless, the two-shot frames and holds them together. Moreover, deep focus indicates people unrelated to the couple behind them in the background at the top of the screen and the noise of people before them off screen. These activities around the couple tighten the sense of their self-enclosure. In their shared pathos, they exist together.

Delayed cinema stills the connection between Antonio and Maria in a two-shot and then shows the significance of their relationship to each other in their faces as they move slowly together. For the first time since the theft of his bicycle, Antonio looks not alone. Also for perhaps the first time, he indicates genuine concern for someone else when he looks at Maria. The depths of her worry and fear show on her face and mitigate his own self-obsession and self-pity. De Sica films them quickly without saccharine emotionalism. Their desperation speaks for itself. Delayed cinema helps to open a new free space-time for them together.

Interestingly, as many students of the film have discussed, Maria disappears from the film after this scene at the public workmen's center. Antonio's relationship with his son Bruno displaces Maria in her absence. The situation relates to and enacts philosopher Emmanuel Levinas's belief in the parental relationship to children as the model of absolute ethical responsibility for the other. Levinas writes, "My child is a stranger (Isaiah 49), but a stranger who is not only mine, for he *is* me. He is a stranger to myself." For Levinas, the child becomes "both my own and non-mine, a possibility of myself but also a possibility of the other, of the Beloved." The film suggests a priority on the father–son relationship over the role and place of the mother. Significantly, in light of the film's abandonment of Maria for Bruno, Levinas's argument for the ethical meaning of paternity has been criticized for diminishing the authority of women and the maternal in the construction of identity and ethics.[16]

Thus, the nighttime scene concludes in a deeper darkness of despair and abandonment as Antonio and Maria fail to get any solid reassurance about the possibility of finding the stolen bicycle and keeping his job. The darkness of the scene foreshadows Antonio's confrontation with the possibility of actual physical death on the urban landscape. Searching by the Tiber River for an old man (Giulio Chiari) whose association with the thief could help in finding the petty criminal, Antonio fears for his son when he hears shouts that a boy needs to be rescued from the river. Realizing that another boy but not his son Bruno was saved from the river, Antonio sees Bruno where he had been waiting by the Monumental Bridge. Once again, Antonio faces death on his search for the stolen bicycle.

Death has been with Antonio from the beginning of the film in the sense of the existential and psychological limitations and boundaries of his life. He has faced nothingness on the streets of Rome and seen his own nonexistence in the face of others. On the riverbank, the waters of the Tiber suggest the paradox of both crossing to the other side to death and to the possibility of baptism and rebirth. Death for Antonio also means surrender to a rigid temporal regime that controls existence until time ends with physical death. As Gordon notes, time and death hover over the film, including the time of such mundane matters as the need to make personal time comport with the public time of transportation and events.[17] Antonio in his encounter with death at the river still remains at an immeasurable distance from a Levinasian notion of death as the relationship with the infinite. Also, caught in the desperate conditions of unemployment and poverty, a sense of shared space and time in life proves remote and impossible to him. The accumulation of events on his search for the bicycle, however, will bring him closer to such a recognition of existence as otherness.

After the incident on the river and unable to find the stolen bicycle, Antonio thinks of death when he decides to spend the little money left from pawning the family's sheets for a good lunch with Bruno. Antonio asks, "Why should I kill myself worrying when I'll end up just as dead?" They go to an expensive restaurant, not a pizzeria, where Antonio's initial pleasure over eating their *mozzarella in carrozza* and sharing a bottle of wine changes with his realization of the momentary nature of his celebration, especially in comparison to a large well-off family and group at a nearby table who are conspicuous with their self-indulgence, oblivious consumption, and sense of privilege. Another family's comfort and security only emphasizes the precariousness for him of his own situation. He doesn't belong in this comparatively expensive restaurant just as he feels homeless on the urban spaces of the city.

Developing the Tiber River theme of death, Antonio tells Bruno, "There's a cure for everything except death." Distraught and miserable, Antonio loses his appetite and takes out a shortened pencil and calculates for Bruno how much money he could be making if he still had his bicycle. Instead, they must struggle, reduced almost to the condition of bestiality like a horse with its feedbag on the street outside the restaurant door.

Interestingly, separated from the violence and disorder of city streets, at least two interior scenes of a domestic or family-related nature suggest the possibility of achieving a different time of renewal and recuperation for Antonio. The domestic family scenes involve the homes of bicycle thieves, the original thief who stole from Antonio and Antonio himself who will attempt to steal a bicycle toward the end of the film.

Reading these interior scenes in terms of the paradigm of spacious temporality and delayed cinema helps to discern the potential in these scenes for a new time and possible redemption. The first scene occurs early into the film as Maria and Antonio enter their apartment after he has told her about the crisis of needing to retrieve his pawned bike in order to assume his new job of gluing posters onto city walls. The couple, we recall, had bickered all the way into their apartment building.

The nature of the relationship between Maria and Antonio changes inside their apartment. The power, energy, and authority shift noticeably. The interior space clearly becomes a domestic, feminine sphere. Not only does the balance of power in their relationship change in the apartment, the filming and editing of the mise en scène aesthetic also changes with an increased intensity upon opening free space-time. Thus, in his discussion of the "several spatial dialectics" in *Bicycle Thieves*, Frank Tomasulo describes the differences between so-called *"social shots"* of a subject in the context of a "mass background or real environment" in contrast to "the spatial construction of interior locations." He notes the setting up of "a structure of inside and outside which reinforces the individual/collectivity antinomy."[18] Gordon also notes the seriousness of the film's "movement between interior and exterior spaces."[19]

Thus, in the apartment scene between Maria and Antonio, De Sica's mise en scène suggests a moment of Maria's existential awakening. In contrast to the exterior filming of urban spaces that depreciate freedom and community, in the apartment, Maria's actions infuse freedom and relation into the space-time of the mise en scène. Maria's existential moment opens the narrow confines of the apartment with a promise of existential possibility.

In her own domestic space of a three-room apartment, Maria acts with determination to resolve the desperate situation of needing to find funds to retrieve the pawned bicycle. Nancy's idea of spacious temporality and Mulvey's delayed cinema help convey how Maria transforms the enclosed space of the apartment into an unlikely environment for sudden existential awakening and presence. Maria and Antonio enter into a hallway that runs through the apartment. De Sica shoots from the end of the hallway. The depth of field and deep focus of the shot enclose man and wife in the extended narrow space. Each enters with one of the buckets of water. Antonio pauses at the end of the hall, while Maria walks through to the kitchen and places a bucket on a table. Antonio takes a few steps forward and rests his shoulder on the wall. He stays frozen at the end of the hallway and in the background of the shot while holding his bucket and looking downward in a pose of continued dejection. Maria drops her bucket on the kitchen table and then turns her back to the stationary camera to walk back down the hall to get the bucket Antonio holds. Antonio looks miserably at her as she takes the bucket.

Without any dialogue, Maria brings life and hope into the scene and apartment. Delayed cinema holds Antonio in stillness and then slowly dramatizes Maria's emerging presence. He moves by himself to the bedroom and sits alone on their bed until she walks in and orders him off the bed so she can take the sheets to be pawned for the money for his bicycle. In the space of their own rooms that she now dominates, she opens space for a time for action. Through her emerging presence, they share time together, as in the concluding shots of their later scene at the people's center. Within the domestic sphere of free space-time, she acts with the existential vitality and authority that life in the postwar public space of Italy tends to deny her. A mise en scène of spacious temporality becomes a mise en scène of relation and existential presence.

Before the second domestic scene at the apartment of the thief who stole Antonio's bicycle, Roman streets do offer some rare moments of joy and pleasure as well as episodic moments of adventure. They occur after Antonio and Maria's retrieval of the bicycle from the pawning warehouse. The bicycle connotes freedom and even a touch of romance. The bicycle brings Maria and Bruno together in the foreground of a scene of happiness and companionship. Antonio and Maria share looks of intimacy and love as she rides with him on the bike. The movie then evokes true excitement on the next morning when Antonio and Bruno go off on the bike on Antonio's first and only day of work. Father and son join other bikers breaking away from slow, old, and over-crowded buses and trolleys in a full-spirited and joyful expression of freedom of movement felt not only by Antonio and Bruno but clearly by the other bikers as well. They all experience a measure of joy, freedom of movement, and escape on Roman streets. Antonio drops off the eight-year-old Bruno to the gas station where he works and goes off to his first day on the new job.

On the third and final day of their story, father and son continue their search for the stolen bicycle. Antonio and Bruno start the day with Baiocco, visiting the most notorious street market at Piazza Vittorio to look for the bike. After several interesting encounters, father and son proceed on to a second market at Porta Portese where they get engulfed in a sudden rain shower that apparently was engineered for the film by the Rome sanitation department. From there they pursue the old man Antonio noticed doing business with the thief who again races off and disappears. They follow the old man to a church service and meal for the poor, a scene that ridicules and excoriates the well-heeled, well-dressed bourgeois people who conduct the service while barely managing to disguise their officious and patronizing attitude toward the city's poor and homeless who should be the objects of care, concern, and love.

Back on the street, Antonio and Bruno look once more for the old man who ran off again, but not without giving Antonio the possible address for the thief at Vicolo della Campanella, 15. Annoyed and frustrated by the day's happenings, Antonio notoriously strikes out at his son who runs off in response to walk by himself at some distance from his father. Antonio's threats and pleadings with his son to obey him and come back to him became one of the film's most famous and noteworthy sequences.

Desperate, Antonio decides to see La Santona, a fortune teller or mystic (Ida Bracci Dorati). Earlier in the film, he had berated Maria for visiting and paying La Santona for help in finding work for Antonio. Elements of this scene clearly seem to have caught the attention of Woody Allen to use them years later to great comedic effect in *Broadway Danny Rose* (1984) when the character played by Mia Farrow visits an Italian fortune teller in New Jersey. Returning to the Via della Paglia, Antonio and Bruno again come across the thief in Trastevere. The thief flees to a brothel on Via di Panico where he seems to be well known. Leaving Bruno behind, Antonio chases the thief, Alfredo, into the brothel. After a brief comedic scene of more chaos and disruption, the two men are thrown out of the brothel onto the street where Bruno has been waiting for his father.

Antonio and Bruno then follow Alfredo into the inner recesses of the thief's neighborhood and dark street of Vicolo della Campanella. A low-angle shot shows a man holding a baby with a wool stocking cap on its head. The man looks with curiosity and concern at Antonio and Alfredo and then quickly retreats into a building. A neighborhood gang of ruffians and local gangsters defend Alfredo against Antonio's manhandling and his insistence that the thief should return his bicycle. The thief's mother shouts wildly from a window above the crowd that Alfredo not only has a clean record and didn't steal anything but that he also needs special attention for his illness. Alfredo, seemingly on cue, then faints dramatically in an apparent fit that Allen also mimicked in his film. The crowd quickly turns into a mob that Alfredo fends off with a plank of wood. He struggles in real danger until a policeman or carabiniere comes to the scene with Bruno who had the nerve and instinctive intelligence to find him. The policeman tells Alfredo's mother that he would like to search her apartment.

A somewhat neglected ensuing scene in Alfredo's apartment with his mother deserves some further study, especially as a counterpoint to the earlier scene in the film in Maria and Antonio's apartment. Both Wagstaff and Gordon note the conditions of true urban poverty in the one-room apartment that the thief Alfredo shares with his mother, an absent brother, and a sister. Gordon writes,

"Here, the working-class Antonio rubs up against a semi-criminal underclass, a subproletariat operating in a world of theft and prostitution, outside the law and according to its own, closed-in systems for regulation and protection."[20] The policeman searches the apartment for the bicycle with Antonio following him while the mother works at her stove, caustically commenting on their intrusion and protesting her son's innocence.

Into this scene of poverty, crime, and corruption, spacious temporality and delayed cinema inject a perspective for realizing the occurrence of a recuperative time. Indeed, delayed cinema accentuates the opening of free space-time in this scene. Accordingly, as Antonio and the policeman look around the apartment and talk, they stop before an open window. Bruno stands in between his father and the policeman, looking up toward his father, who incidentally had struck Maria as looking like a cop with his own official cap for his poster job, perhaps suggesting a contrast of iconic images of masculine paternal authority as opposed to maternal sensibility. In the bicycle thief's apartment, a stilled image opens a mise en scène of free space-time that develops the binary contrast between male power and female care. A woman with a child in her arms appears in a window in the building directly across from the thief's apartment. The child wears the same cap as the child in the man's arms at the beginning of the scene. The disappearance and absence of the man who had been holding the baby suggests some illegal complicity on his part, and perhaps the woman's as well, whether regarding the stolen bicycle or other nefarious activities. The mother and child in the window appear in a direct line above and across from Antonio, the policeman, and Bruno. Her gaze from her window upon the activities in the thief's apartment adds a new dimension and complexity of meanings to the scene. In this scene's depth of field, the multiple levels of action complicate levels of meaning in the film.

The woman stares, an unnoticed observer for the other characters of the scene. Neither Bruno with his back to the window nor the two men engrossed in their conversation notice her. For them, she exists as an invisible presence. She embodies the deep mystery of presence and absence, being there and not there. She becomes a ghostly presence but on another register of meaning that contrasts with Antonio's lost being on the streets of Rome. She suggests a spiritual force and vision. Her silence adds to the ambiguity of her gaze, as though such silence and her sense of invisibility open to an infinite, transcendent possibility. A momentary maternal tenderness and power can be seen and felt in her image across the street as she watches over the scene from a position of maternal care and authority. From her distant place of close observation, she bears witness to a scene of corruption that suggests and holds within it a promise of possible redemption and renewal. Delayed cinema facilitates the work of her look in opening the space of the scene to the possibility of a new temporality.

Figure 1.1   *Bicycle Thieves*: A mysterious maternal gaze as a young boy seeks paternal guidance and care

From her position as observer and possible participant, the mother figure in the window must realize that the violence and cruelty of the original crime of bicycle theft gets compounded by the reaction of the thief, his family, and the people of the neighborhood. The hope for legal resolution to the situation fades as the policeman talks softly and persuasively about the difficulties of satisfactorily settling the whole matter of the stolen bicycle given the support of the neighborhood for the thief and his family. The gendered gaze on the scene by the mother in the window and the gendered tensions of the scene reopen concerns that Maria's role and place in the film originally raised about women in the film and in the culture.

Without ever being noticed by the two men and the boy in the thief's apartment, the mother across the street silently closes the windows and the shutters of her apartment. Her silent withdrawal contributes to the sense of mystery regarding her presence. Does she abandon the scene, or has she marked it with her gaze and blessed it or both? Spacious temporality and delayed cinema serve to open the scene to a complexity of meanings.

As Antonio and the policeman and Bruno walk from the window toward the door to leave the apartment, the policeman holds the door open for the reentry of the mother, who had been asked to leave during the inspection and the conversation between the men. The sullen mother enters followed by

Figure 1.2 *Bicycle Thieves*: A young girl suddenly changes the ethical and existential dynamic in a crowded urban setting

the daughter with her first appearance in the scene. The unnamed daughter walks in between Antonio and the policeman and Bruno at the door and turns slightly to the left to observe the policeman. She is not much taller than Bruno who looks up at her with some childish curiosity. The policeman and Bruno disappear outside the door and go down the stairs.

The daughter enters further into the one-room apartment passing below the taller Antonio. She looks up over her right shoulder toward him as he looks back. She then moves toward the center of the visual frame. She moves directly toward the camera that shows her to be a nubile and attractive teenager. With her body in front of the camera, she turns slightly to her right to see the mother at the stove. The girl carries wood blocks for the stove and thrusts them in a box. As her arms complete the forward gesture of throwing the blocks, she executes a reverse reaction of turning to her left to see Antonio staring back through a narrow space of the closing door. In its brief entirety of a few seconds, the girl completes a kind of rhythmic little dance gesture. Her movement concludes with her look at the door as Antonio finishes closing it, still looking at her through the slightest crack of the door before it closes. Again, she also looks. An exchange of gazes occurs. In a plain short-sleeved sweater that shows off her body and with her hair neatly combed and braided, she becomes a figure of presence and significance.

Figure 1.3 *Bicycle Thieves*: An exchange of looks and the gaze suggests existential revelation and encounter

The exchange between Antonio and the daughter has the effect of continuing and completing the gendered gaze of the mother in the window. Delayed cinema and spacious temporality has opened a mise en scène of existential otherness between the girl and the man Antonio. Otherwise anonymous and unknown, the girl achieves emerging existence presence. Her look offers the possibility of an escape from her environment. She looks toward the other for meaning. Likewise, Antonio looks back at the girl in a flash of existential self-recognition. Antonio and the film leave the girl behind but not before enacting a mise en scène of presence and otherness as made manifest by delayed cinema and open space-time.

Bicycle Thieves also puts Antonio back on the street in all his misery with Bruno. Becoming a bicycle thief himself, Antonio gets stopped and beaten by a crowd that prevents him from getting away on the stolen bicycle. Only Bruno's appeal for his father saves Antonio from arrest. Listening to Bruno, the owner of the bicycle lets Antonio go free in spite of his attempted theft. The gesture of compassion from one city stranger to another that has been largely missing from much of the film from the beginning finally occurs and makes it possible for Antonio and Bruno to overcome the pain of loss and defeat through the modest action of holding each other's hand as they walk together. Father and son in their shared humiliation and mutual compassion and love for each other discover the otherness of existence as they fade into the urban crowd—together.

NOTES

1. Jean-Luc Nancy, *The Experience of Freedom*, trans. Bridget McDonald, foreword Peter Fenves (Stanford: Stanford University Press, 1988), pp. 18, 19. All future references to this book will be to this edition and will be included parenthetically in the text as *EF*.

2. Jean-Luc Nancy, *Birth to Presence*, trans. Brian Holmes et al. (Stanford: Stanford University Press, 1993), p. 155. All future references to this work will be to this edition and will be quoted parenthetically in the text as *BP*.

3. See Laura Mulvey, *Death 24x a Second: Stillness and the Moving Image* (London: Reaktion Books, 2008). All future references to this book will be to this edition and will be included parenthetically in the text as *D: 24*.

4. Jean-Luc Nancy, *Being Singular Plural*, trans. Robert D. Richardson and Anne E. O'Byrne (Stanford: Stanford University Press, 2000), pp. 61, 62; emphasis in the original. All future references to this work will be to this edition and will be included parenthetically in the text as *BSP*.

5. Jean-Luc Nancy, *Adoration: The Deconstruction of Christianity II*, trans. John McKeane (New York: Fordham University Press, 2013), pp. 24, 31, 14; emphasis in the original. All future references to this work will be to this edition and will be included parenthetically in the text as *A*.

6. See Peter Bondanella, *Italian Cinema from NeoRealism to the Present*, New Expanded Edition (New York: Continuum, 1995), pp. 53, 55, 31.

7. See Philip Mosley, *The Cinema of the Dardenne Brothers* (New York: The Wallflower Press, 2013).

8. See Pasquale Iannone, "Vittorio De Sica: Beyond Neorealism," *Sight and Sound* (September 2015): 46.

9. Robert S. C. Gordon, *Bicycle Thieves* (London and New York: BFI Palgrave Macmillan, 2008), p. 62.

10. Nancy discusses and quotes from, Hannah Arendt, *Between Past and Future* (New York: Penguin, 1968), p. 148.

11. See Lorna Collins, "Jean-Luc Nancy, Art and Community," in *Nancy and Visual Culture*, eds. Carrie Giunta and Adrienne Janus (Edinburgh: Edinburgh University Press, 2016), p. 168.

12. Gordon, *Bicycle Thieves*, p. 14.

13. Christopher Wagstaff, *Italian Neorealist Cinema: An Aesthetic Approach* (Toronto: University of Toronto Press, 2007), p. 398; emphasis in the original. Wagstaff quotes De Sica from *Cinema senza tempo*, RAI documentary. For a somewhat different emphasis on De Sica and realism, see, Godfrey Cheshire, "A Passionate Commitment to the Real," in *Current: The Criterion Collection*, February 12, 2007.

14. See Gordon, *Bicycle Thieves*, pp. 71, 108.

15. See Wagstaff, *Italian Neorealist Cinema*, pp. 311, 359, 350.

16. See Emmanuel Levinas, *Totality and Infinity: An Essay on Exteriority*, trans. Alphonso Lingis (Pittsburgh: Duquesne University Press, 1969), p. 267; emphasis in the original. For further and a greater detailed discussion of this subject of ethics and paternity, especially regarding the secondary status of women, see my *Levinas and the Cinema of*

Redemption: Time, Ethics, and the Feminine (New York: Columbia University Press, 2010), pp. 164–167.

17. See Gordon, *Bicycle Thieves*, pp. 53, 78, 110–111.

18. See Frank P. Tomasulo, "*Bicycle Thieves:* A Re-Reading," *Cinema Journal*, vol. 21, nos. 2–13 (spring 1982): 5. Tomasulo makes a larger point about visual structure and design that "compositional masks" displace a needed concentration on class struggle in the film.

19. See Gordon, *Bicycle Thieves*, p. 72.

20. See Gordon, *Bicycle Thieves*, pp. 84–86 and Wagstaff, *Italian Neorealist Cinema*, p. 385.

CHAPTER 2

La Demora (2012)

THE NUDE

The film *La Demora* [The Stay] opens with a tight close-up of an old man's partial profile. Fittingly for an old man in the early stages of dementia, the frame of the close-up cuts off the top of his head. Stopping the frame makes it apparent that the image could be called "The hanging," hanging for the position of his slightly drooped head and neck; hanging for the flabby flesh of his cheek and neck, including the flesh of his double chin that forms two small breasts with his chin; and hanging simply for the suggestion of aging flesh and impending death. The tip of the man's nose also appears suspended from the top of the frame, contributing to the sense of fragmentation in the image. In the stilled image, rivulets of water drip down from his face. Director Rodrigo Plá also practices delayed cinema and holds the camera on the old man in this position for at least twenty seconds. The gray-haired chest of the old man trembles slightly in reaction to the water pouring over his head. The water running from an off-screen faucet can be heard but not seen. The visual absence of the water source adds sensory disruption to the uncertainty of the scene.

Plá's camera cuts for several seconds to a shot of the man's left hand resting on his left knee, indicating that he sits in the process of showering. The tight shot focuses on his knees, hand, and lower thighs. Water drips onto and bounces off his knee as though dropping onto an inanimate object. As in the opening take, the scene indicates bodily fragmentation and disjunction. Body parts stand in for and represent the whole man and his being. After several seconds of this long take, the camera cuts again to a close-up of his gray, wet, chest hair. In this opening take the man's identity, situation, and story remain unknown. The scene conveys dependence, vulnerability, uncertainty.

Figure 2.1 *La Demora*: Struggling with age and infirmity

Another cut to a shot from behind the man shows someone's hand at work washing and scrubbing his hair. The camera stays on the back of his head as the hand rather roughly but thoroughly washes around and in his right ear. Then he tilts to the right for the washing of his left ear. He leans forward for the soaping of his back. The camera shows only the hands of the person bathing him. Both hands work at washing the man.

Two knocks on a door interrupt the noise of the dripping water. A woman cries out in Spanish "Not now" to whoever was knocking on the door. Outside the door a young person complains, "Mom! Nani won't get up!" Still scrubbing the man, the woman in the bathroom says, "Tell him, I'll kick his ass out of the bed." Unclear voices from children can be heard from outside the door, as the woman, who remains faceless at this point, says, "What is it, Dad? Not feeling well?" He shakes his head no.

Then a cut to a two-shot shows the woman, María (Roxanna Blanco), leaning over the left shoulder of her father, Agustín Suarez (Carlos Vallarino) to look into his face and check on his condition. Handing him a small scrub brush, she says, "Do it yourself. I hold you," meaning for him to clean the rest of his body himself. As she leans into the man from behind to help and hold him up, the camera pulls back to reveal the details of the setting. He sits on the side of bathtub in a steam-filled, small, narrow family bathroom. With his chin on his chest, he tells his daughter, "Go outside, I'll finish up." In response, she leans back and in a somewhat berating tone of obvious tension and exasperation says, "What if you fall? Who'll look after you if you break a bone?" Touching his shoulder almost gently, sadly, she then says, "Use the blue towel" and leaves her father.

The perfectly mundane specificity of "blue towel" demonstrates the genius on many levels of *La Demora*. The words "blue towel" describe the towel almost everyone living in the modern world can find in his or her bathroom or

Figure 2.2 *La Demora*: Dutifully bathing her elderly father

closet. The specific detail brings home the scene to anyone with a blue towel, including someone from a background and environment thoroughly different from the poor, working-class life and culture of this film from Montevideo, Uruguay. Plá's extended concentration on naked Agustín involves more than simply making an honest photographic and artistic exhibition of advancing decrepitude and infirmity. In *La Demora* the director's focused attention on the elderly man goes well beyond merely conveying his condition and the accompanying frustration and difficulty for a family of caring for someone elderly and infirm.

The economy, efficiency, and immediacy of the visual and verbal language of *La Demora* achieve an art form of beauty that uses utter simplicity and directness to develop complex characters at the center of genuine moral and ethical crises. In the honesty, authenticity, and transparency of its realism, the film helps to define contemporary neo-realism. From the very beginning, Plá's direction, María Secco's razor-edge black and gray cinematography, and Laura Santello's pointed and pungent screenplay create a neo-realistic mise en scène aesthetic of freedom and relation.

In *La Demora* a mise en scène of deep focus, long takes, and depth of field creates, in Nancy's term, a free space-time for existential emergence and ethical responsibility. What Nancy calls "spacious temporality" opens depths of meaning and happening to enable rethinking experiential time on the screen.

Left on his own in the bathroom, Agustín grasps onto a fixture on the wall above the tub and rises in all his sagging, elderly, and aging nudity. He stands with his side to the camera, exposing his naked hip and right buttocks. He reveals a body of folds of wrinkled flesh. He soaps his bottom and front. Held for study in a stilled or delayed frame, the visual image resonates with the photos and paintings in Jean-Luc Nancy and Federico Ferrari's *Being Nude: The Skin of Images*. They propose different "tonalities of the nude," including "the divine nude" and for contrast the nudity of the "naked sin" and the "naked skin." They say,

> The preoccupation occurs in different registers, from the horror of bodies thrown into the charnal heap to the desperate desire to make bodies their own icons, and it always leads us back in the direction of stripping bare and coming undone. This ambiguous proximity is also an opportunity for thought, if, for thought, it is a matter above all else of remaining stripped bare of all received meaning and figures that have already been traced.

Nancy and Ferrari express a kind of metaphysics and ontology of nudity as a case for seeking and asserting new and honest thought. They write, "The nudes of painters and photographers expose this bareness and suspense on the edge of a sense that is always nascent, always fleeting, on the surface of the skin, and on the surface of the image."[1]

Rather than being merely a stark and taut beginning of a dark film at the expense of an old man's privacy and modesty, the nudity that opens *La Demora* constitutes a prologue and encapsulation of the film's artistic purpose and style of intense ethical and existential realism. Skin and surface, even an old man's, project the sudden and shocking newness of the modern. The nudity strips away history, context, essentialism. An old man's nudity in the very beginning of the film dramatizes, to repeat Nancy and Ferrari's critical metaphor, a "stripped bare" cinematic code and aesthetic creed of seeking authenticity in rendering Plá's unique and original vision of reality. In *La Demora*, Plá persists in looking for and articulating what he sees as the naked truth by eschewing embellishment and intrusion into the visual and cinematic text.

Moreover, the significance of Agustín's nudity in the opening of the film compares to Nancy and Ferrari's analysis of a different nude image and context as "a disturbing of the senses." They write, "More than simple vision and more than an activating of the sense of sight, the nude is, therefore, a disturbing of the senses, indeed, of all the senses and in all senses of the word" (*N*: 92). For them, the disturbance of nudity engenders new thinking about the body, relations, and experience. In *La Demora*, the old man's nudity, especially as exposed in body fragmentation, creates sensory disturbance. The disjunction between sight and sound, between visual images and off-screen sound exacerbates the disturbance. Such disturbance in *La Demora* initiates a process of new thinking just as Nancy and Ferrari propose.

Thus, the disturbance of the senses in the opening of *La Demora* initiates a sensibility revolution. Following Nancy and Ferrari's argument, Agustín's nudity establishes new thinking about spatial and temporal relations in

La Demora. At first, the naked old man seems isolated and confined to the enclosed space of the small bathroom. In fact, the nudity works like an explosion of sensibility with implications for everyone involved in the film.

Agustín's presence and occupation of the bathroom removes its accessibility for other apartment members for a prolonged—even painful—amount of time. His occupancy deprives others. For a time, he removes the bathroom visually and physically for the family. Weak, old, and powerless, his presence affects the use and arrangement of space and time in the apartment. The scene suggests the need to remove the old man to make room for others. Agustín's prospective absence would radically alter spatial relations for others. The alteration of spatial relationships necessarily changes the use and manipulation of time for those in the apartment. As Nancy and Ferrari write about another image, "Thanks to nudity, the presence of the other moves spaces; presence in this case is uncanny, disquieting" (*N*: 92).

Agustín's nudity compels consideration of the relationship of his body to time as well as space. His body injects a crucial spatio-temporal dimension to the scene. The aging of his body signifies the lost past and uncertain future. His loss of memory and his confusion in his dementia implants lost time into the scene. At the same time, as a father and grandfather, his bond with his family members instinctively remains intact and never leaves his mind even in his darkest moments, perhaps as his strongest emotional anchor and hold onto reality. His nudity displays and confirms the connection to the family of flesh, blood, and spirit. Throughout the film, the children, especially Brenda (Julieta Gentile), the pre- or early teenage daughter and oldest of the children, recognize their inescapable connection to the old man. They treat Agustín with courtesy, respect, and genuine affection, at times actually countering the impatience exhibited sometimes by María who bears most of the burden for his care.

Thus, seemingly isolated and marginalized from others and restricted in his movements, Agustín's nudity signifies his existential place in a network of spatial and temporal relationships. Even in his old age, Agustín embodies and animates, to repeat Nancy and Ferrari's term, "a sense that is always nascent" (*N*: 4), as in the stage of emerging existential presence. For Agustín nascent sense means overcoming chronological time with its certainty of death by looking for a time of renewal with others, an existential time of emergence. His nudity becomes a statement and an enactment of life. His existential self and emotional being persist because of the freedom of his actions in his relation to others, including strangers who actively demonstrate concern for him that he appreciates. He also expresses genuine love for his daughter and grandchildren.

FAMILY DISORDER

A mise en scène aesthetic of free space-time and relation describes Plá's cut from the bathroom of the apartment to a foyer that becomes a center of activity of children and family life. Delayed cinema again facilitates opening free space-time for the existential drama of finding time and space for the self in relation to others. Sensory disturbance and disruption also continue for encouraging and cultivating new thinking about experience and relation.

As in the bathroom scene with her father, María's back remains to the camera as she continues working, this time with her children as they prepare for school. Throughout *La Demora*, Plá repeats this shot from behind the subject. The shot not only accentuates dramatic uncertainty about the subject; it also raises metaphysical and psychological questions about vision, concealment, reality, and identity. The shot from behind suggests that without a visible face, the character remains distant, ambiguous, and alienated. The camera position creates a kind of visual and spatial suspension, a temporal interruption that instigates a time of uncertainty with the potential for the new.

Not showing the subject's visible facial reaction to the scene insinuates an aura of mystery and obscurity into the vision of the scene. This mystery complicates Plá's new realism. Plá's neo-realistic mise en scène aesthetic of long takes, deep focus, and depth of field focuses on the family drama of events, happenings, and interactions. This film art enables delayed cinema and spacious temporality to uncover details of the dramatic scene for deepening insight into the scene. The fluidity of space and time in delayed cinema frees the tempo, tone, and rhythm of relations in the scene to propagate a new temporal regime. In a sense, delayed cinema and free space-time inject a new scene and story within the mise en scène. Delayed cinema and spacious temporality intimate a different temporal regime for events and characters. Space and time change as though offering a play within a play that can become a kind of choreographed dance of rigorously coordinated and organized movements to alternative visual and audial rhythms. Details of moments, events, and happenings in the scene take on a new significance. Delayed cinema sustains a close reading of the open space-time of the family dynamic. Thus, delayed cinema and spacious temporality open a mise en scène of freedom and relation that expresses the unseen or neglected in the search for the naked truth.

In the scene, María stands guard by the closed bathroom door to remain near her father. The children surround and engulf her. Brenda in front of her complains about non-matching school clothes as María turns to look over her left shoulder to tell Nani (Fecundo Segovia), the older boy, to go pee in a bottle since his grandfather's presence denies access to the bathroom.

As Brenda walks off, a younger brother Fabri (Thiago Segovia) appears through a glass partition seated at a table eating his breakfast. A cut shows

María at the end of a foyer standing by the bathroom door with her hand on the doorknob. Nani races down the hallway with a slight laugh over the urgency of needing to go to the bathroom. Brenda emerges from the bottom left of the frame and goes past the camera in a blur just as the younger Fabri comes from a door at the top of the frame and walks toward the camera.

The synchronized action in the enclosed space conveys the commotion of family life. Singular individuals become part of the family order as time and space shift in the mise en scène with the movement and inter-relations of individuals.

Brenda contributes to the disorder with her teasing remark as she passes off screen, "I bet twenty pesos you pee all over." Nani, also from off screen, responds, "Deal!" as María calls out, "Brenda, get him a jar!" As María peeks in on her still-naked father, Nani complains, "This bottle's not good." He cries out, "Get me a bigger one. Quick, I'm peeing myself." Another voice, probably Brenda's, exclaims, "Gross!" and from the opposite end of the hallway, Fabri turns in the direction of his mother to announce, "Mom, Nani used a pot!" The boys exchange banalities recognizable to anyone with children or who remembers their own childhood. Nani commands, "Shut up, stupid" and the younger one immediately responds, "Mom, he called me stupid!"

The camera returns to the silence and relative calm of Agustín still dressing by himself in the bathroom. He has managed barely to get a top on but the rest of him remains naked and exposed to the camera as he rises up. The indistinct muttering of family voices can be heard from inside the bathroom. Pulling down on his shirt and then holding onto the wall, Agustín turns slightly, fully exposing his behind to the camera. He struggles with his pants, awkwardly and pathetically bouncing from the left wall to holding out his right arm for balance and stability on the right wall. The camera stays on him and his naked behind for several seconds before returning outside the bathroom door to a solid and expressive two-shot of mother and daughter.

A high-angle shot from slightly above the mother and daughter focuses on Brenda in front of the camera with her head slightly down and key lighting on her forehead as she works on something that turns out to be her school bag that she raises up from the bottom of the frame to put across her shoulder and back. Behind her in profile, María looks down at the sandwiches she prepares for her children. Mother and daughter squabble a bit over money that Brenda needs for a school trip. María promises to have it the next day and appeals, "Help me out, Brenda."

Brenda then walks down the hallway and stops. She glances off screen to her left and then to her right. She knocks on the glass separating her from Nani to get his attention. While she sees Nani, he remains barely noticeable at the extreme left of the frame, again demonstrating Plá's style of revealing things in fragments in order to create sensory disjunction that leads to fresh thinking.

Referring to an item that never gets truly explained or revealed, Brenda exclaims, "It's under Grandpa, dumb ass." She then continues walking toward the camera.

Freezing the frame shows Brenda's pretty face in the upper-right corner of the frame. She then cuts diagonally across the frame and once again passes in a blur before the camera to go out of the left side of the frame. The combination of the previous shot and scene with her mother and the shot of her passing in a blur before the camera suggests her transitional stage of adolescence between immaturity and adult womanhood. Brenda in her adolescence struggles to find her identity for herself and as a member of the family. As María enters from the top of the frame rushing with school bags in both of her hands, Fabri enters from below, saying, "You wet everything!"

Finally out of the bathroom and seated on a chair, Agustín moves a bit forward to enable Nani to pull out something from under him. The boy says, "Excuse me, grandpa" while Brenda goes to give him a goodbye kiss. With all of the children clamoring and squabbling at the door to head for school, María says to her daughter, "Take Fabri's hand, Brenda!"

The commotion over urination humorously underscores in a different register the fluidity of spatial structures and relationships in the opening of *La Demora*. Even with a bathroom door as a sign of attempted separation and privacy, the bathroom occupied by grandfather Agustín intrudes upon the other spaces of the apartment. The door proves porous. The obsession by the children on bodily functions and body parts turns the bathroom door into a metaphor for the porousness of the body itself that so struggles to control its own functions. Inner and outer domains, inner and outer spaces seem quite reversible and exchangeable. The door only accentuates the connection between what occurs on both sides of the door.

The details of the children's movements and activities in the scene articulate choreographed spatial manipulation and organization. As the children come and go, their use and occupation of space reopens space for fresh perspectives and imaginative thinking. The humor of their interactions like the effect of sensory dissonance challenges conventional thinking and relationships. A mise en scène style of deep focus, depth of field, and long takes maps the spatial interconnections involving the family, particularly the children. Spatial positioning and movement act something like a mobile stage for carrying the expression of the relationships between the children, as when Fabri stands by a door and informs on his brother for going in a pot or when Brenda walks by and bets against her brother's accuracy when urinating and later passes through again and calls him a dumb ass. Such expression of relationships conveyed through spatial malleability, movement, and alteration necessarily intimates a flexibility involving time.

Thus, the early scenes of *La Demora* suggest that the openness of free space-time of freedom and relation occurs in spite of conditions of economic impoverishment and social enclosure and restriction. Concerning the children, Plá brilliantly balances the insecurity of economic uncertainty with the emotional security that their rough but loving and dedicated mother provides.

Delayed cinema enables closer analysis of the details that go into constructing the relationships of spacious temporality in *La Demora*. Spacious temporality opens time and space for the otherness of existence, including for the children in their interactions with one another and with their mother and grandfather. Delayed cinema also allows for closer investigation of the fluidities of time for the otherness of emerging existential presence and space-time. For example, holding the frame on the two-shot of María and Brenda in the kitchen illustrates their bond in the same frame as mother and daughter. At the same time, holding the frame highlights that Brenda and María also have contrasting and conflicting roles, purposes, and motivations. Mother and daughter maintain different positions and stances in the frame; they look away from each other, indicating movement toward different directions for that very day and in life. Brenda worries primarily about getting the few pesos necessary for her school trip. She obsesses about it, putting pressure on her mother who earns money for the family as a freelance seamstress doing piece work at home. She sews what appears to be denim pockets that she takes to a factory where her work gets carefully examined before she gets paid.[2]

MOTHER

María worries about everything and everyone. Sewing on her machine, María watches and hears the mistakes of memory and mind made by Agustín as she clearly makes the case in her own mind for sending him to a nursing home. He forgets that he heard in the distant past about the death of a friend. He loses count of the sugar he puts in his coffee and then with embarrassment tries to rationalize his confusion by saying that he likes it sweet. He makes life more difficult and uncomfortable for everyone else in the crowded apartment, taking up needed space and sleeping on the couch.

Worst of all, on that same day, he goes off on his own and gets lost. María comes home during a driving rainstorm and must go out looking for him. A neighbor tells her the obvious: Agustín shouldn't be left by himself in the apartment. The comment and its inappropriate delivery by someone who appears marginally and briefly in a doorway and can hardly be noticed in the film frame again shows Plá's subtlety as a director. The brief appearance of the neighbor adds a disruptive and emotionally charged note to an already chaotic and anxiety-ridden situation. The insensitive comment works as a painful jab at María.

The lost Agustín eventually comes across an old neighborhood friend, Néstor (Oscar Pernas), who takes him home and waits for María's return from looking in the rain, apparently in hopes of beginning a relationship with her. In fact, Nani on the next day gets mildly corrected and chastised by María for inappropriate language and rudeness when he says that Néstor wants to "fuck" her. María says that it is a "bad word," although one that she frequently uses herself. Brenda interjects that "Words are not good or bad," evidencing her precociousness and intelligence. Her look suggests her pleasure over her response and smartness.

When María gets home soaking wet only to find her father, Néstor, and the children at the family table playing a game, she loses her patience and hope for her father. A wonderful shot from her perspective shows Néstor seated at the family table with his back to the door and the camera while Brenda and Agustín look at María, their expressions acknowledging that the head of the household has returned and is not happy. María fires questions at Brenda about what happened to her father in a way that not only demonstrates her anger but also punishes Agustín. She acts as if he is not there or is not capable of speaking for himself. María asks if her father's wet clothes have been changed. Brenda answers, "Sí." A shot of Agustín's profile with a wool stocking cap on his head and a sheepish expression on his face indicates the tension of the situation.

Demonstrating the depth and intensity of her frustration, María comments, "He'd better not give more trouble today, or we'll put a cowbell around his neck so we know where he is." Her words arouse an immediate response from Brenda in defense of her grandfather. With real alarm and sympathy for Agustín, she cries out, "Momma, take it easy!"

A close-up of Agustín's face with his eyes lowered and his face in shadow with the light behind him suggests a death mask.

An incident at María's factory on that same day helps explain her mood and proves pivotal in describing her character, situation, and motivation. It occurs after she gets paid for piece work at the factory and has been warned about new policies that will make getting fair compensation for her work even more difficult. Plá again uses depth of field and deep focus to spatialize, so to speak, María in this factory where she cannot even find full-time employment as one of the regular seamstresses. Transitioning from the sounds of her single, small sewing machine at home to the factory sounds of many machines roaring away, the film puts her in a position of painful subservience as she submits her work only to have some of it called and rejected as "flawed." The camera shows her at the end of a long hallway banked by sewing machines. It then focuses on María's stonily still face as a woman talks to her about her work and the new "rules." Apparently, the only real actress in this cast of non-professional and ordinary people, Roxanna Blanco, who plays María, brilliantly holds her pose as the woman talks. She conveys the depth of María's pain. Her eyes strike a glance at the woman, further suggesting María's vulnerability and bitterness.

The film then returns to a bathroom. Enclosed in a stall in the factory bathroom, María uses a covered toilet as a seat. She goes there for privacy to count the money she has made. A cigarette hangs from the side of her mouth. María sometimes smokes even in her own home bathroom and apparently tries to hide that activity from her children by hopelessly attempting to wave off the smoke and smell through a ceiling window.

In the factory bathroom, María's roughness as a worker and woman shows itself. Her facial expression, gestures, posture, and constricted movement all emanate a kind of physical combativeness and rough independence. Nothing about her in that pose and situation suggests domesticity or the softness of motherhood. Even tucking away some money in her socks that turns out to be for Brenda's school trip has the initial appearance of being for some kind of illicit or nefarious purpose.

As María sits in the stall, she overhears two other women talking by the sinks in the bathroom. The camera rises above the stall and shows the women in conversation about the factory. Amazingly, the wall of the bathroom is a long window enabling observation of the employees in the lavatory. From inside the bathroom, rows of machines and equipment appear in deep focus on the other side of the window. The women complain about outsourcing and about the temporary workers like María who make it hard for the regular employees to strike and get higher wages. A reverse shot from the other side of the window puts boxes and factory shelves between the camera and the woman at the sinks washing and brushing their teeth,

María leaves the stall and the camera shows three women at the sinks and then cuts to inside the bathroom for a long shot of the three women in a row at the sinks. Delayed cinema again proves necessary to accentuate the significance of the shot. Three women lined up in a factory bathroom. Behind them and to the left of the screen the stall doors stay open. To the right of the frame, the window wall of the bathroom forms a line the length of the bathroom from the top of the screen to the bottom right making for an interesting balanced shot of a strange kind of enclosed environment. The women wash their hands and rinse their mouths.

Looking down at the sink and her hands, María says, "Us fucking temps, as you said . . ." The camera holds on the three as the two women look up and turn toward her. Still looking down, María says, ". . . have worked here for five years. No benefits, health, nothing." She looks directly at the two women who now exhibit some concern and embarrassment. "Your union doesn't give a shit." María steps back and looks down again. "No comrade, collective bargain covers temp workers." María reaches down for her bag and starts to leave. With her back to the camera, she says, "Comrade my ass."

The two women look toward María as she leaves the bathroom. A stilled frame shows the women's eyes following her through the door and María's back on the other side of the door. At the top of the frame, to the right, a glimpse of the factory at work catches a woman hunched over a work space.

In her confrontation with the other workers at the factory, María achieves an empty personal and moral victory. The scene really reveals and accentuates her sense of impotence and alienation over not being able to change her life. Not just a statement about unions and politics and inequity among the poor and working class, the scene subtly expresses María's psychological and ethical isolation and abandonment. Responsible for everyone at home and without social and community support for her life and work, María endures a truly alienated existence. Throughout the factory scene, delayed cinema and a neo-realistic mise en scène of deep focus and long takes again suggest an aesthetic for the opening of free spacious temporality.

Accordingly, María's painful experience at work helps to explain her bitterness and frustration that evening at home upon learning of Agustín's absence in the rain. Eventually with Néstor's departure that evening, the family settles into preparation for bed. Simplicity, care, and assiduous attention to detail continue to characterize the filming to develop character, narrative, and emotional intensity. Careful lighting and dark interior colors establish the mood and tone for the scene as Brenda patiently and sweetly helps put Agustín to bed. She helps make up the sofa for his bed and gives him his medicine. He repeats the regimen for his medication, but the deftness of her hands indicates how often she has performed this task. Wearing his wool hat to bed, he also keeps his clothes on, as do the other members of the family, signs of poor heating in the apartment. The camera concentrates on him and parts of Brenda that show her activity in helping him. He follows her movements.

When Agustín asks why Néstor had come to the apartment, Brenda patiently reminds him to bring him home, as though he already had forgotten in his state of dementia. Without any special drama, Agustín quietly shows more than memory with his continued sense of responsibility, feeling, and concern as María's father. He says, "I know that. He waited for your mom, that's why I ask." Without pursuing the subject of Néstor's interest in her mother, Brenda concludes putting her grandfather to bed and turns off the light by the couch. She then hears her mother shout, "Fuck" from the bathroom.

Leaving Agustín, Brenda walks through another excellent shot of the apartment in darkness to the glass bathroom door with a hazy light passing through it. She asks what's wrong and her mother says on the other side, "Fucking shit!" Entering the bathroom, Brenda sees that her mother has hung up soaking wet pesos with clothes pins on a string to dry. She had hidden the money in her socks in the drenching rain. This would be the money for

Brenda's school trip the next day. Mother and daughter proceed together to dry the bills. Interestingly, the bathroom again becomes a key setting for the family, visually emphasizing both the artistic dedication of the film to naked truth but also the physical and psychological reality of the body as the first home of the existential individual.

The scene has importance for its restrained but clear depiction of the affection and love between mother and daughter. María calmly and touchingly assures her daughter that it will work out. The scene accentuates that with all her duties as provider, worker, and caregiver, María's role as mother and protector of her children dominates her mind and actions. The scene conveys this with literary and visual self-control that avoids excessive melodrama or intrusion of manipulative forces into the story, such as non-diegetic narration or soundtrack. Thus, the next morning when María speaks to Brenda about the dried-out money, she tells her to "put it somewhere safe." Brenda cutely and smartly says, "In my shoe," teasing with a smirk to herself about where her mother originally hid the money in her socks. The mother snaps back, "Don't get wise!" but the rapport and comfort that the mother and daughter have with each other comes through clearly and strongly.

Before finally going to bed on the previous night, María found Agustín awake and restless and searching for old photographs and family papers. After some casual banter, another evocative shot from behind both of them shows them seated on the sofa with elbows touching. His face remains hidden, but her cheek and a slight smile can be discerned with key lighting from a lamp over her right shoulder and behind him as they look at a photograph from their past.

Shot again with great care for nighttime colors, balance, and tone, the scene emphasizes that even while commiserating with her father, María struggles to forget the past in order to concentrate on the present and the future for her children. As though to make the point about her priorities, María reminds her father about the paperwork to be done the next day for finding a nursing home for him. Again in a subtle way, the scene drives home the point of the order of priorities that demand María's attention when Nani, the middle child, appears at the door unable to sleep because of bad thoughts. Finished attending to her father, María allows the boy to sleep with her saying, "Okay, come to my bed." He dives in. "Just for tonight, OK?" she says. They both wear daytime clothing to bed under heavy blankets.

The next morning Agustín appears in a suit all dressed up in order to make a good impression that he thinks will help María find a nursing home for him. They go together to a public center to apply for a place in an appropriate facility, but it proves impossible to place him since the facilities really exist only for the homeless and destitute. It turns out that María's meager income and small apartment disqualify her for such assistance.

Leaving the public agency, María's desperation intensifies with each step she takes. A series of brilliant long shots shows her walking by herself before a background of gray city buildings. She walks well ahead of her father until he finally loses his breath and has to stop. She seats him on a public bench to go for water for him. Looking at him from the distance of a small store, she gets the idea to leave him so that he can be picked up by authorities and placed in a public shelter for the homeless. She gambles that he will be spotted by authorities and that she will be able to find him later. She races to her bus. Her physical bearing suggests that an invisible and inescapable stabbing guilt has begun replacing the original agony of having to care for her aging father under difficult conditions. On the bus, her face steadily intimates an inner recognition that she has entered into new and dangerous unchartered moral and ethical territory with the possibility of seriously unintended consequences for her father, her children, and herself.

At first, Agustín sits rather comfortably on the bench situated in the midst of a large apartment complex called the Buceo project. It takes a while for him to become concerned over the lengthening delay of his daughter's return.

THE FACE: THE ART OF THE CLOSE-UP

From this point on of Agustín's abandonment in *La Demora,* Plá and his colleagues create a visual poetry of close-up images of Agustín and María in their separated and distant places. The flow of images takes on a distinct resonating rhythm and power. The progression of close-ups becomes an exchange of looks linking father and daughter throughout their separation.

The organization of the film after the separation of María and Agustín involves two tracks of very different kinds of movement. Agustín remains largely stationary. Sitting by himself, he soon becomes something of a focal point of attention from concerned strangers, most importantly from a truly kind woman named Estela (Cecilia Baranda). He feels compelled, however, to resist efforts to move him to a more comfortable, safer place and environment out of fear of missing María upon what he thinks will be her imminent return to him. He stays fixed to the bench waiting for his daughter. As the day gets darker and colder and becomes night, Agustín takes on a touch of King Lear being an elderly man abandoned by his daughter to the elements and the outdoors—but in contrast to Lear, Agustín never complains or becomes combative and hostile. Instead, he remains humble and loving, even as he becomes more frightened. In his troubled state of mind, he seems primarily concerned about his daughter and grandchildren. He worries about what María's delay in returning to him may mean regarding her safety and the well-being of the children. He stays grounded in family.

In contrast, on a second track of narrative action, María after leaving her father appears to be in a state of constant flux, activity, and distraction. When she gets home she immediately starts working at her machine, saying "No work! No food!" and fending off questions primarily from Brenda about Agustín's situation. She lies to the children that Agustín has been placed in a comfortable, friendly home and that they can visit him. Brenda points out that she wanted to accompany them to the home and even young Fabri misses his grandfather. When Brenda suggests a loss of appetite in the absence of her grandfather, María tells her that the situation does not warrant going on strike. With all of her frenetic activity and distraction, worry remains on her face. She sends the children out for pastries, retires to the bathroom for a cigarette, taking the telephone with her. She then anonymously calls the police to report an old man on a bench at the Buceo project who appears in distress and needs to be picked up and helped by the authorities.

María soon begins a journey through the night in search of her father. It turns out to be not as simple as she had hoped.

The overall design of the film in its entirety, the thought behind individual shots and scenes, and the structured care of the narrative lines continues to ingest complexity, intelligence, authenticity, and depth into *La Demora* so as to make the film a serious cinematic work of art. Delayed cinema also continues to provide a mechanism and theory for examining the art of individual images and frames in the overall context of the moving image. A dynamic interconnection of close-ups and looks of father and daughter reorganizes the urban landscape by compressing time and space. Looks and close-ups externalize the internal psychological realm of pain and fear and internalize the external landscape of separation. The inner pain María and Agustín feel over the emotional and physical distance between them shows on their faces.

THE FACE

Cinematically, the close-up becomes especially important in the final phase of the film with María separated from Agustín. The cinematic theory and experience of naked truth that begins *La Demora* carries over to the film's final phase with a concentration on the nudity of the face. The movie goes from the artistic realism of the nudity of the body in the bathroom to the ethical existentialism of the nudity of the face. The idea of the nudity of the face plays a central role in the philosophy of Emmanuel Levinas, a thinker of some considerable interest to Nancy.

Levinas sees the "naked nakedness" of the face as the link to infinity. He argues "the nakedness of the face" breaks from regular chronological and synchronic time and becomes the term for ethical experience and demand.[3] He says, "This nudity which is a call to me—an appeal but also an imperative—I name *face*. It is doubtless necessary to insist on the concrete figure in which the notion of alterity acquires its meaning." He insists on linking the face and its nudity to the absolute ethical imperative of the relationship to the other. Levinas says, "The ethical attitude takes on a meaning that I call the face of the other man: nudity, exposition unto death, and in the being of I, infinite obligation and obedience to the imperative."[4]

Nancy apparently regards Levinas's "call" to the ethical demand of the face of the other a kind of *"waiting"* or *"vigil"* that proposes "the divine is inscribed at the heart of our experience." He writes, "For Levinas, this waiting, this vigil traverses, perishes (transit), and pushes to the breaking point consciousness, man, the self, being, and philosophy."[5]

In the light of such thinking by Levinas and Nancy, the close-ups of Agustín's face suggest the nightmare of "the delay" in waiting for María at the Buceo. The delay becomes a form of call or vigil for the ethical imperative of the naked face in relation to the other. An uncertain amount of time passes from María's abandonment of her father to a high-angle close-up of him that focuses on the top of his head and strong nose.

The camera stays on him, indicating his sense of dignity, self-control, and passive reserve. It holds that peculiar angle for a close-up of the man from the top of his head without showing his full face with a straight on close-up. It provides a partial shot of the face as though emphasizing the self-divided man's precarious situation and condition.

An off-screen voice gets Agustín's attention. The camera holds the angle of the close-up as Agustín turns to the sound, revealing the front of his face. In natural outdoor light without obvious make-up or studied-dramatic expression, the face appears naked to the world: rough, scruffy, human, an old man squinting into the sun and the face of another.

Switching to his perspective, the camera looks up into Estela's face as she explains that from her window above in the nearby building, she could see Agustín by himself on the bench and wondered if he was alright. Levinas describes such a happening as "the law of the stranger." He discusses "the biblical formula: 'Thou shalt love the stranger.'" He writes that when "someone for whom I do not have regard regards me; that is the very paradox of the law of the stranger." Estela's concern for Agustín follows this law, while also conforming to an idea of "the little act of goodness" that Levinas develops from the works of the Russian author and journalist Vasily Grossman. For Levinas such acts of kindness become "the sole refuge of the good in being."[6]

Moreover, the scene between Agustín and the woman also relates to another topic of interest to Levinas. Estela expresses concern that Agustín has exposed himself to too much sun. She explains the heat of the winter sun can be deceptive and can burn. He sits without a hat but with a scarf pulled tightly around his neck, indicating the cold weather. He resists Estela's advice to move to another, shadier bench out of fear that upon her return María would not be able to find him. Developing Pascal's metaphor, Levinas repeats throughout his work about the need to surrender one's "place in the sun" for the other. He writes, "I am thinking above all of the for-the-other in them, in which in the adventure of a possible holiness, the human interrupts the pure obstinacy of being and its wars. I cannot forget Pascal's thought: 'My place in the sun.' There is the beginning and image of the usurpation of the whole world."[7]

Inquiring about the time—3:30 in the afternoon—Agustín asks Estela to check the little store where María had gone for water. From behind Agustín, the camera shows Estela returning from the store across the grassy field of the complex to report, no María. Without any show of emotion or anxiety, Agustín drops entirely from the bottom of the frame as though losing his grounding. He returns in a full-face close-up shot from the camera's previous high-angle position. Agustín vaguely ponders a possible explanation for his daughter's absence. He imagines she had to go on an important errand as Estela tells him good afternoon.

FATHER AND DAUGHTER INTO THE NIGHT

The camera then cuts to a sharp, powerful long shot of the Buceo at dusk. The rectangular building of the project occupies the deep background while in the middle of the frame and to the right a strange circular structure pushes up and disappears through the top of the frame looking somewhat like a leaning Tower of Pisa. Barely noticeable in the growing darkness and in the shadow of the higher structures, Agustín stands by himself. The art design and structure of the shot and its suddenness mark more than a simple jump in time.

Planting Agustín so pathetically in the midst of the shot dramatizes how time has changed for him. In his mental state and in his situation of abandonment, chronological, synchronic time such as 3:30 becomes meaningless. He has become like King Lear on the heath, part of nature and the external environment and landscape. The facial landscape of the close-up and physical landscape of the project meld and cohere into a different order of space-time. Fully clothed, he stands naked to the world. In the distance of the long shot, he wavers on his feet.

A sharp cut to a close-up of his face breaks him off at the neck at the bottom of the frame with the project building behind him. He swivels slightly to the left and moves directly into the camera. Without any marked change of expression or externalization of emotion, he looks to the right at his surroundings, still in close-up and cut off at the neck at the bottom of the frame. Framing and visual design present and dramatize existential fragmentation and disjunction.

In the deep darkness of the night, emergency services that had been contacted anonymously by María arrive to try to help Agustín by offering to take him to a shelter. Estela reappears to assist while a curious project guard (Néstor Guzzini) also observes the action. All are bundled up heavily against the cold night. In this scene, Agustín exhibits his first real physical agitation and distress with his resistance to being forced to leave his place on the bench where he wishes to wait for his daughter. A patient, sensitive, and resourceful emergency nurse (Emilia Diaz) urges him to leave but ultimately relents. The nurse asks for his address and identification. He vaguely remembers leaving his identification card with María at the public offices for his assignment to a nursing home but cannot recall his address. Touchingly, he shows a picture of his grandchildren that María had given him the night before.

With some ambivalence, Estela and the guard qualifiedly support Agustín in his resistance to being moved. Later that evening, Agustín painfully tells Estela, "If you can't remember where you live, it's like not having a home." Mind, body, and home prove empty for Agustín. The harsh sound of the police emergency vehicle suddenly starting up to leave the Buceo inserts a sense of deepening abandonment into the scene.

At an unknown but ever familiar hour of the night at the Buceo, a crane shot visually positions Agustín at the bottom of a deepening abyss of abandonment. In a long shot, he sits at the bottom of a visual crevice created by a tree and a pole. A streetlight shines on him at a bench and table at the bottom of the shot. At the table, he sorts through papers he takes from his wallet as though trying to find his missing identification and identity in these scraps from his life, some of which fly off in the wind without his notice. His face searches for answers. When Estela returns one more time with something warm to drink that includes a "dash" of brandy to help against the cold, he tells her, "Go home. I'm good." She stays as they sip together, becoming two strangers struggling to be human and real while facing the uncertainties of the night. She tells him that she would be afraid to be alone on the street at night. When she comes back with her car to take him to a shelter, she sees that he has hidden from her, leaving her blanket neatly folded on the public table.

Still later, Agustín's body fails him. He shouts "Hey" to the guard at the Buceo who sits in an enclosed post while listening to a blaring radio. Agustín explains, "I peed myself" and am cold. He finally succumbs to his confusion, asking what to do, explaining he cannot leave because of María, and wonders if the guard knows her. Without any overly dramatic expression or gesture, Agustín's naked face appeals to the guard and the camera for understanding. He says of María, "Would she be mad at me? Could you call her?" After the guard gives him an old pair of work pants, Agustín says that he no longer can feel his hands but insists on staying. He looks off into the night.

La Demora becomes very much of a film about the night.

THE MASK

The cinematic close-up as a means for expressing the ethical imperative of the Levinasian face that exceeds visible expression along with the suggestion by directorial geniuses from Jean-Luc Godard and Ingmar Bergman to Woody Allen that the close-up reaches the inner soul raises intriguing questions about reality, representation, and ethics.[8] For Plá in *La Demora*, the close-up can be seen as key to a mise en scène aesthetic of the opening of spacious temporality. The close-up opens interior and exterior spaces for new thinking about time, ethical freedom, and relation. Agustín's expressionless, undramatic face contrasts with the mask that María's face becomes when she gets home from abandoning her father.

Brenda with her adolescent-like mixture of innocence and precocious intelligence sees through her mother without completely understanding. María works at her sewing machine with effective insouciance regarding her father's absence. Her prevarications steadily become more extreme but less believable, such as claiming that the nursing home looks so comfortable with so many nice people that her father may even find a girlfriend.

La Demora for the last time returns to the bathroom with María in the shower. The camera focuses tightly on her back. As with her father in the very beginning of the film, the water pours down her head, hair, neck, and back. The bathroom remains the place for the naked truth, for coming clean. It signifies the precariousness and vulnerability of the body with all of its openings and porosity as the home for the soul and the self. The camera holds for many seconds on María's back as the water beats down on her. Plá then cuts to a truly agonizing exposure of María. With her head down and hair soaking wet, her back and shoulders hunched over, and her neck pinched, her face evinces unmitigated torture. The pose holds for many seconds and delayed cinema accentuates and examines the tension. She looks frozen and dead, a figure of the terror and the agony of inescapable guilt.

Finished with her shower, she packs a leather case of belongings, including medicine, to take to her father under the assumption that the authorities have brought him safely to a nursing home. To her surprise, she finds the youngest child, Fabri, awake and looking to give her things to take to the old man. The sick look of guilt and shame on her face worsens when Brenda appears. The exchange of looks between mother and daughter turns into a sad appeal from María for silence, understanding, and love. Brenda says, "Tell him I send a kiss."

Taking a taxi in the middle of the night to the nursing home, she compels attendants to let her enter in spite of rules against allowing such after-hours visits. To her dismay, she learns that Agustín never made it to the nursing home. She breaks from the attendants and races through the facility in hopes that a mistake was made and she will find him only to come across another old man so sick he misidentifies María as Aurora his own family member. On her way out, she gets a list of other shelters from the attendant. María apologizes, "This isn't like me."

Unable to find or pay taxis to other shelters, María calls and receives help from Néstor who drives her. At another shelter, she confesses to Néstor about her father and the day's events that "He didn't get lost. I abandoned him," making it the second confession that night of her abandonment of Agustín. She previously confessed to a shelter worker. She says to Nestor, "See? You don't know me either." Obviously, María's search for her father becomes a search for knowing and finding herself. In the absence of any mention in the film of the father of María's children, it seems significant that she makes her confession of abandonment to a man who apparently finds María and her family attractive in spite of being married himself.

Throughout the film, including the night of the search for Agustín, María feels compelled to turn herself into a fortress of strength. In order to protect and sustain her family as their sole provider, she battles any internal impulse toward softness. In the family, at work, and on the street, she tries to be both mother and father. Without any sign or memory of her husband at the house, she tries to fill that gap. The only adult male in the house, her father, has been reduced by senility to a form of infancy as opposed to paternal authority. Accordingly, in a sense, her search for her father parallels and enacts the search to compensate for the absence of a masculine presence or role in the family. To some extent, the renewal of María's old friendship with Néstor clearly helps ease her anxiety on the search. The idea of a missing male figure in the house also may be on María's mind when she informs him that the children think he wants to "fuck" her. Her comment unsettles and embarrasses him to her apparent pleasure. Hints that he provides about his unsatisfactory marital situation also suggest the possibility of a future relationship between them.

Not finding Agustín at other shelters, María and Néstor go to the Buceo. The camera pauses on a long open shot of the vacant, unpopulated nighttime street. Interestingly, María steps into the empty frame, as though signaling her need to fill a gap in her life and in the life of her family. The camera does a slow, wide scan of the field and the project. It then comes back to María and holds on her back. She turns to the right so her face shines in key lighting. She sees the distant figure of her father asleep on the ground getting some cover from the apartment building.

María runs to him and wakes him, saying "Dad" and tries to raise him from the ground by herself. He says, "You took so long." He tells her, "I was going to go home but I waited for you." She says, "Good, Dad. You did good." He asks, "Did something happen? I knew something happened." She rubs fiercely at his frozen hands and then blows her breath on them. He asks, "The kids?

Are they all right?" Key lighting brightens her face as she looks with some sense of awe at his selflessness and concern for others and answers, "Yes. Come on." As she tugs at him, helping him to get up, he says, "Wait. There's a lady I need to thank." She answers with what amounts to a new commitment to her relationship with him, "Let's go home. We'll come back. I promise. Let's go." She rises and pulls him up.

The camera cuts to a shot of the project in the dark with some lights shining from some apartments like watchful eyes. She says, "Are you cold? You're frozen. You feel bad?" He answers, "I'm good. A bit tired." They walk together from deep into the frame forward to the middle. She says, "Come. Néstor is waiting with the car." They stand together in the middle of the frame. She holds his left arm with both of her hands. She places her left hand in her pocket as they continue to walk right to the camera and block the apartment complex behind them. They walk out of the frame and Plá holds the camera on the dead space of the Buceo. One light shines brightly from the building.

From the beginning of *La Demora,* director Rodrigo Plá's visual art, command, and intelligence express and enact an acute moral and ethical intelligence. Plá's artistic vision merges with his unique insight into the human condition. His film art opens space-time for emerging presence and the ethical imperative. The elements of his film art—close-ups, visual design and structure, neo-realistic mise en scène of deep focus and depth of field, timing—construct and comprise the open space for the ethical imperative of the engagement with the other. The art of the film opens fresh ethical space for the face and intervention of the other. Throughout the film, María plays the role of the engineer keeping her family running on time. At the end, she perhaps opens herself and the family to another temporality, the time of the other, which in the end involves the kind of unconditional love that her father apparently embodies, especially in his descent into childish dependency.

NOTES

1. Jean-Luc Nancy and Federico Ferrari, *Being Nude: The Skin of Images,* trans. Anne O'Byrne and Carlie Anglemire (New York: Fordham University Press, 2014), pp. 3, 4. All future references to this work will be to this edition and will be included parenthetically in the text as *N.*

2. For a brief but informative discussion of *La Demora,* see Leo Nikolaidis, "Sounds and Colours," http://sounds and colours.com/articles/Uruguay/la-demora-18913.

3. See Emmanuel Levinas, entre-nous: *On Thinking-of-the-Other,* trans. Michael B. Smith and Barbara Harshaw (New York: Columbia University Press, 1998), p. 57.

4. Emmanuel Levinas, *Is It Righteous to Be: Interviews with Emmanuel Levinas,* ed. Jill Robins (Stanford: Stanford University Press, 2001), pp. 115, 117; emphasis in the original.

5. Jean-Luc Nancy, "Of Divine Places," in *The Inoperative Community*, ed. Peter Connor, trans. Michael Holland (Minneapolis: University of Minnesota Press, 1991), p. 120.
6. See Levinas, *Is It Righteous to Be,* pp. 59, 206, 207.
7. Ibid., pp. 207–208.
8. For a more detailed discussion of this philosophy of the close-up see my *Levinas and the Cinema of Redemption: Time, Ethics, and the Feminine* (New York: Columbia University Press, 2010), pp. 77–86.

CHAPTER 3

Existence and Ethics in the Dardenne Brothers' *Two Days, One Night* (2015)

THE DARDENNE BROTHERS AND THE CINEMA OF FREE SPACE-TIME: BACKGROUND

At the beginning of Jean-Pierre and Luc Dardennes' *Two Days, One Night* (2015), Sandra Bya (Marion Cotillard) awakens from a deep sleep to learn that a death sentence hangs over her in the form of being fired from her job. This news at her awakening sparks the beginning of a journey of initiation on many levels. On one epistemic level, she learns about the realities of an economic and political system that values people according to their economic worth as opposed to their contribution to society as moral and ethical beings. She discovers the force within herself to engage and overcome that system with her own acquired values of sharing her time and place with others. She also undergoes a journey of existential identity that culminates in a revelation of existential freedom through her new relations with others. In her existential encounter with her own inner darkness of alienation, worthlessness, and non-being, Sandra awakens to an ethical demand of infinite responsibility for others that enables her to achieve her place in a new temporal regime that challenges a way of being and a world view based on death. She proposes an alternative way, an existential and ethical commitment to life.

Two Days, One Night comes as a recent addition to the long-celebrated work of the Belgian filmmakers and brothers Jean-Pierre and Luc Dardenne. In this film and in their work in general, the Dardenne brothers commingle a contemporary neo-realistic mise en scène with an ethical philosophy of existential presence. Over several decades for film critics and scholars, the films of the Dardennes have marked a continuation and a culmination of a style, art, and philosophy of filmmaking and editing that go back to mid-century Italian neo-realism and French art cinema. The Dardenne brothers' established and widely acclaimed body of work has contributed to this film history with their innovative development of a unique, postmodern, neo-realistic cinema.

The Dardenne brothers clearly see the connection between their work and Italian neo-realism, the film movement of basic importance to the brothers' significance and influence on a postmodern, neo-realistic mise en scène aesthetic that grounds their ethically attuned cinema. They see their work as advancing and updating the older school of neo-realism. In the conversation with the brothers on the DVD of *Two Days, One Night*, Luc Dardenne makes such connections through television. He says, "I think there's a connection between our film and reality TV. It's not one of copying the other but there's a connection. I think I would find 'the way' of doing it." Luc relates this interest in reality TV to the classic neo-realism of such figures as the major neo-realistic writer and director Cesare Zavatini who worked so closely and so often with Vittorio De Sica. Luc says, "Of course there was Zavattini and neo-realism and following with the camera. But how to really follow someone without interrupting in a sequence shot, I think that that comes from reality TV and video games. I think there's a connection." Continuing his discussion of the realism of the film, he says, "As far as filming, we shot the film in chronological order and Marion and the other actors really liked that. And we really needed that. It allows the character to live her life because she matures."

Thus, in their extensive filmography of achievement, the Dardennes also can be seen as advancing what has been described in this study as a cinema of spacious temporality that engages the philosophy and language of Jean-Luc Nancy to conceive and propose a film aesthetic and mise en scène of free space-time, freedom, and relation. In this context of the thought of Nancy, the Dardenne brothers' mise en scène of opening free space and time for ethical and existential engagement constitutes a major aesthetic and philosophical achievement.

Moreover, this mise en scène aesthetic of free space-time opens the door for the ethical philosophies of such thinkers as Emmanuel Levinas and Julia Kristeva for their work on the centrality of time in the struggle for the soul and the ethical relation to the other. With widely different philosophies and approaches, both thinkers proffer insights that can inform and enlighten the drama of existential and ethical engagement at the heart of *Two Days, One Night*. Like Nancy, both Levinas and Kristeva engage and counter the ethics of the same that occurs in chronological clock time with an alternative temporal order that places ethical and moral priority on the relationship with the other.

The tight conjunction of art and ethical thought in *Two Days, One Night* reinforces the Dardenne brothers' achievement and place in modern world cinema. Film critics and academics have discerned elements in *Two Days, One Night* and in the Dardennes' overall body of work that taken together provide the basis and force for the brothers' special version of a cinema of existential freedom and relation.

In other words, discussion and analysis of the recent *Two Days, One Night* and the Dardennes' work in general tend to highlight aspects of their films that parallel and sustain the argument that their films forward a film aesthetic and mise en scène of free space-time, freedom, and relation. Such writers discuss the Dardennes in terms of existentialism, realism, ethics, mise en scène, and time, among other factors, that comport with the application for film of Nancy's philosophy of spacious temporality and freedom.

Thus, A. O. Scott in a *The Sunday New York Times* article in anticipation of the release of *Two Days, One Night* wrote that "for the past 15 years or so, cinematic realism has been virtually synonymous with the name Dardenne, as in Jean-Pierre and Luc, Belgian brothers, now 62 and 60, who have twice won the Palme d'Or in Cannes." In his subsequent review of the film, Scott repeats that the brothers "practice an austere and democratic style of realism."[1] The Dardenne films that won the coveted Palme d'Or are *Rosetta* (1999) and *L'enfant—The Child* (2005).

Providing additional historical and critical background for the realism of the Dardennes, Philip Mosley notes, "As European auteurs, their films owe much in content and form to an auteurist cinematic tradition that includes French poetic realism of the 1930s and especially Italian Neo-Realism of the late 1940s and early 1950s."[2] Mosley also astutely maintains the importance of a mise en scène aesthetic to the artistic and intellectual success of the Dardennes' films. He says, "Though they work out a script carefully before shooting, everything including the ending depends on the *mise en scène* to which changes may be made on the spur of the moment."[3]

Both Scott and Mosley emphasize the significance of modern and post-modern thought and philosophy for understanding the brothers' films. Scott notes the "existential theme of their work," while Mosley asserts that their "cinema of responsible realism" intellectually "draws them to the French philosopher Emmanuel Levinas," among others.[4] Mosley generously and correctly recognizes that "the most thoroughgoing application of Levinasian thought to the Dardennes' films has come from Sarah Cooper (2007) whose idea of 'mortal ethics' suggests that the brothers challenge the very being of cinema."[5]

As evidenced by the film's lead reviews in the mainstream media, *Two Days, One Night* constitutes something of a breakthrough into mainstream cinema and popular culture consciousness for the Dardennes, partly as a result of the unprecedented casting in their work of an Academy Award winning star for the film's lead, Marion Cotillard. As Joe Morgenstern writes in *The Wall Street Journal*, "For almost three decades the Dardenne brothers, Luc and Jean-Pierre, have been making movies their own way, with unflagging dedication and increasing distinction—impeccably crafted dramas, set in working-class neighborhoods in their native Belgium and focused on plain people living on the economic and moral margins of contemporary Europe."

Morgenstern goes on to focus on the significance of having Cotillard as the lead in the film. He writes, "Until now the brothers haven't seen fit to use well-known actors, let alone movie stars, but they changed that policy by casting Marion Cotillard in 'Two Days, One Night.'"[6] Cotillard won the Academy Award for best actress in *La Vie en Rose* (2007), the story of the great French singer Edith Piaf.

Cotillard plays Sandra Bya who felt compelled to take a leave of absence from her work because of depression. She works for a small business in a rather typical Dardenne brothers Belgian setting of a factory involved in making solar-panels. Preparing for her return to work, she learns that the company management felt that production and efficiency considerations during her absence proved that she was not necessary at work. The management gives the sixteen other men and women in the factory the opportunity to vote to choose between getting a bonus of 1,000 Euros or allowing Sandra to return to work.

The story reads like a fable or fairy tale as Sandra must try to convince a majority of the workers to vote to give up their bonus and endorse her return to work. Convinced by a true and generous friend, Juliette (Catherine Salée), that the vote against her was conducted unfairly because of pressure placed upon the workers by a foreman to vote against her, Sandra gets a reprieve from management for a second vote. She has the weekend, Two Days and One Night, to persuade the workers individually to change their votes in her favour on Monday morning.

The factual and historic background for the making of the film about the crisis in the life of an ordinary worker testifies to the concern and commitment of the Dardenne brothers to the kinds of economic and social issues that historically have motivated filmmakers working in the area of cinematic realism going back at least as far as Italian neo-realism. Discussing the genesis of the character of Sandra and the story, Jean-Pierre told Scott of *The New York Times,* "'She is a person we had thought about for ten years. The idea of a worker forced to bargain for her job not with management but with her fellow employees was a potent metaphor for the state of modern capitalism to begin with, but in the wake of the financial crisis of 2008 and its harsh, prolonged aftermath it took on particular relevance.'"

Thus, the economic crisis compelled the brothers to return to the story. Luc told Scott, "'In 2010, 2012 we really began to see the social and economic consequences and that was what brought us back to this scenario, and convinced us to make the film. There were a lot more people out of work in our area, and not only in our area.'" He informed Scott that since the film's release "anecdotes that mirrored Sandra's predicament became more common" so that "in the spring, three companies in Belgium and France had subjected their employees to similar choices."[7]

The brothers discussed the sources and origin of the film with Larry Rohter also of *The New York Times*. Jean-Pierre said, "'Ten years ago or so, there was a book edited by Pierre Bourdieu, a series of sociological studies called "The Weight of the World: Social Suffering in Contemporary Society." The book had probably 15 case studies and analyses, and one of these stories was a worker cast aside because of the influence of managers, who got the other workers to agree to push him aside. This worker was probably a little less productive at his job, and therefore that team was never getting its bonuses.'"

In the same interview, Luc noted that at that time "'we were working on another screenplay, but then, with the repercussions of the economic crisis that came in 2008 but really started to show up in 2011 and 2012, there were industries that started to shut down, not just in our region, but in France, Spain, Italy, Greece, all over Europe. That's when we said to ourselves, 'It's timely to do this film now.'"[8]

In addition, on the DVD of *Two Days, One Night*, the Dardenne brothers claim that a classic film by Satyajit Ray, *The Big City* (1963), also served as a source and inspiration for the film, especially regarding the film's storyline and conclusion.

FRAMING

Framing invariably acquires extraordinary significance in the construction of the mise en scène aesthetic of Dardenne films. Discussing their *La Promesse* (1996), E. Ann Kaplan notes how "the Dardenne brothers stage the frame in several key sequences" of the film to develop plot, character, and relationships.[9] Cooper's perspicacious and astute discussion of framing in Dardenne films "from *The Promise* onwards" also applies to the emphasis on mise en scène in *Two Days, One Night*, especially in regard to filming Marion Cotillard. Speaking of the Dardennes' film practice in general, Cooper writes, "Their framing brings fictional lives into being but can never fully contain them: their characters' bodies overflow the edges of the frame, rather than being contained within the shots" (Cooper: 72).

A mise en scène style and art of concentrating on framing the body and face of Cotillard as Sandra Bya conveys the film's story. With Cotillard's brilliant performance, the framing becomes more than the mere staging and designing of an effective mise en scène of setting, lighting, costumes, and actors, among a variety of other elements. The Dardennes' framing primarily of Cotillard creates a living, dynamic space for ethical encounter and engagement as the basis for existential transformation and renewal.

Thus, throughout *Two Days, One Night* framing the face and body of Marion Cotillard becomes the platform for a mise en scène aesthetic for the opening of space-time. The story of *Two Days, One Night* could be described in terms of Sandra's relationship to the film frame she inhabits and transforms.

In finding herself, Sandra rarely actually escapes the boundaries of the frame. In such moments, the directors position her firmly within the frame, often looking outward to off-screen people, happenings, distractions, and relations. In these moments, Cotillard inexorably deepens the frame. She opens the space to new meaning of Sandra's identity and relationships and to a mystery of meanings that challenges simple description and easy articulation.

Thus, Sandra's relationship to the cinematic frame becomes the way to imbue the film's art form and style with meaning. Film art interweaves thematic content into the fabric and form of the film. The frame in the Dardennes film encloses a question, a problem, a mystery but not a final answer, certainty or conclusion. The focus on the frame compels the film's confrontation with what Cooper calls the "film's soul" that requires in Levinasian terms the overcoming of the stultification of both cinematic and ontological sameness (Cooper: 77).

DELAYED CINEMA AND STAR POWER

Two Days, One Night opens with a tight close-up of Sandra's face in profile as she sleeps soundly in spite of the ringing of the telephone. The directors hold the enframed face for approximately thirty to forty seconds. The utter simplicity of the face and the image in the frame prove mesmerizing but difficult to describe and explain.

Holding the frame in this fashion in the very opening of *Two Days, One Night* suggests the practice by the Dardennes of their own form of Mulvey's delayed cinema. The image not only testifies to the ubiquity of delayed cinema but also to Mulvey's insight into the power of stars. Mulvey writes, "But the great achievement is an ability to maintain a fundamental contradiction in balance: the fusion of energy with a stillness of display . . . The delayed cinema reveals the significance of the pose even when the 'something has passed.' The halted frame, the arrest, discovers the moment of immobility that belongs to the frame and allows the time for contemplation that takes the image back to the brief instant that recorded 'the real thing.'"[10]

The directors halt the frame to demand contemplation of the face. The mystery of the face compels further delay in moving the image. Cotillard's genius as a proven and acclaimed actress of brilliance and ingenuity to perform the role so convincingly and movingly of an unsophisticated, rather ordinary and plain woman makes her performance both the driving force and the center of stability in the film that keeps it together, thereby enacting Mulvey's star balance of stillness and animation.

Explaining their decision to break from the Dardenne brothers' usual insistence on avoiding stars in their work, Jean-Pierre told Rohter, "It's true, at the start, we did want to work with a star. We wanted to see if it was possible to integrate a star into our family and to see if she would be able to function as a member. We'd seen her in a number of movies, but said we have to meet her."[11] The widely acknowledged success of Cotillard's performance and of the film as expressed by critics, scholars, and the general public indicate the brilliance of the directors in getting Cotillard to star in the film. Certainly her triumph must be considered to involve more than the exploitation of putative international star fame and celebrity.

The delayed stillness of the frame of the opening seconds of the film opens a depth of potential meaning and complexity for the framed image as a cinematic moment that at first seems quite simple and obvious. Some prolonged study of the image, however, insinuates the need to resist the reduction of the meaning and artistic form of the image and frame to formulaic descriptions and categories. The difficulty of the attempts by reviewers of the film to describe and convey Cotillard's performance indicate the deeper complexity of the apparent simplicity of her successful rendering of the character of Sandra.

Thus, Scott writes that Cotillard "accomplishes a breathtaking transformation." He says that "Ms. Cotillard moves past naturalism into something impossible to doubt and hard to describe. Sandra is an ordinary person in mundane circumstances, but her story, plainly and deliberately told, is suspenseful, sobering, and, in the original, fear-of-God sense of the word, tremendous."[12]

Similarly, Morgenstern writes, "What Ms. Cotillard brings to the enterprise is her own depth of understanding, an intricate web of skills, observations and instincts that's enhanced in this film by her special version of worker solidarity." He goes on to acknowledge the mystery at the core of her achievement. He writes, "She is a luminous star at every moment she's on screen (the moments are few when she's not), but she is also, quite mysteriously, a plain woman who serves the story as a whole—a perfect fit with the film's style, and with the actors working around her."[13]

Anthony Lane endeavors to encapsulate the complexity of Cotillard's physical and mental achievement with details of her performance that also fail to encompass the mystery that Cotillard also suggests at the core of her character's being and drive. He writes, "Cotillard looks dwindled and drained, leached of allure by the unkind pallor of the lighting. Anxiety and depression are made flesh, implanted in muscle and breath; hence the involuntary gulps and gasps with which Sandra punctuates her speech."[14]

DEATH ON THE SHOULDERS OF TIME: LEVINAS AND THE DARDENNES

The phone rings and rings in totality for more than half a minute it rings with a slight pause for the caller's second try at getting an answer. A small sound from a cell phone that seems to get smaller and more distant with the urgency of its agitated repetition, the ring sounds doomed to failure in its mission to awaken the sleeper. The small off-screen sound of the phone creates an unsettling sensory disjunction consistent with the style of the Dardennes to disrupt and disturb through partial visual and auditory presentation.

No sleeping beauty with blonde curls and locks and shiny red cheeks that intimate sweet dreams of love and cozy warm nights under protecting covers for snuggling, the sleeper's diminutive features suggest a fragile vulnerability and smallness to match the sounds of the phone. Not so much immersed in the softness of her pillows, Sandra Bya seems part of the bedding. The soft red and blue and brown colors of the pillow cases make her part of a greater graphic design of the setting that nearly absorbs her.

Sandra finally rises to the call of the phone, shaking off her sleep. She wears a blue tank top over red brassiere straps. The small-boned structure of her shoulders, chest, and arms maintain the impression of her smallness and vulnerability. This small-bone structure of her upper body and the openness of her face without a sign of pretense or make-up suggest a kind of nudity to her, of inexorable exposure. The camera hugs her tightly in intimate close-up as she walks directly into it. Answering the phone, she embodies simplicity. Without at first naming or identifying the caller, Sandra explains she was resting—at which point a timer goes off. A pinging timer—indicating that a pizza for her children is ready—drags her into a small kitchen.

The Dardennes squeeze Sandra into a tight kitchen entrapped within a space between the stove and the refrigerator so that only part of her body appears in the frame, thereby continuing their practice of suggesting through the frame a lack of totality for Sandra's character and identity. Her awkward, partially concealed body in the frame and the lack of immediate confirmation concerning the caller, the issue, and the crisis involved in the call accentuate the disruption and fragmentation of the scene.

On the surface, *Two Days, One Night* centers on a woman desperate to save her job and find her identity and self-respect. It seems at points almost a case study of classic left-wing economic thinking about capitalistic injustice and inequality as a cause of existential alienation and desperation. While that ideological and psychological interpretation rings true throughout the film, the opening moments signal another sphere of meaning that also is consistent with the complexity of other works by the Dardenne brothers.

As some reviewers and writers have noted, with the ringing of a telephone call to wake up and the dinging of a timer, it seems safe to assume that time and awakening have important thematic significance in the film. Jonathan Murray notes, "Right from its outset, Jean-Pierre and Luc Dardenne's latest feature is a story about what people do when they cannot avoid asking or acknowledging for whom the bell tolls." Murray goes on to claim, "The real domestic alarm that rouses Sandra, however, is not that which forces her to quit her bedroom on one given day. Rather, it is the wake-up call that threatens to confine her to bed for countless days to come: the Friday evening message from friend and colleague Juliette (Catherine Salée) that delivers the devastating news that Sandra has lost her job."[15] The title of the film itself, it can be noted, also suggests the significance of time in *Two Days, One Night*.

The pungent urgency to rise and awaken in the film stems from the prevalence of death in *Two Days, One Night*. Death hangs over Sandra. Especially given her history of depression that caused Sandra's extended absence from work in the first place and that keeps her on a steady diet of Xanax pills (anti-anxiety medication) during her recuperation, the threat of her loss of work accentuates her wish for death as a refuge from life. Crying with her husband Manu (Fabrizio Rongione) about how others at work regard her, Sandra, in a depressed state and on her way to bed at 7 p.m., complains, "I'm beat. I'm too beat." She says, "No one but Juliette and Robert [Gianni La Rocca] thought about me. As if I didn't exist. They're right. I don't exist. I'm nothing. I'm nobody."

As she cries, Manu stands between her and the camera with his back to the camera. He insists, "You do exist. I love you. You exist for them too." In a genuinely touching moment and image, Manu faces her and places his hands on her shoulders, consoling her with genuine compassion and love until she raises her left arm and places her hand over his right hand on her shoulder.

Manu's love and care momentarily fail before the onslaught of humiliation Sandra first feels in her appeals to the other workers. In what amounts to a ritual of suicide and death, Sandra, after one especially humiliating encounter, says, "I'm not pissing anyone else off." She says good-bye on the telephone to the kids who are away from home. She gets them sandwiches. She straightens things out at home, including the children's beds.

In her bedroom of red and blue colors, Sandra in a red shirt closes the red curtains. The light through the window gives a kind of red radiance to the curtains as though signaling an ominous and extraordinary change in the air. She then goes to bed to die after consuming a combination of pills, only to have Manu call up to her about a visitor. Anne (Christelle Cornil) comes to say that she has changed her vote. Anne says, "I came to say I'll vote for you on Monday."

Reticent and calm as performed by Cotillard, Sandra still feels overwhelmed by Anne's decision. Later Sandra will learn that in part because of her example of fortitude and independence, Anne decides to leave her brutish husband. Anne reports, "It's the first time in my life, I've made a decision on my own."

With Anne's announcement of her change in her vote, Sandra looks gratified and then confused and ashamed. Sandra says, "I just took the whole box of Xanax." Manu asks, "And your pills?" She answers, "*Oui.*"

Telling Anne to call an ambulance, Manu takes Sandra to the bathroom to throw up. Following her release from the hospital, Sandra persists in her fight to change votes and keep her job. As Manu had said, "The only way to stop crying is to fight for your job."

Thus, in *Two Days, One Night*, time involves more than a call to arms against both economic and psychic forces of debilitation. Put crassly, time means more than schedules. The film demands a rethinking of time and its relationship to death. It calls for fresh understanding of awakening as the opening to new thinking on time. As Cooper says, "the spiritual dimension" in the Dardennes films means linking the "physical" and the "metaphysical." She says, "The physical and the metaphysical are closely linked" (Cooper: 78).

Levinas's notion of awakening relates directly to the beginning of *Two Days, One Night* with the film's suggestion of an awakening to death as opposed to life. Levinas chooses, "An awakening that never stops." He prefers "an awakening by the infinite" meaning "an awakening that is produced concretely in the form of an irresistible call to responsibility."[16]

Levinas challenges what he considers to be the misunderstanding and misuse of death that serve as an excuse to fail to recognize the infinite relationship to the other. He disdains "an awakening wherein the unknown, wherein the nonsense of death, is the impediment to any settling in to some kind of virtue of patience, and wherein what is dreaded looms up like the disproportion between me and the infinite" (*GDT*: 23).

For Levinas, death as "nonsense" means that it becomes an opportunity to surrender the struggle for meaning and purpose in life. Death of the self too easily justifies abandonment of the absolute responsibility to the other.

Accordingly, Levinas considers a true awakening as new thinking of a new recuperative time that makes death the access to the infinite. He writes, "Time is not the limitation of being but its relationship with infinity. Death is not annihilation but the question that is necessary for this relationship with infinity, or time, to be produced" (*GDT*: 19).

Engaging Heidegger directly over this issue of time and death, Levinas wants to renegotiate the balance and tension in life between death and time. In contrast to Heidegger as he understands him, Levinas proposes "to think death on the basis of time rather than time on the basis of death." He writes, "Can one seek the meaning of death on the basis of time?" He thinks this "meaning" of time should be "understood as a relationship with the Other, rather than seeing in it the relationship with the end" (*GDT*: 106). For Levinas, the focus of life should be on the infinity of time in the ethical relation to the other rather than its conclusion with the physical death of the self.

"A SPIRITUAL OPTICS" MAKING THE INVISIBLE VISIBLE

The Dardenne brothers' opening segment of *Two Days, One Night* places Sandra Bya's existential journey on a level of metaphysics and ethics. Sandra sees time in terms of her own demise. She lives life as a death sentence. The brothers refuse to let her settle for that answer to her life. They insist on dealing with this existential crisis of belief.

Accordingly, as in their past films, the Dardennes proffer a Levinasian response to the paradox of finding meaning in life through a new understanding of death as a confirmation of a time of infinite responsibility and care for the other. The challenge the brothers face in *Two Days, One Night* that they faced numerous times before in other films concerns the question of how to create what Cooper terms a "spiritual optics." They need to find the means to make the invisibility of the spiritual visible. Cooper writes, "The question for the filmmakers, with a Levinasian point of departure in mind, however, is how to make optics and the visible world speak what is essential to ethical human relations but which cannot be encompassed by vision." She summarizes the issue with a question, "In short, how can their filmmaking give form to the spiritual optics of Levinas's ethics?" (Cooper: 69). Thus, the Dardenne brothers in their commitment to a "spiritual optics" invariably employ disjunctive and disruptive filming in order to resist what Cooper terms "totalizing gestures" that "reduce alterity" and "shrink otherness to self-sameness" (Cooper: 69).

For the Dardennes, the solution to their dilemma as filmmakers of making the invisible visible, of creating a living "spiritual optics," can be found in a familiar place, the face and the body. As Cooper writes, "Like Levinas, then, these filmmakers are seeking a way out of the impasse of being in order for alterity to emerge. The escape route is through the human body, which testifies to the limits of thinking and speaking, as we have seen" (Cooper: 76).

As Cooper sees the influence of Levinas on the filmmaking practice and genius of the Dardennes, "it is not the body of the thinking subject that takes them to the limits of thought, but somebody else or, rather someone else's body" (Cooper: 76). She suggests that for both Levinas and the Dardenne brothers, the physicality of the body of the other and the face of the other provide a means for escaping the sameness of consciousness and intellectuality so that "the unthought that we encounter here is the ethical relation" (Cooper: 76).

SKIN DEEP: THE INFINITE NUDITY OF THE FACE AND BODY

In *Two Days, One Night*, it could be argued that the body and face of Marion Cotillard as Sandra provides an escape route and access to the alterity and otherness necessary for a Levinasian ethical awakening. With Cotillard, the brothers film what Cooper dubs "the topography of the body" so that "the Levinasian face speaks through the movements of the bodies in the diegetic space" (Cooper: 74). In the film, Sandra could say with Levinas, "Thanks to God, I am another for the others."[17]

Perhaps the genius of *Two Days, One Night* comes down to the way Cotillard and the Dardennes create a framed mise en scène of her body, skin, and face that becomes a space for existential awakening and ethical engagement. They manage from the opening close-up of her face to maintain a distance and to establish a free space-time of spacious temporality for ethical interaction.

Accordingly, to a considerable extent, the Dardennes shaped their film around Cotillard—definitely not so much Cotillard the star and celebrity but Cotillard the actress, focusing primarily upon the body of the actress. In their DVD conversation, Jean-Pierre says of Cotillard, "What a gift she gave us. What a gift, what extraordinary finesse" to which Luc adds, "Marion Cotillard leaves behind the body she had in other films. It calls for extreme finesse. It's all between the lines. That's what Marion did and what we expected of her too.

Figure 3.1 *Two Days, One Night*: Marion Cotillard appeals for support

That Marion Cotillard leaves behind the body she had in other films, in ads for Dior and so on. That she takes on a different body."

The brothers also relate the centrality of the body to the entire filming process. Noting how they "rehearsed for six weeks" to find the right "moments and shots and a lot of time on costumes," Jean-Pierre stops speaking to agree with Luc on the significance of the body for the "choreography of the camera." Luc says, "In our rehearsals, we always begin with the scenes where the body has the most important role." He says, "[T]his is how we find the rhythm and build the shot."

Cotillard transforms the space of the framed body from a domain of entrapment, enforced enclosure, self-deprecation, and death to an opening of spacious temporality. She effects a transmogrification from being a figure of embodied despair and lifeless loss to a person of power and authority. She becomes an agent of Levinasian ethics, moving from the death and sickness of self-absorption to being the force for ethical engagement. Her body and her face in the Dardennes' frame effectuate and dramatize Julia Kristeva's belief that "[b]eauty is the soul made fully visible like a flower in summer light."[18] As a being of such beauty, Sandra awakens in a time and new body and in the glow of an enlightened face to find meaning in life through the freedom of her relations with others. She becomes something like the bird she admires while sitting with Manu and hearing and watching this bird in the tree chirping and singing in all its innocence, taking in life's experience and meaning through its physical existence.

Sandra learns that instead of focusing on finding and identifying and naming herself, "it is," as Levinas says, "the priority of immediate exposure to the Other" that demands attention. He writes, "To signify is to signify the one *for* the other" (emphasis in the original). Instead of accepting the nudity of her own innocence as the end and totality of her existence and meaning, she realizes the nudity of the other in the form first of the nudity of the face of the other. Levinas writes, "It is impossible to elude the other man in his exigency, in his *face*, which is extreme immediate exposure, total nudity—as though the other were from the first, without protection, the wretched, and as such, from the first, entrusted to me" (*GDT*: 138). She achieves this ethical clarity through her existential experience and her moment of awakening.

But she begins with cherishing sameness. Learning from Juliette's phone call that she would be losing her job because of the vote by her co-workers, she retreats upstairs, drinks water from the faucet, and goes to her bed, burying herself ever deeper into the covers. Eventually, at the bottom of the stairs of her home, she lingers on the phone, urging a worker Kader (Ben Hamidou) to support her. The camera concentrates on the isolation of her appeal. Holding the frame during the conversation for about two minutes, the Dardennes secure her isolated loneliness and abandonment, especially since only her side of the conversation can be heard. She remains small and defeated in the frame. At one point in a brilliantly controlled gesture, Sandra's fear and dread cause her to stop in the midst of the call, dredging up what little energy and courage she has to continue her appeal to Kader who simply wants to abstain from voting. She appeals, "Abstaining won't work. I need you." And then breathes with gratitude and nervous relief. "*C'est vrai. Merci! Merci!*"

The brothers hold the frame in a similar fashion when Sandra takes a bus at the beginning of her journey to find and appeal to all of the workers for their vote. She gulps repeatedly at a water bottle during this phase of her extended journey. The thirst clearly signals deeper needs. The thirst signifies internal impoverishment and the need for not only physical sustenance but psychological and moral nourishment as well.

On the streets looking for different addresses, long and medium shots continue the diminution of her size as indicative of her alienation and isolation. One worker refuses to answer Sandra's buzz from the call box at the front door, leaving Sandra especially demoralized and intimidated. In another encounter of special moral and ethical discouragement, one weeping co-worker Timur (Timur Magomedgadzhiev) confesses that he cannot support her even after recalling that Sandra had taken the blame for him for something at work in order to protect him. He says, "I'm really glad you came by. I feel so ashamed."

Music prompts two moments of existential relief for Sandra following the idea of Nancy and others of the relationship between music and the potential for revelation and epiphany.[19] In the car with Manu, Sandra complains that Manu now treats her like a child, protecting her from anything that may disturb her, such as the song on the car radio, the French version of a 1963 Petula Clark song, translated into French as "*La Nuit n'en Finit plus.*" As the music surges forth, Cotillard has Sandra break into an amazing, spontaneous smile that resonates with the promise and potential of Sandra's inner resources for regeneration. The brothers recall the moment in their discussion of Cotillard as an example of her intuitive genius and spontaneity as an actor.

The turning point in Cotillard's development of Sandra's character starts with Anne's arrival to Sandra's house to report that she will vote for Sandra. This occurs at the time of Sandra's attempted suicide. The relationship between Sandra and Anne becomes one of mutual resurrection. Obviously under the influence of Sandra's example, Anne finds the courage to leave her husband. Anne and Sandra develop the relationship of mutual support and respect that Sandra fortunately finds in the constant love and persistent attention of her husband Manu and to some extent through the support of her co-worker Juliette.

As Levinas sees it, such relationships exemplify "*copresence,*" a term that seems quite compatible with Nancy's philosophy of the otherness of existence as co-presence when Nancy writes, "Presence is impossible except as copresence."[20] Levinas writes of *"copresence"* as "their position in regard to one another, the relativity in which they become signs of each other, and the regrouping of significations—or the structure, the system—that are intelligibility and disclosure itself" (*GDT*: 146). For Levinas, such copresence entails the encounter and recognition of the face of the other as the sign of absolute ethical responsibility for the other.

At night, after her brief stay at the hospital following her suicide attempt, Sandra finishes another attempt at persuading another coworker and walks past Anne on the phone. The brothers shoot the scene in darkness with what appears to be a red wall as background. Anne's cell phone lights the scene and brightens the redness of the wall. Skin and evening darkness blend together in redness, redolent of the redness of the curtains in Sandra's bedroom at the time of the suicide attempt. Anne can be heard apparently talking to her now estranged husband, saying, "After seven years, it's tough for me too."

Anne and Sandra emerge from the darkness and redness together to join Manu in the Byas' car. Together in the car, the threesome boisterously and joyfully join together in following and shouting to Van Morrison's 1964 version of "Gloria" on the car radio. This constitutes the second instance of the importance of diegetic music to the film as a sign of rebirth and a new time. Again, Sandra's renewed energy and faith animates the joyous scene. "Gloria" becomes a kind of celebration and religious invocation to declare their joint journey of renewal as individuals and as a small community of care. Their unity typifies Levinasian "proximity" that entails the responsibility of "substitution" for the other as opposed to facile identification and empathy. Levinasian "substitution" espouses standing in for the other and maintaining "proximity" to the other but without acquiescing to a social, psychological and ethical conformity that suffocates the other with the reductive impulse toward totalization that imposes sameness.[21] Thinking of their abiding relationship to Levinas, Cooper says, "The Dardennes brothers' cinema is not one of empathy through conventional identificatory routes, but is one of proximity" (Cooper: 84).

TO MURDER OR NOT TO MURDER

Two Days, One Night opens with a scene that introduces the theme of time and death. Sandra's feelings about her life and her relationship to death force her coworkers to awaken to their own feelings on these matters. Considering Sandra's existential condition and psychological state, the coworkers must choose between surrendering their bonus and supporting Sandra or at least on a figurative, symbolic, and ethical level, murdering her. With their votes to abandon her, they choose to figuratively complete the suicide that Anne and Manu prevented when they literally saved Sandra.

At one point in the film, a worker, Julien (Laurent Caron), who resists Sandra's appeal for support in order to keep his bonus, says, "Put yourself in my shoes." In fact, the manner in which Julien makes his own appeal to Sandra for some reciprocal identification, understanding, and even sympathy from Sandra, the actual and very real victim of the situation, constitutes a profound ethical and philosophical failure. It suggests a kind of solipsistic and narcissistic view, as though Julien can only perceive his own existential crisis and ethical dilemma without regard for the other.

In effect, Julien perhaps commits his own version of the great moral crime throughout history of complicity in murder through silence and inaction. He declines responsibility not only for the other but for his own actions and decisions. He suggests the situation of the bonus gives him no choice but to condemn and doom Sandra. Julien thereby tests Levinas on the meaning of murder, leaving it up to Sandra ultimately to correct the universe. Levinas writes, "This infinity, stronger than murder, already resists us in his face, is his face, is the primordial *expression*, is the first word: 'you shall not commit murder.'" Levinas continues, "The infinite paralyses power by its infinite resistance to murder, which, firm and insurmountable, gleams in the face of the Other, in the total nudity of his defenceless eyes, in the nudity of the absolute openness of the Transcendent."[22]

Interestingly, the brothers Dardenne contrived the startling conclusion of the film with that same idea in mind of putting one's self in another's shoes, but they transform its dramatic significance and ethical meaning, making it the tipping point in the film's philosophical argument and the path to the conclusion of the narrative. As Jean-Pierre on the DVD interview says, "Luc showed up one morning and said, 'I think we need to put Sandra in the same situation as the others.'" In the same position as Julien, Sandra triumphs morally and ethically.

The dramatic conclusion marks the ethical culmination of the film with the marvelous revelation of Sandra's ethical and moral triumph.

The conclusion also marks the full flowering of Cotillard's performance with her portrayal of the transformation of Sandra's role and meaning for the film. Sandra returns to the factory for a second vote on restoring her position. After the boss Dumont (Batiste Sornin) sets the rules, Sandra must boldly overcome her discomfort with the stares from all the workers literally assembled as a gauntlet before which she must pass. As she waits for the news of the vote about her, she also confronts Jean-Marc (Olivier Gourmet), the foreman who lobbied against her retention at work. She stands up to his bullying, his lies, and deceit. She directly contradicts his lies, expressing the truth of his actions. She says, "You're heartless," a beautifully fitting phrase coming from one gaining heart and functioning morally from the heart.

In another brilliant framing of an extended close-up, Sandra waits patiently for the results of the vote. In the psychologically long wait, she embodies patience, resolve, and quiet determination evidencing her victory over the fears that once crippled her. She learns that a tie vote of 8–8 means that she has lost her bid. After thanking the workers who supported her with poise and dignity, she gets summoned from the locker room where she gathers her possessions to see Dumont the boss in his office.

The Dardennes' brilliance at the realistic cinematic compression of plot, character, meaning, and filming achieves climactic fulfillment in this brief scene. The boss Dumont encapsulates everything that the film opposes about modern life with his values, attitude, and bearing. He represents the opposite of all that Sandra comes to suggest in her own ethical and existential spontaneity. His officious and indifferent treatment of a secretary as personnel matches his attitude toward Sandra as an economic factor involved in his production costs and his factory's efficiency. After directing the secretary to check into some business matters, saying, "Ask them to explain these figures," he responds to the secretary's question about what to say if the people she asks wish to speak with him. Dumont casually says, "I'll be free in ten minutes."

Such a casual comment in such a casual way expresses volumes. He gives Sandra and her life and her value exactly ten minutes. The time once again becomes central to the film. He deems Sandra worthy of and values her for ten minutes. Dumont the time study expert makes people into figures. He controls the future by scheduling and programming his time for her, eliminating the possibility of the unexpected. Similarly, he tells her where to sit as though a prescribed seating plan exists for the occasion. "Sit down here," he says in an emotionless voice and way.

Seeing how much support she garnered from the workers and fearing discontent in their ranks, Dumont proposes a seemingly acceptable conclusion to keep Sandra on sick leave and then to decline to renew the contract of a fixed-term worker. This would put Sandra in someone else's shoes, placing her in the same position the other workers had filled with their vote on her situation. Dumont says, "In September, I will let a fixed-term contract expire, and you can come back. For now, you'll be temporarily laid off."

Dumont's proposal puts the dramatic spotlight on a humble fixed-term worker. In an earlier scene, Sandra persuaded the worker, Alphonse (Serge Koto), to change his vote to support her. Alphonse enacts a mini-drama, a play within the play, that repeats and reinforces Sandra's crisis but with the added element of Alphonse's race as a black man. He tells Sandra, "I'd like to vote for you tomorrow. It's what God tells me to do." He says, "I should help my neighbor." He then adds, "But I'm afraid of the others."

Significantly, Alphonse resists his identity as different and the other. He admits that Jean-Marc urged him to vote for the bonus if he wants "to fit in" with the others. Besides wishing to fit in and be like the others rather than achieve his own existential identity, Alphonse also worries about losing his job as a fixed-term worker, a fear that turned out to be justified given Dumont's ultimate proposition to Sandra. Thus, Alphonse's decision to change his vote for Sandra constitutes an outstanding ethical triumph in that he votes against his own interest. As Levinas says, "The fact that in existing for another, I exist otherwise than in existing for me is morality itself."[23] Alphonse's decision fulfills and dramatizes Levinas's ethical demand of taking responsibility for the other as the priority in human experience and relations.

Alphonse's decision to vote for Sandra comes as a result of the clarity and strength of Sandra's personal appeal to him. Sandra's confidence and certainty in her scene with Alphonse suggests the extent of her growth and maturity. Cotillard's understated and reserved performance makes Sandra's transition to moral authority and presence believable and credible.

In her scene with Dumont, Cotillard again exhibits extraordinary physical poise to match the maturing verbal acuity of her character, Sandra. Moreover, in this scene the Dardennes not only fulfill their own plan of placing Sandra in another's shoes to show her difference from Julien and her own moral triumph, but they manage—in an amazingly brief space and time—to establish a tension between two totally different ethical and moral regimes. Sandra and Dumont dramatize this tension between them as they sit across from each other. In spite of his exertion of his own superior position as the boss, Sandra conveys a sense of equality in her opposition to Dumont.

Dumont says, "In September I will let a fixed-term contract expire, and you can come back. For now, you'll be temporarily laid off." Dumont says, "There—that's my good news. You're staying with us."

Sandra snaps back at Dumont with mental and physical agility and authority, seeing through his moral obfuscation to the truer ethical problem Dumont's argument reveals. At first, Sandra felt a false moment of joy when Dumont opened their talk by saying that he would allow her to keep her job and will let the workers have their bonus. She then immediately changes her position when Dumont completes his proposition with the plan to end Alphonse's contract.

Sandra says instinctively without any hesitation, "I can't let someone be laid off so I can come back." Her action and position gain added authority through the authenticity of her language as a worker, as a member of the working class. In contrast to Sandra, Dumont makes arguments that remove people and the consequences of his decisions upon people from his consideration. He answers Sandra with legalisms that disregard human reality and daily life. He says, "He won't be laid off. His contract just won't be renewed."

Sandra's response turns their brief exchange into a boxing match of words and meaning that leaves Sandra standing and triumphant. The exchange becomes a time of epiphany and revelation for Sandra. She achieves a new existential presence in her confrontation with her boss. She fires back at him, "It's the same thing." He says, "No, it's not," insisting on arguing in abstract terms of language and legal authority as opposed to human reality.

She simply says, "Good-bye Mr. Dumont." The brevity of her response resounds in emphasizing an existential moral position that exceeds language and that goes beyond being to an ethical argument for moral responsibility to the other. As in Levinas's argument for ethics as a first philosophy, Sandra convincingly places ethics over being.

The final scene may be studied and considered as an example in film of a classic tracking shot that keeps Sandra in a moving frame to dramatize her emerging ethical and existential presence. The sustained enframed tracking shot gives her ownership of her achievement of her moral authority. In the tracking shot, Sandra again remains fixed in the frame as she walks and talks on her cell phone. As usual, the Dardenne brothers create a kind of disjunction and disturbance by articulating only Sandra's part of the conversation, inserting a degree of incompletion into the drama that creates a space of freedom in the scene for interpreting it.

Significantly, in this frame, Sandra's face and the movement of her body express freedom and joy. She has given up her job but has gained the beauty of her soul. She has not only found her identity and mental health but also found her place in a greater reality and time that allows for psychological and ethical recuperation and existential freedom.

Talking to Manu and reporting on the results of her meeting with Dumont, she says, "Yes, it's going to be tough, but I'll start looking today. At noon." Responding to something Manu says on the other end of the line, presumably an expression of his love for her, she answers, "Yes, me too." She starts to end the conversation, but her face changes with a sense of instinctive sureness and awareness. Her look suggests the wisdom of Levinas's visage as expressing the unspeakable. Her face enlightens the scene while her walk and body exhibit new strength and confidence. Sandra jumps back to her conversation saying, "Manu, are you there? We put up a good fight." Her smile cracks her old patterns and ways of thinking and living and opens a new life for herself and others. She says, "I'm happy."

In the final shot she walks off to a new life, showing her back to the past.

Together, the Dardennes and Marion Cotillard make a modern masterpiece of neo-realism. They consistently and persuasively enframe and position the body of Cotillard in a new kind of mise en scène of moral and existential engagement. The film itself as an art form animates and employs Cooper's term of a film's "soul" (Cooper: *77*). Rather than verbally expatiating upon

Figure 3.2 *Two Days, One Night*: Cotillard striving for identity, dignity, and power

the moral crisis and existential dilemma of the film, *Two Days, One Night* realizes the linkage of the material and immaterial through the realism and art of the filming of the restrained performance of Cotillard. The film does not expound upon the Levinasian theme of the responsibility to the other or propagate Nancy's case for the otherness of existence and togetherness. It becomes and materializes those philosophies of the other through Cotillard's embodied realization of Sandra's existential moment of truth and the ethical priority of the other. Cotillard's face and body open space and time in the Dardenne frame for freedom of thought, action, and interpretation. Under the Dardenne brothers' direction, Cotillard becomes the time and space of the frame. Art form and thematic content cohere. Sandra's final words, "I'm happy," encapsulate and resonate with the film's achievement of simple complexity.

NOTES

1. See A. O. Scott, "Cross Cuts: Specializing in Ordinary Ordeals," Arts & Leisure, *The Sunday New York Times*, p. 1. See also A. O. Scott, "What's More Important: My Job or Your Bonus?" December 12, 2014, *The New York Times*, p. C1.
2. Philip Mosley, *The Cinema of the Dardenne Brothers: Responsible Realism* (New York: Wallflower/Columbia University Press, 2013), p. 13.
3. Mosley, *The Cinema of the Dardenne Brothers*, p. 5.

4. Scott, "Cross Cuts: Specializing in Ordinary Ordeals," p. 16; Mosley, *The Cinema of the Dardenne Brothers*, p. 3.

5. See Mosley, *The Cinema of the Dardenne Brothers*, p. 17. See also Sarah Cooper, "Mortal Ethics: Reading Levinas with the Dardenne Brothers," *Film-Philosophy* (August 2007), pp. 66–87. All subsequent references to this essay will be to this text and will be included parenthetically in the text as Cooper.

6. See Joe Morgenstern, Morgenstern on Film, "Dark 'Night' of the Soul, With a Luminous Star," *The Wall Street Journal*, January 9, 2015, p. D3.

7. See Scott, "Cross Cuts," p. 17.

8. Larry Rohter, "Respect and Awards, but Still No Oscar: The Dardenne Brothers Discuss 'Two Days, One Night,'" December 30, 2014, *The New York Times*, p. C5.

9. E. Ann Kaplan, "European Art Cinema, Affect, and Postcolonialism: Herzog, Denis, and the Dardenne Brothers," in *Global Art Cinema: New Theories and Histories*, eds. Rosalind Galt and Karl Schooover (Oxford: Oxford University Press, 2010), p. 296.

10. Laura Mulvey, *Death 24x a Second: Stillness and the Moving Image* (London: Reaktion Books, 2006), pp. 162, 163.

11. Rohter, "Respect and Awards," p. C5.

12. Scott, "What's More Important?" pp. C1, 8.

13. Morgenstern, "Dark 'Night' of the Soul," p. D3.

14. Anthony Lane, The Current Cinema, "Good Fights," *The New Yorker*, January 5, 2015, p. 80.

15. See Jonathan Murray, review of *Two Days, One Night* in *Cineaste* (Winter 2014): 50.

16. Emmanuel Levinas, *God, Death, and Time*, trans. Bettina Bergo (Stanford: Stanford University Press, 2000), pp. 22–23. All future references to this work will be to this edition and will be included parenthetically in the text as *GDT*.

17. Emmanuel Levinas, *Otherwise Than Being or Beyond Essence*, trans. Alphonso Lingis (Pittsburgh: Duquesne University Press, 1998), p. 158.

18. Julia Kristeva, *Hatred and Forgiveness*, trans. Jeanine Herman (New York: Columbia University Press, 2010), p. 57.

19. See Jean-Luc Nancy, *Listening*, trans. Charlotte Mandell (New York: Fordham University Press, 2007).

20. Jean-Luc Nancy, *Being Singular Plural*, trans. Robert D. Richardson and Anne E. O'Byrne (Stanford: Stanford University Press, 2000), pp. 61–62; emphasis in the original.

21. See Levinas, "God and Philosophy" in *Emmanuel Levinas: Basic Philosophical Writings*, eds. Adriaan T. Peperzak, Simon Critchley, and Robert Bernasconi (Bloomington: Indiana University Press, 1996), pp. 129–148.

22. Emmanuel Levinas, *Totality and Infinity: An Essay on Exteriority*, trans. Alphonso Lingis (Pittsburgh: Duquesne University Press, 1961), p. 199.

23. Ibid., p. 261.

Western Spaces: Landscapes of Denial, Death, and Freedom

El Viaje:
Tommy Lee Jones and the Violent Times of the Mission to Mexico

"TIME IS VIOLENCE"

Jacques Derrida argues that the aporetic impossibility of time and of living outside of presence condemns time to violence. Derrida writes, "There is no experience which can be lived other than in the present. The absolute impossibility of living other than in the present, this eternal impossibility, defines the unthinkable as the limit of reason." This impossibility invariably commingles time with death and violence. The slippery present moves into loss and absence or fades into smothering abstraction and definition. Derrida writes, "The living present is originally marked by death. Presence as violence is the meaning of finitude, the meaning of meaning as history." This impossibility of presence and time means that for Derrida "then time is violence."[1]

The "living present" of death also means that presence and time commit violence against meaning. The instability and fluidity of time challenge the quest for meaning. Arguing that "time *is* that which erases . . . time," Derrida maintains that "[t]ime has already been suppressed at the moment one asks the question of its meaning, when one relates it to appearing, truth, presence, or essence *in general*." He says, "Time is a name for this impossible possibility."[2] As Levinas argues, time and the search for meaning can become entrapped in suffocating sameness.

Levinas, as previously noted, sees presence as "the time of the Same" that encircles meaning and encloses consciousness into a self-affirming "correlation and equality between what is thought and thinking itself."[3] Levinas strives to go beyond the synchronicity of presence toward a diachronic temporality that overflows and bursts out of the known, the same, and the thought to a realm of transcendence and the infinite responsibility toward the other.

Tommy Lee Jones in *The Three Burials of Melquiades Estrada* (2005) turns the Western into a drama of the violence and impossibility of time in its engagement with meaning. The landscape becomes a scene of perennial, inexorable temporal contention. Rather than the spatialization of time through endless expansionism on the virgin American frontier, Jones presents a boundlessly open malleable space of borderline Texas and Mexico that undergoes continuous reconfiguration by a distant, fluid horizon that stretches toward the infinite unknown. The film moves steadily through this temporally shifting space. Time functions as a player in the film in combat for survival with other temporal players. The open space of the landscape becomes a mise en scène of embattled temporality.

The initial temporal battle in the first part of the film occurs between the so-called ecstasies of time: the past, present, and future. As both director and star, Jones displays a form of delayed cinema inventiveness as he activates film's ability to manipulate time. He deviates radically from narrative coherence to mix up the present with the past and the future.

In a second phase of *The Three Burials of Melquiades Estrada*, time and space meld into a kind of vast spatial openness that absorbs and swallows time and presence. Time transmogrifies and resonates with Julia Kristeva's analysis of the Freudian *zeitlos* or "lost time" that she compares to dreams and intra-psychic operations and disorder. She writes, "The term *timeless*, which I analyzed in *Intimate Revolt*, is a Freudian notion that applies to the time of the unconscious: the unconscious is not aware of time; it is *zeitlos*, timeless, outside time."[4]

In *Intimate Revolt*, Kristeva sees "an unbound time: *zeitlos*" as part of the experience of the death of the other, especially the analyst. About this *zeitlos*, she says, "this infinity is pulled between the impossible temporalizing of the drive and the openness of working-throughs to come." For Kristeva, "being absorbed in unbound time" engenders "this experience at the crossroads of time and the timeless." She speaks of being situated in "this temporality of a double infinity—an infinity of impossibility and openness."[5]

Thus, for Kristeva the infinite impossibilities of linear time's efforts to encompass psychic drives engage the infinity of lost time's peregrinations into the unknown. Kristeva's struggles with time persist throughout her work.

Tommy Lee Jones's cinematic time experiment not only explores this highly complex domain of temporal dissonance and disjunction; it makes that journey into time by also engaging the issues and questions of ethics, morality, meaning, and belief that the encounter with the aporetic time entails. He creates a postmodern narrative masterpiece in cinema about the search for the human soul and for meaning in existence. The violence of the narrative manifests the greater and deeper temporal violence the narrative intimates and conveys. Jones uses the inherent fluidities of cinematic time to express these complexities of form and content. In the face of the dilemmas of time, *The Three Burials of Melquiades Estrada* enacts emerging existential presence in a space-time of freedom to assert the priority of the ethical imperative for struggling toward meaning in existence.

LA FRONTERA: TRANSNATIONAL BORDERLAND

The ideology and myth of the virgin American West clashes dramatically with the narrative, culture, and history of the borderland Southwest, the setting for *Three Burials*. The myth of the West proclaimed "the virgin land" as a frontier for the renewal of time and the rebirth of the white Anglo-European man into a new man, the American, who begins history over again.[6] In contrast to this vision of a pristine wilderness open to conquest for national expansion, the frontier of the borderland Southwest has been described as *"la frontera,"* a transnational borderland consisting of a diversity of peoples, including Native Americans, Mexicans, Mestizos, and Anglos.

In his analysis of *Three Burials,* Matthew Carter turns to scholars and writers such as Patricia Limerick, Gloria Anzaldúa, and Richard Etulain to explain the relationship of the concept of the ethnically diverse *la frontera* to the film.[7] Carter argues that the film illuminates the contrast between the myth of the America West and the idea of *la frontera* as a concept of cultural complexity and diversity.

In contrast to the notion of the West as free and unoccupied wilderness space for the Anglo-American's exploration and conquest, the Southwest of *la frontera* should be understood as geographic and cultural space filled with a diversity of cultures and peoples. Carter maintains "the film does depict the borderlands as an in-between space, one that is not simply defined as a line drawn between two distinct and wholly different countries, societies, cultures. Instead, it is depicted as a space with its own character and meaning, one that is inseparable from history and myth." Carter acclaims the film's attention to the details of cultural and racial identities in the borderland. *Three Burials* also dramatizes the significance of more than a century of domination of these ethnic groups by Anglo elites. Carter writes, "By applying the concept of *la frontera* to *Three Burials,* we can interpret the film's ideological agenda as one that explores the traumatic 'legacy of conquest' by which the U.S.–Mexico border has been historically and geo-politically constructed asymmetrically along cultural and racial lines."[8]

In the light of scholars and writers of the modern Southwest, the *la frontera* of *Three Burials,* as seen by Carter, offers a vital alternative to what at least in an earlier phase of American history was the standard story of the American West as propagated by Frederick Jackson Turner's "frontier thesis" of the superiority of frontier values and experience in shaping American character and culture.[9] Turner's hegemonic theory of frontier values contrasts starkly with Carter's description of "Anzaldúa's language" of borderlands reality and *la frontera* sensibility. Carter says she "elicits a powerful imagery of the border as an open wound—*'una herida abierta'*—her emotive language exploding the repressed history of the U.S.–Mexico border."[10]

The culture, history, and even the violence of *la frontera* suffuses the making and meaning of *Three Burials* as a cinematic industrial production and as a work of art. The story itself, as reported by Aitor Ibarrola Armendáriz, grows out of the relatively recent history of violence in the borderland "when a young man of Mexican descent—but the holder of an American passport—was accidentally killed by three Marines who were chasing some drug traffickers" around the time of the beginning of this century.[11] Manohla Dargis identifies the young man as "an 18-year-old Texan, Esequiel Hernandez, Jr., who lived and died near the border; he was tending goats when he was killed by a marine patrolling for drug smugglers."[12] In his comprehensive and authoritative article, Carter carefully describes how the film assiduously strives not to repeat the mistakes and depredations of the past by being a transnational film in its incorporation of both American and Mexico peoples and elements in its art form and in its production processes. Carter writes,

> Aside from the collaboration of U.S. and Mexican personnel on the film's production—the screenwriter Guillermo Arriaga, a number of the actors, creative contributors, and technicians are Hispanics—there is a stylistic acknowledgement of transnationality in the fact that the film's dialogue is in both English and Spanish. The same is true of the chapter headings that announce the sections of the film. It can also be considered transnational in its presentation of cultural identity. In part, it deals with the various ethnic groups—Hispanic, Chicano, Mestizo, and Mexican—that the "official" history of the borderlands so often neglects, and that, so the charge goes, the frontier mythology and the Western genre often reduce to Orientalist, unflattering, or outright insulting stereotypes. Not only does *Three Burials* explode such stereotypes—it explodes the whole notion of a "border" through its presentation of various characters and their relationships, all of which cross "borders" of one kind or another: marital, lawful, political, social, economic, cultural, or racial.[13]

In spite of the intensity of the effort that goes into arguing that *Three Burials* proves the artificiality and inauthenticity of geographic and national borderlines separating Mexico and Texas, the significance of *la frontera* borderline differences persists. As Tommy Lee Jones told Scott Simon of National Public Radio about *Three Burials*, "It's a study in social contrast and study of how things are the same on both sides of the river and how things are different. And what the implications confronting an international through the middle of a culture might be."[14] On the borderland of *Three Burials,* "social contrast" and "things" that are the "same" and "things" that are "different" often break into violent extremes of both difference and sameness. The history and the current reality of contention and violence remain an inescapable part of the scene and the story of the borderland in *Three Burials.*

In fact, in addition to the significance of the geographic border between countries, the concept of borders and borderline, as others suggest, remains pervasive on many levels in *Three Burials.* My discussion elsewhere of Kristeva's association of borders with the modern condition applies and resonates with considerable relevance to *Three Burials.* Her notions, as noted above, of "unbound" time and time at a "crossroads" feed into her description of modern "borderline personalities" and "border states of mind" that evoke "subject/object borders" and the "border region" of reality and fantasy of "psychosis" (*IR*: 7, 9, 10). She describes modern man as "a being of boundaries, a borderline, or a 'false self'" in a culture of a "growing number of narcissistic, borderline, or psychosomatic patients."[15] These terms help to define character and the human condition on the borderland of *la frontera* in *Three Burials.*

A DIFFERENT TIME: DIACHRONICITY AND LINEARITY

In regard to ethical thinking, Levinas, we recall, speaks of "this tearing of the Same by the Other" (*GDT*: 111). He writes, "Here we are speaking of a bursting of the Same, whom the Other disturbs or tears out of his repose" (*GDT*: 195). Tearing apart of sameness for the ethical encounter occurs from the beginning of *Three Burials.* In *Three Burials,* such tearing accentuates the priority of ethics and responsibility over convenience and opportunism. Tearing means separating from others for a moral and ethical stand. It means dividing from one's self to consider and act on an ethical calling. It involves challenging conformist thought and behavior. It suggests the necessity sometimes of taking a path deemed deviant, abnormal, even subversive and dangerous in order to follow the implications and consequences of an eccentric inclination or extremist vision. For Levinas, this tearing of the same for ethical subjectivity becomes necessary to establish the relationship of responsibility of the self or same to the other.

Tommy Lee Jones makes the violence, pain, and injustice of *la frontera* the background to violence and disruption on other frontiers of meaning and existence. Anzaldúa's "open wound—'*una herida abierta*'" cuts deep and in many directions in this film of *la frontera.* Jones shifts the film from the geography and history of *la frontera* to a metaphysical and ethical plane of examining

Figure 4.1 *The Three Burials of Melquiades Estrada*: Tommy Lee Jones makes Barry Pepper his prisoner

the value and meaning of the human experience. *Three Burials* elevates the narrative to an overarching transcendent dimension that examines the indispensability of ethics for a meaningful life.

Thus, the violence of geographic and national borders and of borders of the mind and experience reinforce and perpetuate the temporal violence of the structure of *Three Burials*. Carter notes how "multiple perspectives" and "disjointed plots have become something of an authorial trademark for Arriaga," screenwriter for the film, who in a similar fashion to director Alejandro González Iñárritu, wrote for *Amores Perros* (2000), *21 Grams* (2003), and *Babel* (2006). Carter writes, "Perhaps the most immediately apparent of *Three Burials'* narrative strategies is the peculiar temporal and spatial disjuncture apparent in the first half of the film. This section of the story is pieced together by interspersing 'contemporary' action with sequences from the past."[16]

Accordingly, the temporal disruption and disorder of *Three Burials* signals the film's commitment to projecting and enacting an ethical and metaphysical adventure into a new time that counters and supersedes the ordinary, linear time of daily events. Levinas, among others, helps to enlighten the time of *Three Burials*. He seeks an "asymmetrical" relationship to the other, one based not on equality or reciprocity but on the absolute responsibility for the other. For him, such a relationship and responsibility also involve the violence of a tearing apart and rupturing from consciousness and synchronic time that Derrida discusses as presence. Levinas avers a time and relationship based on an infinity that exceeds and devastates ordinary time and comprehension. He writes, "The relationship with the infinite is an untenable question: it is unrepresentable and without a punctuality that would let it be designated; it is outside of the compass of comprehension in which the successive is synchronized" (*GDT*: 110).

Jones in *Three Burials* employs such an uncertain "compass" as the only guide available for a search and journey that cannot define its teleology or purpose with absolute clarity because of its commitment to an infinity beyond ordinary understanding. In the face of such uncertainty, the obligation for the search persists. Levinas writes, "Infinity, nevertheless, does not exclude searching, that is, its absence is not a pure absence" (*GDT*: 110). He says "searching" would then become "the relation with the singular, a relation of difference" (*GDT*: 110). This search approaches the infinite in a way that ordinary synchronic time of sameness cannot. It involves a time of diachronicity, of disorder, and disruption from ordinary, regular synchronic time. Levinas writes, "As relation would nevertheless remain, and this would be diachronicity itself. It would be for us to think of time as the very relation with the Infinite [*l'Infini*]" (*GDT*: 110).

Jones and screenwriter Arriaga contrive a simple and economical dual narrative structure for *Three Burials*. Offsetting the disjuncture and disruption of a diachronic temporal regime in the film's first phase and the timelessness of the second phase, they employ the classic narrative form of the journey. The journey structures much of the film. In response to a teasing remark by NPR's Scott Simon that *Three Burials* resembles "a kind of road picture, not to compare it to Hope & Crosby," Jones described the film, saying

> Yes, a journey picture, really; which is an old, narrative form and classical structure wherein Mr. Hero begins in a way mundane, a rather possibly bad or evil place, and is compelled by circumstance to take a long journey through various other places. Usually there's an oracle somewhere along the way. Until finally, he winds up in a good place where he's able to relate more gracefully to the world around him having learned something and lead the audience and possibly learned along with him, or experienced the feeling of having learned something.[17]

Suggesting something of the education he gained as a Harvard undergraduate, Jones went on to say, "It's a road picture, yes, in the same sense the Odyssey is or Don Quixote is."

Thus, director Tommy Lee Jones joins philosophers Levinas and Kristeva who suggest that a non-linear diachronic temporality develops difference and disjuncture at least in part through the encounter with a temporal regime of greater structure and linearity. In the form of a binary oppositional relationship, a non-linear diachronicity can express itself against a regime of temporal structure and order. The narrative journey in *Three Burials* functions as a line to map the disruptions and disjunctures of the story's diachronicity.

The linear journey in *Three Burials* involves the search for and discovery of the undiscoverable and the impossible. The journey structures the search for a transcendent time of ethical responsibility. As Levinas writes, "A searching as a questioning, and a questioning arising prior to every question about the given. *Infinity in* the finite. A fission or a putting in question of the one who questions. That would be temporality" (*GDT*: 110; emphasis in the original). Levinas helps to explain the search for finding an impossible Infinity in the finite.

DESERT LANDSCAPE: NORTH OF CHIHUAHUA

The time of the journey in the *Three Burials* includes passage through a landscape, as suggested above, of lost time. The landscape of *la frontera* to the north of Chihuahua in *Three Burials* extends endlessly without definition toward a horizon into a greater unknown. The landscape portends a violence against time and presence as profound as the temporal violence of the disruptions of the first part of the narrative. Several commentators highlight the importance of the cinematography of Chris Menges in rendering the awesome endlessness and ingrained violence of the landscape. Roger Ebert, for example, notes that the "doomed landscapes" of this part of the film provide the workable and credible setting for the multiple complexities that the film dramatizes.[18] Ordinary linear time gets lost and consumed by the voracious emptiness and death of the landscape. The shadows and shapes of the landscape obscure meaning and direction.

The landscape of *Three Burials* realizes Jean-Luc Nancy's description of the landscape that absorbs all presence as its endless horizon creates strangeness and absence to the point of dislocating the "landsman" on a lost land. The landscape tears and shatters, divides and disrupts, challenging any temporal regularity and coherence.[19]

In a sense, Jones depicts a journey through this density of nothingness for the purpose of bringing life to the bareness of this high, deadly desert. Jones insists on an interaction with the void and emptiness of the landscape to create new life on the human level of personal interaction and on the transcendent level of ethical and moral relation. The interaction gives the journey a fresh meaning as the search for the sacred in the emptiness of the desert. Thus, Jones suggests "a catch phrase for *Three Burials*" might have "something to do with the consideration of the mechanics of faith." Thinking of the writer Flannery O'Connor, he returns to her understanding of faith as "what you know to be true whether you believe it or not."[20] Jones apparently wrote a thesis at Harvard on O'Connor.[21]

The landscape of death exists on both sides of the border of *la frontera*.

"DEATH MASK": TIME AND THE PHOTOGRAPH

The journey cowboy foreman Pete Perkins (Jones) undertakes stalls, suspends its momentum, and almost expires over a photograph. This photograph involves temporal violence comparable to the disjuncture and disjointedness of the first phase of the film and the lost time of the landscape in the second phase. The photograph impels Pete to confront time itself as well as loss, death, and the incommensurability of experience. It accentuates the learning and maturing trajectory of the journey and propels the narrative toward its climactic conclusion of ethical, psychological, and spiritual revelation. The photograph deepens Pete's growing awareness of his own vulnerability and weakness.

On an empirical and practical narrative level of experience, Melquiades "Mel" Estrada (Julio Cesar Cedillo) had told Pete that the photograph was of his wife and family back in Mexico at a place called Jiménez. At the time, both men during a rare break from cowboying sat peacefully and comfortably together under a shady tree not far from water. The photograph in strong light shows a woman and three children lined up according to age and height and facing the camera. A man, presumably Mel, stands somewhat in the background but also facing the camera. Mel, speaking with some emotion in his voice, told Pete the names of the children and the woman. He says, "The oldest is Elizabeth. She must be 14. And Yesenia is probably 12. And this little guy is Aaron. He's going to be a damned good cowboy." The picture shows a young boy with a great smile and a big sombrero pulled down to his ears and over his forehead. With a pause and a clear sense of appreciation and respect in his voice, Mel pointed out the woman he called his wife. In doing so, he turns from Pete and looks off in the distance, indicating how much he cared about and missed his wife. He says, "And this is Evelia Camargo, my wife."

Instead of affirming and solidifying Mel's place and position in the world with his wife, family, and community, however, the photograph in the last phase of the film raises not only questions about Mel's real identity and history but also undermines and impugns the purpose and meaning of Pete's journey.

Thus, when Pete and Mike reach the town that Mel described as his home, no one recalls or admits to ever knowing Mel. In a small local store, people break into laughter over Pete's persistent questioning about Mel and his family. They insist that they never knew such a person. A man in the story picking happily on a toothpick identifies the woman in the photograph but says her name is not Evelia, as Mel told Pete, but Rosa (Cecilia Suárez). Pete then goes and finds Rosa whom Mel described as his wife and she denies knowing Mel. Pete thrusts the photograph before the woman, forcing her to look at the picture of her, the children, and the man who stands in the background of the group shot. She grows increasingly agitated over Pete's persistence. Exhibiting genuine alarm and anxiety over the situation, the woman draws away, saying, "What are you doing with a photo of me and my kids?" She says, "Don't talk foolishness because you'll get me in trouble with my husband Javier Martinez." Rosa claims no knowledge of the man in the photograph. She leaves Pete in a state of total confusion about the real identity of Melquiades and his relationship to the woman and her family and about the implications for his journey over these sudden questions and developments.

The crisis created by the photograph leads Pete to change from being an agent of belief and power to becoming a figure of faith, an adherent of what Jones describes as the "mechanics of faith." Jean-Luc Nancy confirms Jones's educated insight into the difference between belief and faith. Nancy claims, "Faith is holding to an assurance about which nothing is sure, which can be neither perceived nor comprehended. Belief is an assurance that somehow gives itself a perception or quasi-perception and quasi-comprehension of the 'reason' for my assurance." Nancy summarizes, "Belief therefore comes down to a representation, even if it is indistinct, hazy, badly determined. Faith, strictly speaking, does not rely on any representation at all."[22] Pete set out on his journey with a photograph in his pocket that he thought represented Mel and his family. By the end of the journey, he must act on faith.

It comes as a matter of great significance that a photograph challenges Pete's system of belief. In a sense, a photograph itself as a form and force constitutes the greater challenge to Pete's world. The ontology of a photograph, as Jones surely knows, encapsulates and highlights the questions of time, death, and reality that the journey raises. A photograph dramatizes the whole issue of the violence of time and presence.

Nancy discusses the photograph and time in a way that helps to explain the significance of a photograph for time, violence, and death in *Three Burials*. Nancy sees the photograph in ways that resonate with Mulvey and Bazin. He sees "the photograph *itself*, as a death mask, the instantaneous and always rebegun image as the casting of presence in contact with light, the casting of a presence fleeing into absence, which one neither captures nor represents, but which paradoxically, one thus contemplates." The photograph fixes "a suspended hesitation" in time. Interestingly, he sees cinema by contrast as "a modality of presence" (*GI*: 99, 101, 106; emphasis in the original).

Accordingly, stuck on hold, delayed by a befuddling and enigmatic stilled photograph, Pete acts like a film rather than the personification of a "death mask." Instead of death, he chooses to continue the journey of existential presence and emerging being. He enacts in the moment of doubt, the tension between the stilled image and moving image. Rather than choosing the "death mask" of the frozen moment, he endeavors to achieve emerging presence in part through the awakening of ethical subjectivity. He follows Captain Ahab's dictum in *Moby-Dick* that "All visible objects, man, are but as pasteboard masks." Ahab tells Starbuck, the forlorn first-mate of the ill-fated whaling ship the *Pequod*, "If man will strike, strike through the mask!"[23] For Pete, suddenly the experience of realizing the unanticipated ambiguity of the photograph toward the end of the film educates him about masks.

The photograph's education of Pete Perkins about time, presence, violence, death, and hidden meaning toward the end of his journey puts everything that preceded it in a new light. The beginning of the awakening instigated by the photograph not only illuminates the past, it also accentuates and informs the occurrences during the journey that intimate the potential for existential revelation and renewal.

THE STORY: "A ROAD PICTURE"

Pete set off on his journey with Mel's dead body strapped across the back of a burro to fulfill the promise Pete made to the living Mel that if Mel should die in Texas, Pete would return his body to Mel's wife and family at his home north of Chihuahua. Mel wished to be buried at home near his family. The journey in fact turns out to be for Mel's third burial.

The first burial occurred when border patrolman Mike Norton (Barry Pepper) killed Mel and buried him in a shallow grave. Sitting on a slope of the open high desert landscape with a copy of *Hustler* turned to "Hot Shot," Norton had intended to masturbate but jumped up instead to the sound of rifle shots that he thought were directed at him. Observing Mel with a rifle in his hands, Mike killed him not realizing that Mel had been firing at a coyote to protect his animals. A coyote later uncovered Mel's grave and died for it when another patrolman shot him.

Following those events, Sheriff Frank Belmont (Dwight Yoakam), over emotional and vociferous objections by Pete, buried Mel for the second time without ceremony or respect, thinking and talking about him as a "wetback." Suspicious from the beginning about details concerning Mel's death, Pete learned from his married girlfriend Rachel (Melissa Leo), who also regularly scheduled sex with the sheriff, that Belmont and border authorities would not investigate the circumstances of Mike Norton's killing of Mel. Grieving over the loss of his best friend and outraged over the injustice of the handling of the killing, Pete kidnaps Mike, leaving Mike's wife Lou Ann (January Jones) bound and gagged in their prefabricated home. He then made Mike dig up

Mel's remains. Following this disinterment, Pete took Mike captive, dragging, pulling, and forcing him on their journey to Jiménez, the town Mel claimed to be his home.

Motivated at first by the desire for justice and revenge over his best friend's killing and committed to a cowboy code to honor his word about the burial, Pete set forth on his journey with a corpse and a kidnapped border patrolman. He also felt compelled not only to punish Mike and make him suffer for his killing of Mel, but—and even more importantly—to reform him, to make him aware of the wrong he had done and the crime he committed. In that sense, as Jones suggests, the journey becomes a classic quest and adventure, a journey of initiation into a new moral order.

Throughout *Three Burials*, Pete acts as a cowboy man of action, power, and authority. He worked as a ranch foreman and lived the lifestyle as such. He built a special bond of friendship and loyalty to Mel based on their shared commitment to cowboy discipline, rigor, expertise, and energy. Pete impressed Mel with his riding skills on Mel's excellent quarter horse to such a degree that Mel made a gift of the horse to Pete. (Interestingly, the horse Mel initially rode had a broad white blaze down its face while the chestnut-colored horse Pete takes on the journey has a star on its forehead.) Pete organized and managed a tryst of a sexual adventure during the first part of the film with Rachel for himself and Lou Ann for Mel. They partied for pleasure and friendship, exhibiting a liberating sexual energy, joy, and freedom with grace and self-respect that their other relationships and activities, including marriage, often denied them.

Pete's masculine code of action and independence led him to erupt with explosive force in his confrontation with Sheriff Belmont over the handling of Mel's death. He acted without fear or hesitation in challenging Belmont. He then took the law into his own hands as he invaded Mike and Lou Ann's prefabricated home and took Mike captive.

Accordingly, a man of proven physical strength and courage with a great depth of character and inner resources, Pete discovers that he cannot bully, rope, ride, or charm his way past a crisis of metaphysics and time, of existence and meaning. He must work his way through this crisis to emerge as a new man.

GLOBAL AMERICA AND THE PEOPLE

After getting Pete to commit to the bizarre promise of taking his body back to Mexico in case of his death in Texas, Mel sardonically said, "I don't want to be buried among all these fucking billboards." In the context of all the history of domination, inequality, and abuse on *la frontera*, the *Three Burials* proffers a scathing portrait of the United States of commercialism, materialism, prejudice, and narrow-mindedness. Jones depicts a society with its greatest commitment to things and gadgets and an oppressive technology as opposed to people.

The personnel and operations of the U.S. Highway Patrol and the local Sheriff's department of Southwest Texas in the oil and cattle lands of the Permian Basin encapsulate the crisis of a country overburdened with self-importance, narcissism, and the surrender of self and responsibility. The border patrol drives six beautifully kept, clean, brightly colored official jeeps and cars like mad over the rough land of the border. They drive together like a herd of teenagers trying to impress one another. The cars and jeeps take on a life of their own, seeming to congregate together like mindless sheep or cattle. The motorized vehicles form a protective shield against the intrusion of different forces and people and the environment itself. The men carry the most modern high-powered rifles with sophisticated aiming devices and firing mechanisms. They have two helicopters buzzing the landscape and checking the Rio Grande. Their sophisticated phones and communications equipment undoubtedly invariably mock them with constant buzzing and pinging sounds that send out useless alerts and messages. With all of their efforts and energy, the authorities lack the depth of character and patience that enable Pete to observe them from afar with the detachment, individualism, patience, discipline, and rigor that enable him to elude their efforts to find him.

As represented in their worst light by Mike Norton, the border patrolmen mostly hate the other, the stranger, the foreigner. The brutality of Mike's treatment of the desperate immigrants making their way across the border even offends and troubles other patrolmen, including his supervisor, Captain Gomez (Mel Rodriguez), who primarily worries about having to take responsibility for Norton's misdeeds. Thus, at the beginning of the film, Norton vigorously chases down some immigrants, grabbing and throwing down one young woman, Marianna (Vanessa Bauche). With a full-bodied blow to her face that breaks her nose, Norton shouts, "Stay down, bitch." The authorities regularly refer derisively to the Mexicans as "wetbacks" and obviously consider them less than totally human.

Julia Kristeva brilliantly summarizes the psychic and social significance of such attitudes toward the stranger and foreigner. She writes, "The foreigner is within us. And when we flee or struggle against the foreigner, we are fighting our unconscious—that 'improper' facet of our impossible 'own and proper.'" She adds that "we are all foreigners."[24] For Kristeva, fleeing from or hating the stranger involves fleeing or avoiding the encounter within our own psyches.

Thus, Jones suggests a society in *Three Burials* of escapists fleeing from confronting inner weakness and vulnerability and external demands for courage in relating to others. Norton's wife Lou Ann typifies such a situation in her boredom and lack of imagination. She limits her world view to a dread of getting fat and to finding momentary fulfillment at the mall. She fears that the highlight of her life may have been her popularity with Norton in high school. The bleakness of the popular culture around her in Texas matches her insecurity and restlessness.

In contrast to the United States, Jones idealizes the life and culture of the Mexicans in the film. He presents them more in terms of a vision of human possibility rather than as a realistic social description. For him, the Mexicans form a genuine community without fear of the stranger and the other. When Pete and Mike come across a little group of three relaxing vaqueros who somehow have set up a television set on the open landscape, the Mexicans not only welcome the two "gringos," they give Mike and Pete meat and a bottle of some kind of liquor. Mexicans find and save Mike after he has been bitten by a rattlesnake while attempting to escape from Pete. Marianna, the woman Mike slugged, operates on his leg to drain snake poison from his wound and nurses him back to health from his life-threatening fever. She then breaks his nose with a hot coffee pot after pouring the coffee on him, shouting happily, "Now we're even, asshole!"

Shown as living at a subsistence level far below the standard of living for most Americans, the Mexicans demonstrate an idealized—even romanticized— alternative to the way of life north of the border.

LOVE AND MARRIAGE

The failure of love and marriage swirls as a force at the center of the void in American culture in *Three Burials*. When Pete and Mel pick up their dates for the tryst that Pete organized, Mel expresses his shock that one of the women, Rachel, is married to the owner of the Sands restaurant where she works and where everyone meets in the small town. With some bravado, Pete waves his arms as they walk to his truck, saying, "So is the other one," referring to Lou Ann, the wife of border patrolman Mike Norton. Ironically, without ever realizing it, in shooting Mel, Mike kills the man who cuckolded him. The ambiguity of Mel's relationship to the woman in his photograph suggests he also may not be immune to committing adultery.

Mike's penchant for, perhaps even addiction to, pornography signifies the confusion of the people in the film over the relationship between love and sexuality. The one sexual scene between Mike and Lou Ann illustrates in a disturbing way the problem of sexuality in the film. After cutting his toe nails with a long knife in a rather gross image, Mike responds to Lou Ann's plans for a light dinner that night by walking behind her and checking out her concerns about weight, deciding that she is not fat. Lou Ann stares at the soap opera on the television as she prepares dinner. She does not seem to even hear Mike say, "You're my red-hot mamma," as he walks closer to her, opens his pants, pulls up her skirt and lowers her panties, and enters her without another word. She bends over slightly resting on the kitchen counter as though undergoing a surgical procedure. Her face registers pain and annoyance with absolutely no sign of pleasure during the brevity of their sex that legitimately has been deemed a rape.

The scene contrasts sharply with Lou Ann's look and behavior with the apparently inexperienced and awkwardly hesitant Mel on their tryst. January Jones transforms Lou Ann into a sparkling, bright, happy American blonde put together for a blind date. Her hair is swept back to the side in a bun. She wears a lacy halter top that reveals her midriff. She presents a charming picture. She smiles vivaciously and moves sprightly. At the motel, she takes the initiative, opening the door for Mel as he fumbles with the key. Watching Lou Ann enter the room, Mel stands outside hesitating until the camera shows her arm extended outside the doorway to bring him into the room. In their room, Mel maintains a look of shy inexperience as though not sure how to behave in this situation with a married Anglo woman. They sit on the bed looking like innocent teenagers. So unfamiliar with Spanish although living in the Southwest, Lou Ann strains to ask if he would like to watch television. She turns on the television only to instantly turn off two porno stations. Then they dance and warm up to each other as she smiles and relaxes and puts her hand on his chest, becoming increasingly comfortable in his arms.

When the couples reappear laughing and singing and enjoying one another's company, her hair has come down and her face beams with new life. She moves with the grace and energy of a cheerleader as she goes back and forth between Mel's truck and Rachel's car to retrieve her pocketbook.

As the scene concludes and the couples break up, however, Jones introduces a sharp, subtle, and disturbing note of dissonance into the pleasure of the afternoon. In a medium shot of Rachel and Pete talking together, Pete gestures with some of his own rare awkwardness, as he seems to be attempting to set up another meeting with Rachel only to be reminded that she has Sheriff Belmont scheduled in the near future. With continued awkward discomfort, he indicates "OK" but then throws in, "What about old Bob?" referring to her husband at the Sands restaurant. She smiles and explains "That's different" being her husband. Jones brilliantly conveys the hidden insecurity and lack of clarity in Pete's connection to and feelings for Rachel.

In a subsequent scene, Rachel's friendly and sympathetic laughter in response to Sheriff Belmont's pained embarrassment over his repeated impotence accentuates the dysfunctionality and disconnection involving love, sexuality, and relationships in the film.

Thus, after Mike has been away with Pete for an extended but vague time, a disconsolate Lou Ann tells a distressed Rachel that she will be leaving Mike to return to Cincinnati regardless of what happens to Mike. She says, "I don't care; the son-of-a-bitch is beyond redemption. I'm leaving him." The perfect intensity and anger of Lou Ann's facial expression and physical position matches the obvious alarm Rachel feels over losing her best friend. With Pete in Mexico, Rachel will only have her husband Bob, the restaurant owner and cook, for company.

The final connection in the film between Pete and Rachel constitutes the strongest and most painful articulation of the faded power of sexualized love and marriage as a historic way of confronting life and death with meaning and purpose. It occurs after Mariana has saved Mike. Pete sits and drinks shots at a small, friendly local bar somewhere on the way to Coahuila, apparently waiting for Mike to get stronger to continue the journey. Throughout the film, Jones has brilliantly conveyed Pete's character to the point of suggesting his interior life as well as his physical authority as a cowboy foreman and man. Jones never seems stronger as an actor in his portrayal of Pete than in showing Pete in his moments of weakness. As Pete sits at the bar getting drunk, age, wear, and tear break through his own mask of invincibility. The phone rings signaling the readiness of a call he wants to make.

Pete gets to the phone and shocks Rachel at the other end. Stunned at the call, she tells him how the border patrol has been looking for him. Pete slurs his words in response. He tells her, "Rachel, I want you to come to Mexico." She asks, "What for?" and he answers, "Marry me—be my wife." Rachel looks at the phone in horror as though seeing through it to Pete. She says, "Are you crazy? I can't do that." He asks, "Why not?" "Because I love, Bob, Pete." Recalling the laughing words she spoke to him after their last sex at the hotel, Pete repeats, "You said I was the only one you loved." Again with anxiety and panic in her voice and on her face, Rachel fires back to the phone, "Pete, you don't understand. I have to go. Take care!" A low-angle shot lingers on Rachel's face looking down at the phone with continued alarm and fear. The look and shot convey the significance of the moment. The look indicates her realization of a change in Pete that exceeds expectations and understanding.

Rachel's use of the words "crazy" and "understand" also resonate. Sheriff Belmont repeatedly called Pete crazy and clearly Pete has not understood a great deal for all his authority, native intelligence, and independence.

BODY AND SOUL: TIME AND THE DEATH MASK OF MELQUIADES ESTRADA

The crisis and failure of love, marriage, and sexuality as part of Pete's search for meaning in the face of death drives Pete forward in the last phase of the film. Pete's proposal and appeal to Rachel dramatize the cost to his psyche and his body of the journey with Mel and Mike. The impossibility of the idea of Rachel leaving her home to live with a poor, aging fugitive cowboy suggests the depth and extent of Pete's psychological and emotional damage.

Drunk so that he stumbles and sways a bit as he walks, Pete leaves the bar and heads to a shed in the back where he unwraps the grotesque face and upper body of Melquiades Estrada. He talks to the corpse for the first time in the film. Pete says, "We'll get you home pretty soon, Melquiades. Any day now." He looks at the ridiculous face that does not resemble anything human. With a note of irony and self-awareness regarding the crazy situation, Pete says, "You look like hell, son." He takes a rough horse brush from the wall by the body and goes to brush Mel's hair. As the hair falls out, Mel looks helplessly at the loose hair and brush and settles back on the floor and the wall of the shed with a gesture of depletion and temporary surrender.

Levinas writes, "We encounter death in the face of the other" (*GDT*: 105). "Death in the face of" Melquiades Estrada stays close to Pete through most of *Three Burials*. Facing death throughout the journey in the face and form of Mel constitutes a constant challenge to Pete to find meaning in both death and life and in his own reaction to Mel's death and burial wish. The disjuncture of time in the first part of the film and the lost time of the second culminate in the issue of time and death. Pete's alienation as a kind of stranger and loner on both sides of the border further exacerbates the tension of his confrontation with death as the last frontier of disjunction. In both the United States and in Mexico, Pete remains the inexorable stranger in the land looking for a home and for a place for his own experience and being.

In dealing with death and time, *Three Burials* moves steadily toward reaching for existential presence in the relation to a diachronic time of infinity. The time of the diachronic relation to the infinite becomes a way to encounter the violence of time and the presence. Levinas addresses the inexorable presence of death in life and time that Mel's dead body expresses. He writes, "Death as annihilation marks being-there. It would imply, as its referent, a time similar to a span that extends out infinitely prior to birth and after death. This time counts, and we count it in everyday life: it is everydayness itself. This time is the dimension in which being unfolds" (*GDT*: 54). Thus, Levinas proffers adhering to "a more profound, or originary, time behind linear time" (*GDT*: 54).

Three Burials hints at various points to such a stretching toward a time of infinity in dealing with the violence of death and time. This effort often entails a religious form of expressing the desire for a time greater than the immediate moment. Captain Gomez of the border patrol, for example, crosses himself at the second burial of Melquiades to the surprise of those around him.

The most impressive and moving direct encounter of Pete and Mike with a religious sensibility of the infinite occurs in their meeting with a blind old man (Levon Helm) who lives isolated and abandoned in his modest cabin on the open landscape. Listening to a Spanish radio station in a language he cannot understand but likes to hear, the blind old man lives like a desert prophet beyond language and words and strained meanings in a realm of a different kind of immediate experience and radical consciousness. He tells Pete he smells decaying flesh. He readily accepts Pete's explanation that they have a dead animal that needs tending. The man soon invites Pete and Mike to eat and stuns them when he says, "Let us pray" and holds up his hands to be held by the two men who then also hold each other's hand, completing the circle of worship. The modesty of his prayer moves both men and suddenly begins to bring Pete and his captive together in an unexpectedly human way. He prays, "Dear Lord: We thank you for this meal and for bringing me these friends and for our daily bread and for all the animals and the beasts in the field. Amen!" Given the situation and tension between the men, the old man's prayer seems to humble them, including with the irony of the word "friends" in their relationship.

The mood of humility gets deeper when the old man informs his visitors that cancer will prevent his son from bringing him the food, supplies, and care that he needs to survive; so the old man says to Pete and Mike, "Kill me!" He says, "I don't want to offend God by killing myself." With clear sympathy, Pete honestly responds, "We don't want to offend him either."

Mel's steadily deteriorating condition and the humorously hopeless effort to preserve the corpse during the journey for burial signify the metaphysical absurdity of the engagement with the violence of time and presence. The gruesome condition of Mel's face and body makes the corpse into a comic figure that mocks Pete's steadfast efforts to maintain him properly. The steadily worsening condition of the physical body suggests the need to find a spiritual meaning beyond the physical to explain and justify the whole journey and burial endeavor. Without verbally articulating a greater purpose to Pete's work, Jones's portrayal of Pete suggests through facial expressions and physical movement that Pete grows steadily aware of working for something greater than the physical that overwhelms his own comprehension. Toward the end of his journey, the effort becomes a matter of faith more than belief. Pete grows increasingly aware of being called on a mission greater than himself.

An amazing scene during the earlier phase of the journey establishes the pattern for the intensity of Pete's existential commitment to completing the adventure. Jones sets up the scene as a beautifully designed setting. It happens at night. As a campfire burns and pops in the night, key lighting develops interesting contrasts of shadow and darkness and light. Pete sleeps to the side of the scene with his head on his saddle as a pillow and without any apparent substantial covering on the ground for his body. Mike tries to sleep propped up against a huge rock that also supports the decaying corpse of Melquiades. The face by then has become blackened and hideous. Mike tries to get away from the smell of the decaying corpse and moves into stronger light in the middle of the screen. Pete, sleeping with one eye open and his pistol in his hand, tells his handcuffed prisoner, "Go back where you was at."

Back against the rock, Mike looks again at the dead man's face. He calls to Pete, "Hey you . . . Hey Pete the ants are eating your friend." Pete jumps up and takes a burning cloth to burn off the ants from Mel's face also managing to burn himself. The burning makes Mel's appearance even more grotesque for the rest of the journey as Pete continues to work on the dead man. In the segment with the blind old man, Pete inserts a tube into Mel's mouth to fill the body with anti-freeze to preserve it. The dead man's eyes stay open as though in bewildered amazement over his condition.

In such scenes, Mel looks more like a puppet than the remains of a living being. The mixture of the comic, the ridiculous, and the grotesque ineluctably reopens the question as to the purpose of Pete's entire endeavor. The face becomes the second death mask of the film to complement the death mask of the photograph. Like Mel's family photograph, his burned dead face seems to freeze time or become what Bazin, of course, dubbed embalmed time.

Pete commits his life to preserving and finding meaning behind the death mask of that face, a mask that appears to ridicule Pete for his efforts. The visual interaction between Pete and the death mask suggests that Pete engages in an interior dialogue with himself over his mission. As Nancy suggests, a death mask in itself instigates and maintains continuous veiling and unveiling in the search for truth behind the mask. He writes, "The final effect of the death mask is to mask the imagination *itself*, even as it uncovers it as dead beneath the mask. Dead and consequently, respectively, *having been*: it will always already have begun to image (itself)" (*GI*: 97; emphasis in the original). Once again, the death mask's relation to time opens a new perspective on time and being. The death mask speaks to the possible impossibility of time and death.

FACE TO FACE: THE LOOK AND THE GAZE

For Levinas, the face constitutes a key for relating to the violence of time and presence by engendering the possibility of transcendence. As I have argued elsewhere, for Levinas "the epiphany of the face" projects the "meaning of the beyond" and the search for transcendence. He says, "The face is alone in translating transcendence. . . . A transcendence that is inseparable from the ethical *circumstances* of the responsibility for the other."[25] In seeking transcendence and the beyond, the face means the human and the responsibility to the human. The human face insinuates a transcendent temporality for the relationship between the subject and the other that animates existence and emerging presence.

The concepts of the look and the gaze help to construct an understanding, analysis, and discourse on the face in relation to time and the other. In his work on the image and presence, Nancy advances the look and the gaze to help focus on the other for emerging presence. He writes, "The other approaches me face-to-face, and thus shows itself as other" (*GI*: 97). The showing occurs through "the look of the other, that is, the look onto the other and the other as look" (*GI*: 97). Similarly, he writes, "such a gaze and such a power" come "face-to-face with the one who sees" (*GI*: 92).

Thus, the look and the gaze project the interaction of the face in relation to the other. Interestingly, Nancy quotes Levinas on the face and presence of the other, thereby bringing both philosophers together in their ideas about time and the face. Nancy quotes from Levinas, "'That presence [of the Other—*Autrui*] consists in coming to us; *making an entry*. Which can be stated thus: the *phenomenon* that is the apparition of the Other is also *face;* or again (to show this entry, at every instant new in the immanence and essential historicity of the phenomenon), the epiphany of the face is *visitation*'" (*GI*: 125).[26]

Accordingly, several crucial scenes throughout *Three Burials* constitute what Nancy dubs a vigorous "crossing of gazes" and also of looks for an existential epiphany of the face and transcendence (*GI*: 111). Understood as the expression of the face in looking toward presence and transcendence, the look and the gaze in these scenes accomplish what both Paul Tillich and Kristeva consider epiphanies of a time of *kairos* when existential presence achieves the transcendent.[27]

Such an epiphany of the face as a Levinasian "visitation" happens at the very beginning of *Three Burials* in the first encounter between Pete and Mel. In the scene, Pete and his cowboys relax in a spacious, modern, and well-kept barn of the ranch. Several practice lassoing and roping. Pete the foreman sits comfortably among his men. They all look up as a cowboy on a beautiful chestnut horse stops outside the open barn door. Behind Mel on the horse an amazing fullness of bright light over the Texas landscape highlights his presence in the door. Pete looks immediately with special intensity and engages him speaking in Spanish. Mel says his horse needs water and he is from Coahuila. In spite of the considerable distance between the men, intense, tight close-ups of the two suggest the intimacy that will come to identify and determine their relationship. Continuing to speak to him in Spanish, Pete asks what he is doing in Texas and what kind of work does he want. Mel moves his head ever so slightly and with a slight smile answers, as Carter knows, "I'm just a cowboy." The sudden and mysterious nature of his appearance gives Mel a mythical quality as though coming from a different and transcendent domain.

At the beginning of their new friendship and relationship, looks and gazes between Lou Ann and Rachel articulate in silence what they wouldn't say to each other in words. Watching Rachel mop the floor as she speaks to her husband through the cook's window of the Sands restaurant, Lou Ann thinks she sees a future for herself that she dreads of loss and meaninglessness.

A powerful exchange of looks that could encapsulate all of *Three Burials* occurs in silence between Mike Norton and Mariana. Mike broke Marianna's nose after chasing her down on the border. Later, she went on to save Mike from snake poisoning and the onset of gangrene before breaking his nose to get even. In the subsequent scene after being healed and then beaten by Marianna, Mike leaves his sick bed to go outside into the sunlight and finds a circle of people, including Pete and Mariana, shucking corn. Limping and still somewhat dazed and wearing a bandage over his broken nose, Mike sits down with the group. He finds himself looking into the face of Mariana with her own bandage still covering her broken nose. The visual exchange marks a tipping point for Mike's journey toward redemption and the other.

Delayed cinema focuses on the epiphanic shock of recognition and revelation in these exchanges of the look and the gaze between Marianna and Mike. Delayed cinema holds the tension of the frame and the image for the thrust and drama of the subsequent moving image. In a way, Laura Mulvey's delayed cinema compares to the tension of presence and death in what Nancy terms "the grounding of the image." He writes that "the ground of every image" intimates "dying as a movement of self-presenting," in a sense the tension of presence and absence in the photograph and cinema (*GI*: 97). Delayed cinema captures that tension of presence and absence in the image. Delayed cinema enables crucial concentration on the image for the interaction involved in the look and the gaze. At times, such delay becomes indispensable for analysis and understanding.

JIMÉNEZ

Making their way over the rough Mexican landscape, Pete and Mike continued their journey, arguing over the existence of Jiménez after being told by Manuel (Irineo Alvarez), the man in the local Coahuila store, "Jiménez? No, not around here," a judgment confirmed by the town's leading citizen, Don Casimiro (René Campero), who tossed down the photo of Mel's family saying, "No, I don't know him" and then about Jiménez, "No, it doesn't exist around here."

Suddenly empowered and reinvigorated by the weakening of Pete's position on his search for Mel's alleged home of Jiménez, Mike still on the burro holds his arms out in exasperation as a gesture to the barren roughness of the landscape, shouting, "Your friend has lied to you." Pete answers with calm determination, "No, he hasn't." Mike screams, "There's no Jiménez, man, wake up. . . The place doesn't exist." Pete refuses to agree, saying, "Yes it does." Mike screams out, "There's no fucking Jiménez, man. Don't you see, there's no Jiménez."

Entering Pete's consciousness, *Three Burials* flashes back to Melquiades' description of Jiménez to Pete. Mel calls it "a beautiful fucking place. It sits between two hills. The air is so clear there you feel like you can hug the mountains with your arms." The close-ups of Mel as he speaks and Pete as he listens add visual resonance and a confirmation of mood and tone to Mel's words. Both men stand over their saddled horses with the horses between them and the camera. As he speaks, Mel looks off into the distance as though picturing Jiménez in his mind. Pete in turn rests his chin and head on his hands that he has placed over his horse's neck. He looks uncharacteristically wistful and contemplative. Then he raises his head, clearly indicating his interest in this place Mel describes as Jiménez. As the camera pans over the landscape, Mel says, "A stream of clear clean fresh water bubbles up right out of the rocks there. If you go to Jiménez . . . I swear to you your heart will break with so much beauty."

After all the dangers, hardships, obstacles, and challenges of the journey to Jiménez, *Three Burials* hinges on questions of vision, belief, and faith.

A long shot cuts to Pete and Mike at the top of a hill. Pete continues to move, pulling the burro and Mike along with him. Pete has pulled both all the way through Mexico—what would be an extremely impressive feat for both Jones and his character Pete. The two come to a place with some trees and rocks that appear to have once been some kind of shelter. Dismounting, Pete declares, "This is Jiménez."

Pete's imagination takes over from his sense of reality as he points out certain aspects of the location that confirm its existence and identity as Jiménez in his mind. He laughs with relief. As Pete describes aloud what he sees, a close-up of Mike shows his sense of horror. Pete finally seems to have fulfilled people's expectations regarding his sanity. The scene compares to other great mad performances in film, including Humphrey Bogart's amazing soliloquy in John Huston's *The Treasure of the Sierra Madre* (1948). Understated and restrained in his acting, Jones plays Pete as bemusedly envisioning the details of what once had been the home in Jiménez of Mel's life and family. Pete points out the house, the water, "the store right over yonder," and the graveyard. He smiles, almost giggles at what he thinks was the garden and the pleasures it provided to the people living there.

Pete then walks back to the burro and Mike, who has been observing everything, and holds the photo up to him. Barry Pepper's responsive acting holds up brilliantly against Jones's lead. Pete tells Mike it all looks just like the contents of the picture; but a shot of the photo reveals that Pete holds it on its side so that it turns and distorts the image's reality. From his place on the burro, Mike looks over the photo and Pete's outstretched hand and into Pete's face, registering not only a touch of humanity but also self-concern over Pete's mental state. He nods in agreement and says calmly but with a touch of wonderment, "You found it, Pete."

A lovely soundtrack accompanies the men as they work to build a kind of sanctuary for Melquiades. They knot branches and twigs together for the shelter. Mike pushes wet dirt into the crevices between the rocks of the shelter and Pete hangs a sign that says "Jiménez Coahuila." Mike nods his approval and Pete walks down from the top of the new structure and sits next to his captive. The two of them sit together with Pete's arm over Mike's shoulders. Pete takes a drink of whiskey from the bottle Mike offers him and then—with a smile and his arm still over and around Mike's shoulders—tells him, "You have a grave to dig!"

All that done, including the third burial, Pete's mood changes. He grabs Mike and pushes him to a kneeling position by a tree onto which he places the photo of Mel and the family. He demands first in Spanish for Melquiades and then in English, "Ask for forgiveness." He repeats to Mike's confusion, "Ask for forgiveness right now or go to hell right now!" He takes out his revolver as Mike protests, "I don't believe in hell." Pete fires over Mike's head into the tree. He fires the gun into the ground all around Mike's kneeling position as Mike screams in terror.

Mike then breaks down, holding out his extended arm to Pete. In this scene, Pepper manages through his acting to transform the perfectly despicable and selfish character of Mike Norton into a sympathetic and renewed human being. Earlier, Mike had evidenced definite signs of trauma over killing Mel, such as deep depression after the event and associating the red of Lou Ann's skirt with Mel's blood. Such moments add psychological realism and complexity to his character. Only at the end with Pete's instigation and violent insistence does the trauma become true mourning and regret. Thus, at the sight of the burial and sanctuary, Mike cries, "I swear to God, I'm sorry." The camera closes in tightly on Mike in agony on the ground. "I swear to God. I swear to God, I did not mean to kill him." He cries on his knees, turning slightly to Pete who looks down on him. Mike appeals, "It was a mistake."

Pete turns and walks away as Mike continues, "I didn't want it to happen." With Pete no longer in the scene or shot, Mike looks up to the photo, saying, "It hurt me. I regret it every single day." He cries up to the picture in genuine sorrow and pain. In a close-up of Mike on his knees, he prays for forgiveness. He holds his arms up to the photo and then with head bowed covers his head with his hands. He says, "Forgive me, Forgive me . . . Melquiades . . . For taking your life, forgive me."

An overlapping fade out shows nighttime and Mike with a blanket leaning fast asleep on the rocks of the sanctuary. The camera moves in tight on Mike finally at peace. The camera tilts up over the rocks and to the hillside above with Pete standing by himself near a campfire in key light and looking into the distance thinking over what has been accomplished. He stands and exists at that moment on an elevated plane, occupying a place between existential fulfillment and spiritual transcendence.

At daybreak, Pete kicks with impatience but not with anger at Mike's foot to wake him. Pete looks down at his captive, saying, "You can go now." Waking up, Mike looks confused as the morning light floods his face. After a beautifully timed long pause and a look of bewilderment, Mike asks, "Where?" Pete answers, "To your wife," and then looks off, understanding the uncertainty of Mike's marital situation and adds—"Wherever." Mike admits, "I always thought you'd end up killing me." Pete, looking down as though speaking to a child, says, "You can keep the horse," and after another beautifully timed pause adds, "son."

Pete walks off, mounts the burro, and enters into the brush and woods as the horse whinnies and Mike moves forward into stronger light with a look of concern on his face that has not appeared there before in the film. Mike then calls out from his deepest being to the disappearing back of Pete, "You gonna be all right?"

Pete and Mike prove Lou Ann wrong; Mike could be redeemed, transformed to believe in something greater than himself and to put the thought of someone else's safety and life ahead of his own. Levinas, we recall, says, "The fact that in existing for another, I exist otherwise than in existing for me is morality itself."[28] Pete has been terrorized and tormented into caring for someone more than himself. Existence in terms of the other for Levinas makes transcendence possible. Mike comes to see Jiménez because he helped to build it; but truly seeing it requires seeing it through different eyes. Here, too, Levinas's words seem worth repeating: "The vision of God is a moral act. This optics is an ethics."[29] If Mike achieves a form of redemption that Lou Ann thought impossible, Pete learns about a paternal love of absolute responsibility and care for the other that transcends the law, common sense, and perhaps even sanity. In the absence of women, the men find redemption through one another. For both men the disjunctive and disruptive time of the other enables emerging existential presence through the transcendent ethical relation to the other.

NOTES

1. See Jacques Derrida, "Violence and Metaphysics: An Essay on the Thought of Emmanuel Levinas," in *Writing and Difference*, trans. Alan Bates (Chicago: University of Chicago Press, 1978), pp. 132, 133.

2. Jacques Derrida, *Margins of Philosophy*, trans. Alan Bates (Chicago: University of Chicago, 1982), pp. 53 n.32, 55; emphasis in the original.

3. Emmanuel Levinas, *God, Death, and Times*, trans. Beettino Bergo (Stanford: Stanford University Press, 2000), pp. 205, 195. All future references to this work will be to this edition and will be included parenthetically in the text as *GDT*.

4. Julia Kristeva, *Hatred and Forgiveness*, trans. Jeanine Herman (New York: Columbia University Press, 2010), p. 285; emphasis in the original.

5. Julia Kristeva, *Intimate Revolt: The Powers and Limits of Psychoanalysis*, trans. Jeanine Herman (New York: Columbia University Press, 2002), p. 40. All future references to this work will be to this edition and will be included parenthetically in the text as *IR*.

6. Classic works for the development of this thesis include Henry Nash Smith, *The Virgin Land: The American West as Symbol and Myth* (Cambridge, MA: Harvard University Press, 1950); R. W. B. Lewis, *The American Adam: Innocence, Tragedy, and Tradition in the Nineteenth Century* (Chicago: University of Chicago Press, 1955); Richard Slotkin, *Regeneration through Violence: The Mythology of the American Frontier, 1600–1860* (Middletown: Wesleyan University Press, 1973); Annette Kolodny, *The Lay of the Land: Metaphor as Experience and History in American Life and Letters* (Chapel Hill: University of North Carolina Press, 1975). See also, the discussion of Wai-chee Dimock, *Empire for Liberty: Melville and the Poetics of Individualism* (Princeton: Princeton University Press, 1989) in the preceding chapter of this work.

7. See Matthew Carter, "'I'm Just a Cowboy': Transnational Identities of the Borderlands in Tommy Lee Jones," *The Three Burials of Melquiades Estrada, European Journal of American Studies*, vol. 7, no. 1 (spring 2012): 2–15. See also Patricia N. Limerick, *Something in the Soil: Legacies and Reckonings in the New West* (London: Norton, 2000); Patricia N. Limerick, *The Legacy of Conquest: The Unbroken Past of the American West* (London: Norton, 1987); Gloria Anzaldúa, *Borderlands-la Frontera: the New Mestiza* (San Francisco: Aunt Lute Books, 1999); Richard W. Etulain, *Re-imagining the Modern American West: A Century of Fiction, History, and Art* (Tucson: University of Arizona Press, 1996). See also Aitor Ibarrola Armendáriz, "On Third Thoughts: The Ambivalence of Border Crossing in Tommy Lee Jones," *The Three Burials of Melquiades Estrada, Journal of English Studies*, vol. 11 (2013): 149–170.

8. Carter, "'I'm Just a Cowboy,'" p. 5.

9. See Frederick Jackson Turner, "The Significance of the Frontier in American History," in *Frontier and Section: Selected Essays of Frederick Jackson Turner*, ed. Ray Allen Billington (Englewood Cliffs: Prentice-Hall, 1961).

10. Carter, "'I'm Just a Cowboy,'" p. 4.

11. Armendáriz, "On Third Thoughts," p. 152.

12. See Manohla Dargis, "Dead Man Rising: An Odyssey in Texas," review of *The Three Burials of Melquiades Estrada*, Film Review, *The New York Times*, December 14, 2005, http://www.nytimes.com/2005/12/14/movies/dead-man-rising-an-odyssey-in-texas.html?_r=0

13. Carter, "'I'm Just a Cowboy,'" p. 2.

14. Jones with Scott Simon on "Weekend Edition Saturday," NPR, January 28, 2006.

15. See Julia Kristeva, *New Maladies of the Soul*, trans. Ross Guberman (New York: Columbia University Press, 1995), pp. 7, 178. All subsequent references to this work will be to this edition and will be noted parenthetically in text as *NMS*. For my previous discussion of Kristeva in these terms see my *Clint Eastwood's America* (Cambridge: Polity, 2013).

16. Carter, "'I'm Just a Cowboy,'" pp. 5, 6.

17. "Weekend Edition Saturday," January 28, 2006.

18. See Roger Ebert, review of *The Three Burials of Melquiades Estrada* in the *Chicago Sun-Times*, February 3, 2006 quoted in Armendáriz, "On Third Thoughts," p. 155.

19. See Jean-Luc Nancy, *The Ground of the Image*, trans. Jeff Fort (New York: Fordham University Press, 2005), pp. 58–61. See also the discussion of Nancy and the landscape in the preceding chapter of this work. All future references to this work will be to this edition and will be quoted parenthetically in text as *GI*.

20. "Weekend Edition Saturday," January 28, 2006.

21. See Josh Hurst, "*The Three Burials of Melquiades of Estrada*," *Christianity Today*, February 3, 2006; http://www.christianitytoday.com/ct/2006/februaryweb-only/threeburials.html

22. Jean-Luc Nancy, *Adoration: The Deconstruction of Christianity II*, trans. John McKeane (New York: Fordham University Press, 2013), p. 88.

23. Herman Melville, *Moby-Dick*, eds. Harrison Hayford and Hershel Parker (New York: Norton, 1967), p. 144.

24. Julia Kristeva, *Strangers to Ourselves*, trans. Leon S. Roudiez (New York: Columbia University Press, 1991), pp. 191, 192.

25. Emmanuel Levinas, *Outside the Subject*, trans. Michael B. Smith (Stanford: Stanford University Press, 1993), pp. 94–95. See also my *Levinas and the Cinema of Redemption: Time, Ethics, and the Feminine* (New York: Columbia University Press, 2010); emphasis in the original.

26. See Emmanuel Levinas, *Humanism of the Other*, trans. Nidra Poller (Urbana: University of Illinois Press, 2003), p. 31; emphasis in the original.

27. See Paul Tillich, *The Eternal Now* (New York: Charles Scribner's Sons, 1963), pp. 126, 130, 131. See also Julia Kristeva, *The Incredible Need to Believe*, trans. Beverley Bie Brahic (New York: Columbia University Press, 2009), pp. 30–31.

28. Emmanuel Levinas, *Totality and Infinity: An Essay on Exteriority*, trans. Aphonso Lingis (Pittsburgh: Duquesne University Press, 1969), p. 261.

29. Emmanuel Levinas, "For a Jewish Humanism," in *Difficult Freedom: Essays on Judaism*, trans. Seán Hand (Baltimore: Johns Hopkins University Press, 1990), p. 275.

CHAPTER 5

The American Way: Time, Death and Resurrection in Iñárritu's Western Masterpiece

THE REVENANT (2015): TEMPORAL DUALITY AND THE "VIOLENCE OF THE IMAGE"

With *The Revenant*, Alejandro González Iñárritu directed a historic revision of the Western genre for our times. Over the history of film, the Western has changed with the creative and intellectual imagination of filmmakers such as Tommy Lee Jones with *The Three Burials of Melquiades Estrada* (2005) as well as with the interests and impulses of the public. Iñárritu in *The Revenant* reimagines and reinvents the Western, positioning it in a new dimension of mythical, mystical, and metaphysical interaction and meaning. Under Iñárritu's direction and Emmanuel Lubezki's celebrated cinematography, the film's innovative and creative audio-visual artistry shows rather than merely states and claims a reenvisioning and rethinking of the historic American grand narrative of regeneration through violence on the frontier.

The Revenant tells the story of scout, trapper, and legendary frontiersman Hugh Glass, as played by Leonardo DiCaprio, on the American high plains frontier during 1823. Iñárritu and Mark L. Smith adapted and co-wrote the screenplay from Michael Punke's novel (*The Revenant: A Novel of Revenge*) (2002), which was based on the real-life exploits of the actual frontiersman. It was filmed primarily on the American and Canadian Northwest but also on other worldwide locations such as Argentina. Apparently, Iñárritu and his crews went wherever enough snow could be found to authenticate the setting, a search allegedly made necessary by the damage done to the climate by global warming, as DiCaprio claimed when accepting the Academy Award for his performance in the film.

Iñárritu's achievement in taking the Western genre to new levels of art and meaning rests to a considerable extent upon the temporal aesthetic he establishes for the film. Laura Mulvey's theory of delayed cinema explains the importance to *The Revenant* of the tension between the stilled frame image and the moving image. Iñárritu creates a careful and rigorous interaction for, in Mulvey's phrase, "the blending of two kinds of time" of stillness and movement. Consistently throughout *The Revenant*, the basic digital technology of delayed cinema demonstrates how brilliantly constructed framed images in relation to the moving image in the film engender temporal and spatial conditions for emerging existential presence. Mulvey writes, "New moving image technologies, the electronic and the digital, paradoxically allow an easy return to the hidden stillness of the film frame." She says that "the frozen frame restores to the moving image the heavy presence of passing time and of . . . mortality."[1]

Filming generally in chronological order and natural light, Iñárritu maintains a precisely timed rhythm between the linear narrative of *The Revenant* and a steady continuum of moving and stationary long takes of extraordinary images and visualizations that compel a balance between detached thought and deeper immersion, something like Mulvey's contrast between pensive and possessive spectatorship (*D24*: 161–196). In his filming and direction, Iñárritu exhibits extraordinary visual command and intelligence in ranging between sweeping and encompassing panoramas and intimately detailed images and scenes. The temporal fluidities of delayed cinema enable close study of stillness and the moving image in *The Revenant*. This temporal dynamism dramatizes emerging existential presence and opens the cinematic image to the infinity that the mortality of the photographic image and absence and presence suggest.

Mulvey almost could be anticipating the raging river, the magnificent forested wilderness, and the cracking and swaying in the wind of gigantic fir and pine trees in *The Revenant* when she writes, "Unlike the photograph, a movie watched in the correct conditions (24 frames a second, darkness) tends to be elusive. Like running water, fire or the movement of trees in the wind, this elusiveness has been intrinsic to the cinema's fascination and its beauty. The insubstantial and irretrievable passing of the celluloid film image is in direct contrast to the way that the photograph's stillness allows time for the presence of time to emerge within the image" (*D24*: 66). Referencing major French philosopher and film theorists, she asserts that "the frozen frame restores to the moving image the heavy presence of passing time and of the mortality that [André] Bazin and [Roland] Barthes associate with the still photograph" (*D24*: 66).

The emphasis on such temporal dynamics and dramatics of stillness and the moving image contrasts with the overt temporal manipulation of other Iñárittu films that were written by Guillermo Arriaga, who also wrote the screenplay for *The Three Burials of Melquiades Estrada*. The earlier three films that involved collaboration between Iñárritu and Arriaga were *21 Grams* (2003),

Babel (2006), and *Amores Perros* (2000). These films exhibited a temporal aggression and disjunction that gets muted in *The Revenant*.

Iñárritu's contrasting temporal regimes in *The Revenant*, as expressed by delayed cinema, make the film into a felt and lived experience on many levels. The film triumphs in conveying the pain, turmoil, terror, and coarseness of life under primitive frontier conditions. Dirt, mud, and filth become tangible and palpable. Danger and death lurk everywhere. Individually and collectively, for the men on the frontier every effort, activity, and action demand energy, commitment, and imagination. Iñárritu's camera intimately details the pain and difficulty involved in the struggle for survival. Truly exceptional filming with enthralling multiple combinations of moving camera shots, sweeping shots, long takes, ground-level shots, aerial shots, close filming, and panoramic views all coupled with an ingenious use of sound reminiscent of Iñárritu's innovations with sound in *Birdman* (2014) make *The Revenant* a genuine achievement of modern filmmaking.

In *The Revenant*, what Jean-Luc Nancy terms "the violence of the image" relates to the concerns of Derrida and Levinas over the violence of time. Nancy's extensive argument about the violence of the image resonates with the violence of time as studied by Derrida and Levinas. For Nancy, "the extreme violence of *cruelty* hovers at the edge of the image, of all images." He says, "Perhaps every image borders on cruelty."[2] As in the case of the violence of time, the paradox of presence plays a central role in the dynamic of the violence of the image. Regarding the struggle of the image with presence, Nancy asserts, "The image disputes the presence of the thing. In the image, the thing is not content simply to be; the image shows *that* the thing is and *how* it is" (*GI*: 21; emphasis in the original). Also like the violence of time, the image engages the complexity of presence. Thus, for Nancy, image operates through self-division based on the difference between the image and thing. He writes, "The image is a thing that is not the thing; it distinguishes itself from it, essentially" (*GI*: 2).

THE TRAPPER AND THE PAWNEE HEALER–I

The concentration on the image as an aesthetic and metaphysical matter of death and life occurs in a particularly interesting extended sequence toward the middle of *The Revenant* with the emergence of fur trapper Glass from a freezing, surging wilderness river. Glass fled into the river and the rapids to escape screaming Arikara warriors. Crippled and hindered with noxiously open and deep wounds from an encounter with a bear, Glass went down the rushing rapid waters like a free-floating human log covered in his heavy bear fur coat and other frontier clothing. Glass moved from the river, stumbled on

Figure 5.1 *The Revenant*: Leonardo DiCaprio struggles for survival and regeneration in the wilderness

to the snow-covered riverbank, and collapsed as part of an ongoing pattern of resurrection in the film.

After a break into another storyline track of the film, *The Revenant* returns to Glass on the riverbank and the emphasis on a series of powerful images that supersede the linear narrative. He builds a fire, marvels at shooting stars falling from the vast sky, and then looks up to observe a horrifying triangular mound of bones much higher than he that turns out to be part of a dream sequence. In the dream, his face then appears from behind and within a death mask of bones that seems to speak directly to Nancy's point about the cruelty of images in time when he notes that "the death mask makes the 'image' of death visible" (*GI*: 24).

As though confirming the significance of the mask for presenting death, Glass's dream cuts to the corpse of Glass's Pawnee wife (Grace Dove) killed in the midst of a raid on her burning village by uniformed soldiers, probably Americans. Glass in the dream points his fire piece at a soldier with blood-soaked upturned hands. Then flickering images of running river water that turn red with blood flow over Glass's sleeping face while the back of his head rests on rocks. He awakens shivering with fever and the freezing cold on the riverbank.

Rising and trembling, Glass goes back into the freezing waters to use a makeshift wooden spear to catch a fish in a little dam of rocks that he con-structed. He eats the fish raw in one of the scenes of wilderness survival and life that has attracted so much attention from critics and viewers for its realism and authenticity.

This series of images builds toward the longer segment that encapsulates the artistic triumph and historic achievement of *The Revenant*. Leaving his fire behind, Glass with the aid of a walking stick, makes his way up the snow-covered incline that rises from the riverbank. In a long take, a beautiful medium–long shot tracks Glass up the hill. Rolling snow-covered hillside and naked brush and tree limbs mark the space between the camera and Glass.

Following a consistent pattern in the film of ground and low-level shooting, the camera conveys a sense of deep immergence into the landscape. The camera zooms in slowly over the rough landscape, keeping Glass to the left of the frame and somewhat blocked out by intervening brush and branches with rising levels of hillside and mediating crevices and crannies to the right of the frame immediately before the camera.

Holding-delaying the frame emphasizes Glass's painful movement and the difficulty of the terrain. Trapper and tracking camera continue up the grade with a magnificent tree momentarily blocking him out completely. The wind howls through the trees, but beneath that sound, another, deeper growl as a kind of undertone breaks through the noise. Glass pulls on branches and limbs to make his way to the top of the hillside to discover the source of the sound.

At the top of the hillside, camera and Glass meet for an amazing close-up. Glass's beard seems to be part of his bear coat. Tangles of dirt-encrusted hair cover his dirt-covered face. In the background of the framed image, light-blue sky with wisps of clouds extends to the horizon.

A freeze frame captures the intensity of Glass's look into the distance. The camera then moves even closer to the face of the trapper and turns to the right to encompass his look. Glass's face in profile appears at the very edge of the frame while almost the entirety of the rest of the image reveals what he sees: a herd of buffalo under attack by wild wolves. Again, freezing the frame emphasizes the tension between the close-up and the contents of the image.

The scene continues to prove Iñárritu's and Lubezki's brilliant talents and gifts for visually designing and constructing amazing outdoor scenes and panoramas that work as part of the cinematic drama and vision without ever becoming mere spectacle and decoration. The special genius of this particular scene that are characteristic of this director and his cinematographer in *The Revenant* concerns the visualization of the tension between Glass and the landscape. As director and filmmaker, Iñárritu humanizes the deadly dangerous landscape and the meaning of the landscape to the human subject by concentrating on the intensity of Glass's perspective and relationship to the environment.

Moreover, coming at the end of the tracking shot up the hill, the stilled frame holds and maintains the intensity of the visual image. The still image then moves to incorporate the sight of wolves overcoming a buffalo that falls to the ground. The camera proceeds to encompass the landscape, ultimately circling back to Glass in an existential moment of revelation. Looking off to the open sky, Glass falls to his knees.

Iñárritu cuts to night-time and holds his shot for at least ten straight seconds on a light in the distant sky that burns in the middle of a circular opening in the clouds, perhaps an omen of significance and recognition for those looking for it. In another tight close-up, Glass sleeps on the ground and snores until woken by the sound of wolves and a man's shouts.

Glass twists around and looks upon another amazing image to match the image that took him to sleep. In a long shot, fires burn around the dead buffalo carcass to ward off preying wolves, at least one of which runs away with flames shooting from its hide. Glass sees a man on the other side of the dead buffalo and begins moving toward him.

The camera again tracks Glass but this time from behind the trapper as he makes his way to uncooked raw buffalo meat. The camera stays with Glass as Iñárritu continues a style of in-depth, deep-focus shooting of a long take. The space-time of the mise en scène creates the visual and psychological tension for existential emergence.

The haunting image of the stilled frame places Glass's back, centered at the bottom of the frame, in desperate tension to reach the middle ground of the frame where the stranger sits eating the fresh raw meat of the buffalo. The stranger sits on the farther side of the buffalo opposite Glass with the stranger's own back to the open space of the landscape at the top of the stilled frame.

A shot from the position of the strange man shows him eating from the cavity of the dead buffalo's carcass as Glass approaches him. At first threatening Glass with his bow and arrow, the man throws Glass a hunk of meat that reportedly, according to Jonathan Romney, was actual "raw bison liver" rather than fake offal at DiCaprio's alleged insistence in order to gain the experience and sensibility for a "convincing" performance.[3] Both men continue to devour their meal from the insides of the dead buffalo.

Showing the man the grizzly bear claws he wears as a trophy, Glass explains about his severe wounds that after being attacked and mauled by the grizzly bear, his men left him to die; they also killed his son Hawk (Forrest Goodluck) who was shown staying on with Glass earlier in the film to protect and help him. Also a Pawnee like Glass's wife and son, the man named Hikuc (Arthur Red Cloud) says, "I lost my family too. Sioux killed my people. I'm going south to find more Pawnee." Hikuc says, "My heart bleeds."

Filmed in a low-angle close-up as he tells his story, Hikuc's rough appearance, facial scars, and gruff demeanor fortunately keep him from becoming portrayed sentimentally as a typically romanticized picture of the classic, friendly Native Americans in film and literature. Red Cloud's genuine Native

American identity and background also give his character, the Pawnee warrior Hikuc, a quality of authenticity.

After telling his story, Hikuc turns sharply to his left and walks with his back to the camera between the dead buffalo and Glass seated on the ground. He then speaks what becomes a key theme and moral of *The Revenant*. He says, "But revenge is in the creator's hands." Significantly, Hikuc speaks these words with his back to the camera. The absence of facial gestures when speaking the lines accentuates and universalizes the spoken words while also depersonalizing and abstracting the statement to a degree. Glass's face in profile, however, remains in the frame with a look of concentration that suggests his consideration of Hikuc's message. He clearly internalizes what he hears from the grieving Pawnee warrior.

Hikuc's words and message pertain with special potency to Glass who seeks revenge and vengeance on the two men who abandoned him in the wilderness and also killed his son. Those crimes of murder and abandonment were made after Glass's party of fur traders were ambushed by Arikara warriors, who also are dubbed "Ree" warriors by the frontiersman. The attack by the Rees and the subsequent flight deeper into the wilderness by the trappers left the frightened men in a state of disarray and confusion about their location and the best way back over the mountains to the fur company's Fort Kiowa with what remained of their fur pelts.

In the midst of such shared fears, an amazing computer-generated bear attack on Glass left him mauled, brutalized, and torn up with gaping wounds, scars, and cuts, and literally on the verge of death. Using his hunting knife to strike madly at the attacking animal, Glass managed to kill the bear but wound up buried beneath the dead carcass. The other trappers had to pull Glass out from underneath the bear. The cries of the dead bear's hungry and abandoned cubs added a touch of accentuated loss and pathos to the scene.

Given the dangerous conditions and the near impossibility of hauling the weight of the stricken scout over the wilderness and mountains in terrible weather, the leader of the group, Captain Andrew Henry (Domhnall Gleeson), decided to leave Glass behind for burial in anticipation of his imminent demise. He placed Glass under the care of two of the trappers, John Fitzgerald, played by Tom Hardy to perfection as the embodiment of pure evil. Hardy makes Fitzgerald into a convincing force of violence and nihilism. Fitzgerald accepted the task for extra compensation, while the second trapper, a very young Jim Bridger (Will Poulter), stayed behind for Glass out of a sense of duty and care. Interestingly, the historic figure Jim Bridger became a truly legendary frontiersman and mountain man with even greater national fame than Glass. Glass's son Hawk stayed on to be with his father.

Hawk had been the object of Fitzgerald's malignant and noxious racist goading even before the Ree attack and Glass's injuries. Worried about the worsening weather and the possible proximity of the Ree, Fitzgerald, without Bridger's awareness and consent, declared Glass dead and just barely covered him over in a shallow pit while still alive. Fitzgerald then killed Hawk, lying to Bridger that the young Pawnee just took off.

At that point, the narrative of the film becomes what Richard Brody terms "a taut, classic double chase" with Glass surviving his burial beneath the bear and his second burial in the ground to pursue Fitzgerald and Bridger back to the home base of Fort Kiowa. At the same time, the Ree chief Elk Dog (Duane Howard) pursues Glass, mistakenly thinking that the trapper joined in with the kidnapping of the chief's daughter Powaqa (Melaw Nakehk'o), who in fact was taken by French traders.[4]

Actually, in one of the film's reductions of the character of Glass to a typical Western hero, Glass rescues Powaqa from a camp of French traders who abuse and rape her. Elk Dog's search for his daughter constitutes a clever reversal of the classic historic American captivity narrative as represented so famously in modern film by John Ford's and John Wayne's *The Searchers* (1956).[5]

Both Hikuc and Glass as two men with experiences of grief, loss, and abuse develop a relationship, with Hikuc assuming a sense of nurturing and responsibility for the crippled, demoralized, and brutalized Glass. They ride Hikuc's spotted white horse together over Western plains and into wintry weather. At a campfire after a day's ride, a ground-level shot shows Glass in the foreground asleep by the fire with Hikuc protectively in the background noticing light snowflakes.

A subsequent image shows a beautiful landscape covered in snow. Seasons and weather measure the time of Hikuc and Glass's journey rather than clocks and schedules. Close-ups of Hikuc accentuate his fierceness, which makes his tenderness toward the injured Glass even more touching and poignant. As Glass in the snow fills a canteen by a rushing stream, Hikuc comes up behind him, takes some sort of indigenous medicine from his own mouth, uncovers the back of Glass's neck, and puts the material on the wound. He says in Pawnee, "Your body is rotten." He goes on, "Need to heal. You could die."

The camera pulls back to show the two men in a strong depth of field shot that conveys the bond of fellowship developing between them. Hikuc walks toward the camera and out of the frame. The delayed image emphasizes their differences and separation as well as their mutual dependence and affection.

In a more conventional narrative order, Iñárritu cuts to the secondary storyline of Fitzgerald and Bridger on horses that they found in a decimated Indian village. The two men come over a hill and, in the distance, they see their destination, the company Fort Kiowa.

ON THE LORD'S SIDE

Earlier in *The Revenant*, Fitzgerald and Bridger still on foot came across a destroyed village occupied at the time by foraging pigs. Dead Native American bodies were strewn throughout the village. Bridger asked who did the violence and Fitzgerald thought that the devastation may have been done by friendly soldiers. He said, "It could be Captain Leavenworth's boys."

Walking through the village and horrified by the death and destruction all around him, Bridger caught sight of a woman hiding in a tepee. Without revealing her existence to Fitzgerald, Bridger left her some food and walked off as Fitzgerald discovered that there were horses still in the village for them to take. Fitzgerald shouted, "We got horses over here. . . The Lord's on our side, kid!"

That evening, Fitzgerald told Bridger the story of how his father in Texas once found God. He began the conversation by asking Bridger, "You all right there, kid? Your head in the right place?" meaning was he allowing his conscience to bother him about the way they had buried and left Glass in the wilderness. Fitzgerald then proceeded to tell how his father on a failed hunting trip found himself starving and prayed to God for help.

In the light of the campfire, Hardy's voice, speech, and facial gestures as he and Bridger partake in their own squirrely meal, perfectly convey Fitzgerald's cynicism and veniality. Fitzgerald's beard glows in the light of the fire. He speaks, eats deliberately, chews over each morsel of meat from his hands, savoring each juicy bite, and nods thoughtfully as he remembers and conveys the story as though reliving it himself. He says reflectively but pointedly to influence and instruct Bridger on ethics and the real meaning of life and religion in the world, "And God, it turns out, he's a squirrel." The light of the fire casts a glow in Fitzgerald's glaring eyes. His expression gives him a devilish look as he finishes his meal and says, "Yeah, a big old meaty one." He laughed over recalling his father's words that "I shot and ate that son-of-bitch."

The story, of course, was intended as a lesson in Fitzgerald's philosophy of life. The story functions as an extended metaphor, a self-serving myth, to justify and rationalize a view of life as a battle for survival in which the strongest and most self-serving win. Fitzgerald turns a dark Darwinian and Spencerian view of life into a bedtime story by the campfire for the young Bridger, thinking it should be part of his education of the young man.

Finally, in sight of their destination of the trapper company's military-style fort, Fitzgerald continues the line of thought and argument that he had been making since the two trappers left Glass in his shallow pit of a grave. Long shots and panoramic shots again emphasize the magnificence of the landscape; but Fitzgerald's words inscribe a textual significance upon the scene that contrasts dramatically with the visual beauty of nature's frozen landscape. Fitzgerald transforms the landscape into a battlefield for the survival of the fittest. Out of selfish self-protection, he continues his efforts to convince Bridger about the ethical justification for their actions based on the conditions under which they were made.

Along with lecturing Bridger in the form of bedtime stories, Fitzgerald tries to put the case in terms of the young man's achievements and manhood. He appeals to Bridger's vanity and pride over how he should feel about his achievement of finishing the journey. For Fitzgerald, the journey marks the younger man's initiation into manhood. Upon seeing the fort in the distance, Fitzgerald says, "Yeah, there she is. We did it. You ought to be proud of yourself, boy!"

Sensing his failure to impress Bridger and assuage the young man's troubled conscience, Fitzgerald then tries to argue the logic of self-survival over ethics as though also rehearsing his story for authorities at the fort in the person of Captain Henry. Fitzgerald says, "We followed orders. We just skipped the funeral part." He then switches to an even more direct and obvious argument for their mutual safety. Looking at Bridger and at the fort in the distance, Fitzgerald says, "Don't go down there and start growing no kind of conscience. For sure as night will come, they will have us both swinging from a couple of ropes."

In effect, Fitzgerald's argument undermines his purpose by suggesting their actual culpability in the death and abandonment of Glass. In the absence of a better or more persuasive story on their behalf over how they left Glass, Fitzgerald correctly fears that Bridger's conscience could kill them both. Fitzgerald looks at him with evil intensity. In response, Bridger's facial expression transparently conveys his lingering doubts and self-torture over the morality of how they left Glass in the wilderness.

The tracking shot to the fort visually encapsulates the asymmetry of the cultural conflict between capitalistic forces of conquest and exploitation and the indigenous populations. Native American children race to the two men on horseback begging for something from the men. The Native Americans on the outside of the fort live in conditions of squalor, displacement, and destitution.

In his office at the trapper company fort, Captain Henry, an honorable and honest almost officious man, questions Fitzgerald and Bridger regarding the circumstances of their alleged burial of Glass. Warily accepting with some uncertainty Fitzgerald's account, the captain agrees to the promised compensation and offers to give Bridger an unexpected reward as well. The tension and discomfort on Bridger's face during the de-briefing reflects the guile and deception of Fitzgerald's words and behavior. Hardy in this scene again demonstrates intense control over the psychological complexity of his soulless character. Bridger, in a kind of outburst of frustration, leaves the office without taking the money, compelling Fitzgerald to explain that he has been beating himself up over the situation for the whole journey back.

The design and construction of Iñárritu's frontier fort graphically depict the inherent and irresolvable tensions in the intrusion into the American frontier by European interests and cultures. The trappers find themselves in a makeshift, somewhat wobbly, and insecure fort of thin logs. The enclosed space becomes a trap and prison as much as a sanctuary for protection. Conditions deteriorate into congestion and overcrowding. Native Americans become reduced to aliens and foreigners in their own environment. They live outside the fort as secondary, almost non-human figures without the resources or opportunities for their own survival and perpetuation. Braves become sub-servient and the women prostitute themselves.

Moreover, conditions at the fort not only dramatize the cost to the Europeans of their repression and domination of the native indigenous peoples, the generation of a slum culture and mentality signifies the exploitation by the fur company of its own workers and people. The economics of the fur company becomes a lesson in capitalism and exploitation. To his shock, Fitzgerald learns that some of the costs for his trapping will come out of his own pay and compensation.

With all the space of the magnificent outdoor wilderness and frontier around them and an open sky above them, the men live in terrible conditions. The fort shows signs of dilapidation. The men drink heavily with one another and with Native American women. They appear listless, agitated, and dis-tressed with themselves and in one another's company.

Iñárritu films the details of the fort so closely, tightly, and precisely as to subvert any romantic illusions about the frontier experience, at least from the perspective of the lives, conditions, and purposes of the trappers and their employer. In that sense, Fitzgerald's corrupt nature and deep cynicism make him a perfect manifestation of the culture and history of the frontier fort.

TWO MEN, TWO STORIES

The scene in *The Revenant* of Fitzgerald's story about his father finding and eating God in the form of a squirrel occurs right before Iñárritu cuts to Glass's emersion from the freezing river after his escape from the Ree warri-ors. Similarly, immediately following the scene of Hikuc's concern about the condition of Glass's rotting flesh, the film cuts to the appearance of Fitzgerald and Bridger in sight of the trapper fort. The cuts between and into differ-ent storylines come at points to dramatize the progress in both chase stories. More important, the cuts occur at pivot points or tipping points that highlight differences between Glass and Fitzgerald and between the nature and meaning of their journeys.

Moreover, Iñárritu not only contrasts the two storylines of Glass and Fitzgerald but also intends to put them in a position of interconnection and interaction, creating something of a reflexive dialogue between them. He also clearly means for this interaction to accomplish more than a litany of clichéd social and cultural themes that add false depth to the film, as Brody chides. Aesthetically, Iñárritu endeavors to achieve more than a story with vivid illustrations, as Brody also asserts.

At the level of narrative and character development, Iñárritu establishes a dichotomous, perhaps even Manichean, contrast between Glass and Fitzgerald to accentuate what separates them in terms of values, attitudes, culture, and character. The men represent opposing views of manhood and heroism with Fitzgerald embodying a creed of selfishness and cynicism and responsibility only to himself. He sees manhood as a code of the survival of the self by whatever means necessary. As tenacious in his commitment to survival and overcoming adversity as Fitzgerald, for Glass, true manhood requires quieter responsibility for the defense, security, and welfare of others. He measures manhood by the extent of doing for others. Glass identifies himself primarily in terms of fatherhood, family, and community in the form of the tribe.

Although seeming to appreciate Bridger's company and enjoy his mentoring relationship with him, Fitzgerald exists as an autonomous self. For Fitzgerald, the landscape, environment, geography, and indigenous people all exist for exploitation and economic opportunism. Glass clearly has a Native American impulse toward a spiritual relationship to the landscape. He merges and melds with the environment and makes the indigenous population his family.

Fitzgerald lives in a world governed by cause and effect and mechanical rules that must be obeyed to survive. Glass searches for a spiritual realm of meaning and purpose to be gleaned from his own Anglo-American culture and from his partially adopted Native American culture as well as in his own pragmatic experience.

Hardy's nuanced, disciplined, and rigorous performance and Iñárritu's creative and intelligent direction save Fitzgerald from becoming a cliché or stereotype of movie-made evil and malevolence. They center Fitzgerald in what amounts to an intolerably cruel and challenging work environment as a fur trapper in the wilderness. Acting, costume, and direction make Fitzgerald human, concrete, and singular in the drama of his struggle to survive and achieve at least a minimum of security and success under overwhelmingly difficult odds. Moreover, the extraordinary cinematography of grandiose mountains and frontier landscapes also positions Fitzgerald in a Western environment to give him credibility and a quality of realism as a genuine frontier figure.

IÑÁRRITU ON TIME AND SPACE: THE METAPHYSICAL QUESTION

Accordingly, of considerable importance, Iñárritu maintains the genius of the visual design, sweep, and intensity of *The Revenant*, while also imagining and creating a temporal design of dual temporal regimes. The linear regime of Fitzgerald's chronology of encounters, dangers, deceits, and deceptions contrasts with the moments of non-linear, non-chronological, and diachronic visionary temporality that Glass experiences.

Thus, Iñáritu and Hardy convey Fitzgerald's story and character in a fairly straightforward way. When Fitzgerald and Bridger on their horses come up from behind a hill to see their fort in the distance, Iñárritu places them in a beautiful setting with an awesome background of snow-covered mountain peaks. The setting provides an outstanding stage for Fitzgerald's continuing fears about the uncertain outcome of the war within Bridger between conscience and the fear of exposure regarding Glass's burial. Carefully timed and positioned close-ups of Hardy enable him to present the ugliness and danger of Fitzgerald's character with powerful consistency and persuasiveness, while Will Poulter as Bridger proves convincing in his reaction shots to the moral and ethical horrors and challenges that clearly threaten to engulf him both physically and psychologically.

Significantly, as directed and filmed by Iñárritu, Fitzgerald, as the embodiment of one example of the immigrant European's physical struggle in the wilderness, could be considered the external manifestation of the Cartesian autonomous ego of domination and exploitation of the environment and indigenous peoples. The cost of the colonialization, commercialization, and commodification of peoples and the environment shows on the faces, the physical bearing, and body movements of the trappers and frontiersmen. Close-ups, facial expressions, just about every step forward and every physical movement by the men intimate the hardships of their situation, condition, and challenge.

In contrast to the filming of the Westerners as the physical expression of a pioneering Cartesian ego of control, power, and appropriation, Iñárritu directs a counter-narrative in a different temporality of the finite flesh and body that for many thinkers animates, energizes, and realizes the potential for the idea of the soul as the happening of emerging existential authenticity and presence.

In the person and figure of DiCaprio's portrayal of Glass, the body houses and projects the existential possibility of the ineffable, the unrepresentable, and the spiritual. Building on DiCaprio's performance, *The Revenant* transforms DiCaprio's body into a stage and space for dramatizing a philosophy of the body as the extension of the soul and the soul as the articulation of the body for meaning and significance. In his violent encounters with man, beast, and nature, DiCaprio's struggles for survival enact the continuous transposition of the self, spirit, or soul and the exteriority of the body, dramatizing what Nancy terms the body as a "wound that doesn't heal" in a relationship of "entelechy" in which "the one takes place only through the other"—"the soul as the entelechy of the body."[6]

Soul and body in the wilderness continually and inexorably interact and transform each other. The finite flesh and body as housing the spirit and the spirit as informing, enlivening, and transforming the flesh resonate throughout Glass's endless ordeals in the film. Body and soul happen for and through each other to counter the divided self of alienated trappers. Animals join in the process. The computerized bear mauls Glass, but a bear also provides the fur that envelopes Glass with warmth and security. The body of a horse taken from perverse French trappers, a beautiful spotted animal that Glass rode at top speed over the edge of a high plateau into giant fir trees below to escape rampaging Ree riders, provides a home and shelter for him against the freezing weather. Bear and horse keep Glass's body and spirit together.

The interaction of body and soul in DiCaprio's performance occurs with the fluctuations between different temporal regimes. Glass undergoes a break from regular chronological narrative time to experience a new time of renewal. Temporal interruption and suspension insinuate a time of emerging being and a coming into presence for Glass as opposed to a fixed linear temporal regime that schedules and programs individuals. The time of the body in its engagement with the soul supersedes the time of the world, markets, and trading.

The wondrous environment in *The Revenant* of endless mountain ranges, open skies, and towering trees that bend and sway with the wind engenders and cultivates the possibility of existential revelation at the same time that the same wilderness demands total commitment and effort in the body's struggle for survival under crushing and dehumanizing circumstances. The time of the flesh welcomes realization, revelation, and epiphany. Such time provokes and cultivates the soul—the soul being the idea of the body as well as the body being defined by the spirit—for his existential coming into being as occurs in Glass's visions of loss, lack, hope, and love. His visions and dreams bring back his murdered son and wife, and the Pawnee Healer and compel him to seek vengeance on his son's killer, Fitzgerald.

Freed from the constraints, mores, and inhibitions of conventional civilization, the existential self in the wilderness can achieve a Thoreauvian vision of nature as the expression of higher laws and meaning, just as the painter Thomas Cole saw nature and the wilderness as God's house. Frequently repeated shots of the shimmering trees of the forest create the impression of the overarching branches as forming a cathedral of nature. As has been widely noted, the amazing cinematography creates a visual rendering of the awesome mystery of nature and the wilderness. Thus, although in markedly different geographic locations and space than the settings that inspired Cole's Hudson

River school of painting, Iñárritu's vision of the wilderness resonates with Cole's words about the wilderness:

> Perhaps the most impressive characteristic of American scenery is its wilderness. It is the most distinctive because in civilized Europe the primitive features of scenery have long since been destroyed or modified—And to this cultivated state our western world is fast approaching; but nature is still predominant... for those scenes of solitude from which the hand of nature has never been lifted, affect the mind with a more deep toned emotion than aught which the hand of man has touched. Amid them the consequent associations are of God the creator—they are his undefiled works, and the mind is cast into the contemplation of eternal things.[7]

Cole's art at the time of the Transcendentalism of Ralph Waldo Emerson and Henry David Thoreau, among so many others, also occurred concomitantly with a different ideology of the Western virgin wilderness that Jefferson called an "empire for liberty" and that history dubbed as the time and geography of America's "manifest destiny."[8]

The Revenant incorporates in its visual and written texts the aesthetic, historical, cultural, and ideological contrasts and conflicts entwined in the difference between, on the one hand, the ideology of an "empire for liberty," and, on the other, the transcendental idea of a pristine land untouched by humankind as evidence of the work, as Cole says, of "God the creator." Both views of the West find representation in *The Revenant*.

While sustaining this diversity and multiplicity of symbol-laden meanings, Iñáarirtu opens *The Revenant* to another metaphysical sphere of experience and understanding to imbue the film with an original dimension of meaning. Compared to Fitzgerald's journey in conventional time, Iñárritu has a different design in mind of a non-chronological, non-linear temporality for the development of the story and character of Glass. He wishes to make Glass a figure of greater meaning on his journey on the frontier and in life that goes well beyond Fitzgerald's experience and consciousness.

THE TRAPPER AND THE PAWNEE HEALER-II

To achieve the metaphysical dimension and expression in *The Revenant* that he seeks, Iñárritu transforms the classic Western roles of the white hunter and the Native American, of the Pawnee Hikuc and the Trapper Glass, by creating a new kind of relationship between them that completes their individual regeneration together. For some scholars, the wars between the Native

Americans and the Anglo settlers became the defining metaphor for the Anglo "regeneration through violence" and rebirth in the wilderness.[9] Iñárritu reinvents that relationship. He transmogrifies "the spatialization of time" on the endless frontier to a temporality that Nancy describes as spacious temporality.[10] In this different spatio-temporal sphere of experience, it becomes possible to achieve a deeper sense of being than the adventure of conquest and domination provides.

Leaving the fort of the frontier trappers with close-ups of both young Bridger and Captain Henry in stark images of moral doubt and uncertainty about what really happened to Glass, Iñárritu returns *The Revenant* to Hikuc and Glass. He cuts to a long shot at ground level of Hikuc's horse in the open landscape in the snow. The shot immediately indicates not only the sparsity of grass but the lack of shelter against the weather. Without any melodrama, the image immediately suggests an element of impending disaster with the exposure to the elements. The horse emanates a kind of dumb bravery in its stillness and resolve. Then a cut shows Hikuc tugging and pulling at grasses and tasting some of the vegetation, seeking medicinal plants for the ailing Glass, and putting them all beneath his clothes to keep them dry for starting a fire or for meager sustenance.

These images set a tone and rhythm for another long shot, this time of the two men on the snowy earth by a totally naked shrub in a snowy landscape on the open plains beneath an endless sky stretched to the horizon. Another stilled image accentuates the sense of time delayed for the men in a frozen, timeless, and dead world.

In the scene, the two men, Hikuc and Glass, become part of nature and the environment in their stillness. Glass wears his fur coat that gives him a resemblance to a beast on the dead, frozen plain. Even at that distance and in that position, Glass's stillness also suggests a certain lethargy and surrender to the sickness that Hikuc worried about when examining Glass's rotting flesh from his bear wounds. A hood covers Glass's head. As he looks off into the distance, his face remains only a splotch of gray without real identity marks or color, reinforcing the image of weakness and depletion. Hikuc, under the tree and to left in the frame, evidences signs of life with his head turned up as he looks toward the sky.

Iñárritu holds the image for several seconds and then cuts to close-ups of the two men that ends with an amazing shot of Hikuc with the great cavity of his mouth open and an impressive length of tongue stretched out to catch some sprinkling raindrops. Glass turns ever so listlessly to watch him exhibiting his beard covered with snow and ice. Hikuc signals with his tongue for his friend to also catch the raindrops. And suddenly two men come alive and slowly break into laughter over the silliness of their situation and efforts.

Throughout the scene, the tension between delayed cinema and the moving image brings out the details of the images of the two men in their desperate existential situation but also the issue of time as both a kind of prison of enclosure and the opening of infinite possibility. The sequence of shots really marks the continuation of the scene that began with Glass's emergence from the river and his first encounter and interaction with Hikuc that were interrupted with the cuts to Fitzgerald and Bridger on their journey and arrival at the trapper fort. The segment as a whole introduces a special temporal regime that forms the relationship between the two men and the special meaning that their relationship acquires. Delayed cinema and the moving image dramatize the achievement for each of the men of a kind of natural existential moment in each other's company as they share the space of the frozen terrain and the gift of raindrops that stiffen their resistance and determination and lighten their burden.

VIOLENCE, THE IMAGE, AND BEING

The sequences of shots and images of the bonding of Glass and Hikuc open the way for a truly remarkable sequence of images that represent Iñárritu's most obvious and strongest effort to fulfill his ambition to make *The Revenant* as a work of cinematic art also a work of metaphysical and ethical imagination. He endeavors through a series of carefully designed and constructed images to intimate a fresh dimension of experience and meaning to the film. The construction and concentration on the time of the individual images as part of the cinematic flow and trajectory of images displace the regular linear organization of a scene or segment with a non-linear, non-chronological temporality of the imagination.

Iñárritu works to place Glass and his story in a metaphysical and ethical realm that encounters and recognizes ultimate existential questions without creating artificial answers that enervate and mitigate the drama of the challenges of existential uncertainty. As Kristeva writes, "What kind of truth are we talking about? Not a kind that may be logically demonstrated, that may be scientifically proved, that may be calculated. It is a matter of a *truth* 'we stumble upon,' to which I cannot not adhere, that totally, fatally subjugates me . . . A truth that keeps me, makes me exist. Rather than being an idea, a thing, a situation, might it be an experience?"[11]

Iñárritu seeks that "kind of truth" that Kristeva describes that "makes" Glass exist in *The Revenant*. Iñárritu told Jonathan Romney that although "he isn't religious," he has "long been concerned with matters metaphysical." He described Glass as "becoming 'a man, a beast, a saint, a martyr, a spirit.'"[12] To create this metaphysical and existential experience for Glass, Iñárritu emphasized the importance of finding and making images that could convey the authenticity of such an experience on the screen, explaining to Edward Lawrenson of *Sight & Sound,* "You can say a lot things but film is about images."[13]

The aesthetic and metaphysical mission that Iñárritu assigns to his images in *The Revenant* returns us to Nancy's notion of the violence and cruelty of the image. Nancy proffers images that intimate emerging presence rather than frozen pictures of presence. He sees the image as "the manifestation of presence, not as appearance, but as exhibiting, as bringing to light and setting forth" (*GI*: 22). This "bringing to light and setting forth" suggests not just interesting pictures and representations of reality for his images but emerging being in the image—the death and the emergence of being.

The violence of the image, as Nancy sees it, demonstrates the energy and dynamism of the image for enacting emerging presence. He says, "No doubt there is violence in all this, or at least there is always the possibility that violence might surface. The image not only exceeds the form, the aspect, the calm surface of representation, but in order to do so it must draw upon a ground—or a groundlessness—of excessive power" (*GI*: 22). The power of creation in the image tears asunder the ground that provides the foundation for the image.

For Nancy, the image should entail more than reflecting or resembling reality; it must involve destructive creation. The image becomes self-sustaining through the imagination. The image feeds on the energy of the disjuncture between presence and absence. He writes, "The image must be *imagined;* that is to say, it must extract from its absence the unity of force that the thing merely at hand does not present. Imagination is not the faculty of representing something in its absence; it is the force that draws the form of presence out of absence; that is to say, the force of 'self-presenting'" (*GI*: 22; emphasis in the original). Nancy writes, "The image is always a dynamic or energetic metamorphosis" (*GI*: 22). Thus, the violence of the image enacts the ongoing "metamorphosis" of experience in the form of the imagined image.

Iñárittu's sequence of images in the Glass-Hikuc segment enacts the violence of time for emerging being in the image. Rather than the time of the mechanical process of linear images that relate a chronological narrative, as in the story of Fitzgerald and Bridger, Iñárritu imagines a time of creative imagination, a kind of imagistic visual poetry. As an imagined construct, the images integrate multiple levels of meaning in its artistic form.

Interestingly, the raindrop sequence with Hikuc and Glass concludes with a long shot of a smiling Glass coming to life as he observes Hikuc trying to catch some more rain on his extended tongue. Glass's face in the shot emerges out of the cover of his hooded fur piece, giving him the appearance of coming to life, of a sudden new birth. His body becomes at one with the animal fur that covers him.

The sharp cut to the next image immediately puts rebirth and regeneration in another context. At eye-level, the camera slowly moves ahead and tilts up to tall whitish birch trees and the open sky above them. The branches of the amazing trees suggest a kind of gothic structure made from nature. At eye-level, the camera holds tight on trees in the immediate foreground that form an entrance or doorway. The deep focus of the shot points to a pathway through the trees and into the natural cathedral. At the top of the birch tree in the center of the image and frame, a nest hangs from a hidden branch as though suspended in mid-air in nature's sanctuary—an empty squirrel's nest redolent of Fitzgerald's vulgar and nihilistic imagery and analogy. Directly below the nest, the blazing light of the sun forms a star. Iñárritu bathes the scene in a kind of sky-bluish-whiteness that gives the scene a tone of awesome uniqueness and mystery.

Delayed cinema sharpens the details of the images but also creates the tension of anticipation as the camera moves forward into the natural church. With the camera tilted up as it moves forward, the trees become an inverted V stretching to heaven. The camera keeps the tree with the nest in the middle of the shot as the center of attention. The whiteness of the clouds form a kind of canopy over the scene. The scene then gets immersed in a blazing otherworldly whiteness of existential uncertainty.

A sharp cut reimagines the previous image. Hikuc's body is planted in the middle of the frame moving forward but his face and body have become darkened, making him into a kind of inky blot. The background of the image and frame turn the landscape into a kind of abstraction of light-bluish whiteness while the trees suddenly have become thinner and scattered and spaced out, giving the whole scene a sense of unreality. The trees no longer suggest a cathedral entrance way and structure but an image of a white wasteland and loss.

In one cut, Iñárritu creates a limbo world of transition into a different time. The lighting, coloring, and spacing of thin trees suggest a fresh danger of a storm. Then, Hikuc leads his horse with an ailing Glass mounted on him. A long shot reveals a scene of abandonment, open stormy sky, and long, snow-covered landscape. The two wander just a bit more until Glass falls from the saddle, too weak to hold onto the animal. The distance of the shot objectifies the fall, saving it from melodrama. The camera holds the image at a distance and then cuts sharply to a totally different, jarring perspective. He shoots from ground level with the camera focused tightly on Glass's face as he lay on the ground unconscious. Hikuc moves behind him and kneels so both face toward the camera. Hikuc leans over Glass into the camera and checks his friend's forehead for fever, a rough but loving motherly caretaker.

In another shot, starting a fire, Hikuc blows into dry grass twisted in his hand that he has kept under his clothes. Making the fire glow and starting the construction of a wilderness shelter, Hikuc drags the unconscious Glass over the ground by the fire. Hikuc works deliberately to build a shelter, chopping down tree limbs and carefully arranging them for stability and durability. The branches and limbs of the birch trees that had been the imaginary natural cathedral will become the makings of a thin but life-saving lean-to and shelter in a storm in the wilderness.

With the camera again tight on Glass's face and forehead, the voice of Glass's dead wife can be heard in a bare whisper, saying in Pawnee (with subtitles), "When there is a storm . . . And you stand in front of a tree . . . If you look at the branches, you swear it will fall. But if you watch the trunk, you will see its stability." With these words in Glass's mind as he lay unconscious, Hikuc nurses and cares for him, putting grass and medicinal herbs on his wounds, taking off the wet bear cover but keeping him warm by surrounding him with grass wrapped around snow that burns for warmth and smokes, turning the shelter into a sweat lodge so that the unconscious Glass will absorb the heat and fumes. Both men stay in the frame with the camera holding at ground level. Then, in the background, Hikuc continues building with only the horse for company a few feet away.

Iñárritu, with a form of Bergmanian imagistic cross-fading, shifts to total blackness on the screen. The transition signals a deeper immersion into a different state of the unconscious, of loss, of death. Iñárritu holds the blackness for several seconds until slowly a light enters from the upper-right corner of the frame—and then slowly a hand appears across a rock wall toward the painted image of a rough, primitive Jesus. The cave-dwelling scene and the image on the wall suggest the influence of the mixed Hispanic and Native American art and culture of the American Southwest. A torch exposes more of the painting, moving down to Jesus's crossed feet nailed together. The faces of sorrowful witnesses appear on the cracked wall in pain over Jesus's crucifixion. A man—Glass—with his back to the camera holds a torch to the wall and reveals a kind of ghoulish figure on the painting, a version of a black death mask with large peering eyes holding a white body extended in a collapsed state before it. A cut to the outdoors shows some crickets together in a kind of love ritual, signifying perhaps the beginnings of life in its earliest state.

Iñárittu then cuts to a low-angle shot of Glass looking up on the same landscape as before the dream sequence but without snow and the storm. He stands and looks on a barren scene of thin naked trees and the remains of a destroyed old church. The design and thrust of the walls of the structure mimic the design and movement of the trees of the natural cathedral of birch trees. Glass walks slowly through the remains of the dilapidated and abandoned structure. He sees a wall at the far end of the structure with a mural, another image of the crucifixion, and a round opening at the top that could have held a window. In front of the wall in a low-angle shot stands Hawk, Glass's murdered son, who turns slowly to look at his father. Solemn music enriches the scene. Father and son look at each other as Hawk turns and walks back through a puddle of water on the ground of the empty church ruins into the camera and toward his father as the two hug. In reverse shots, the camera tightens on each of them with their eyes closed in their desperate, unbreakable embrace of each other.

Then, holding tightly on to Glass's face with his eyes closed shut as though afraid of losing what he imagines and clutches, the camera cuts to a crane shot of Glass on the same landscape and in the same ruined church but hugging a naked burned-out tree. At the top of the screen, a church bell rocks back and forth but without a sound.

Scratching and tearing noises and grunts reveal Glass buried in the shelter created for him by Hikuc. Like a bear, he has been hibernating to get well and heal his wounds. He undergoes yet another resurrection. Pushing twigs, grass, and coverings away, Glass emerges into the light and the same snowy landscape on to which he had collapsed. He finds the rations and clothes Hikuc had left for him but not finding the Pawnee healer he soon starts walking at a slow, hesitant, and handicapped pace, until he sees Hikuc hanging from a tree, lynched by French trappers who put a sign over him saying, "*On est–tous des Sauvages.*"

The images of Glass's dream come from the unconscious, beginning with the soothing, comforting words of a Native American mother and wife who counsels and practices wisdom and patience in the face of danger and adversity. The dream enacts Kristeva's analysis of the *zeitlos* or the lost time of the unconscious. She sees the lost time, to reiterate her argument, as "the expression of a new relationship to time" that opens and even unleashes the repressed power of the inner psyche. For Kristeva, the unconscious and the lost time, especially as manifested in dreams, provide an energized link to what she terms "this state of grace."[14]

Kristeva could be using the dream sequence in *The Revenant* as a practice exercise to illustrate her theory of how lost time "passes through the image of dreams and through the hallucinatory image."[15] Lost time in the dream and the image achieves both verbal articulation or its expression as "grace" and "*kairos*" as the time of revelation that breaks from regular, chronological time.[16] Similarly, Kristeva could be describing Glass in *The Revenant* when she discusses the mixture of boundary and borderline crossings entailed in the search for the sacred. She writes, we recall, "What if the sacred were the unconscious perception the human being has of its untenable eroticism: always on the borderline between nature and culture, the animalistic and the verbal, the sensible and the nameable?"[17]

The imagined images of the lost time of Glass's extended dream sequence exist in their own reality. The dream sequence intensifies and accentuates the pattern at least since his river emergence of telling his story in a slower cinema of images in a non-linear temporality that suggests delayed cinema. A time of deep space and depth of field predominates for Glass. The temporal regime of the dream sequence accentuates the parallelism between the fluidity of film and Glass's steady existential emergence.

The images of the sequence impel a search for meaning: an empty squirrel's nest atop nature's cathedral once again recalls Fitzgerald's God as a meal for a miscreant; an empty bell over a church in ruins rocks in silence as lifeless and barren as the nest and the landscape below; a crucified Christ shares a mural with a devil-like figure in an unidentified cave; a dead son approaches his father walking to him through symbolic water in the dilapidated church; Glass's imaginary reunion and hug for his dead son shows him embracing a burned-out tree situated by a burned-out church; and the discovery of the lynching of Hikuc the Pawnee healer as a perverse human sacrifice.

The images of *The Revenant* point in the direction of a desolate, abandoned landscape in a world without meaning, hope, or God. The spirit of the times seems to belong to Fitzgerald. The cynicism, selfishness, and corruption of the Fitzgeralds of the world run things. But Hikuc, speaking in Pawnee about his family murdered by the Sioux, offers an alternative view, saying, "My heart bleeds. But revenge is in the creator's hands."

In classic long shots that he has used throughout *The Revenant* to dramatize and accentuate the reduced and diminished size and significance of the human being in the vast natural wilderness, Iñárittu shows two men barely discernible among the snow-covered rocks, trees, and rushing river water fighting to the death with a hatchet and a knife. In closer shots, Fitzgerald and Glass butcher each other, stabbing, wounding, and cutting. Blood soaks the white snow with a seeming permanent stain of hatred and violence. Set in the midst of such wondrous, natural beauty, the slaughter and mayhem of the men testifies to the absurdity of the human condition. A cacophony of sounds, a mixture of noise, clatter, and disjunctive music punctuates the scene of destruction.

Finally succumbing to Glass's refusal to be denied his revenge against Fitzgerald for killing his son, Fitzgerald looks up to Glass, who holds him down on the ground with his bloodied, bare hands. Fitzgerald groans, "You came all this way, just for your revenge, huh? Well, you enjoy it, Glass. 'Cause there ain't nothing gonna bring your boy back!" Glass looks deeply into the killer's face. Fitzgerald says, "No, it won't." Digesting those words, Glass looks up to the sound of approaching Arikara warriors with Elk Dog reunited with his daughter Powaqa. He also hears in his imagination Hikuc's words in Pawnee, "Revenge is in God's hands . . . not mine."

With that revelation, Iñárittu begins his final series of slow, long takes of images to suggest questions rather than final answers to the mystery on so many levels of Glass's journey. Glass drags Fitzgerald still alive and gives him to the river, which takes him to the awaiting Arikara party and Elk Dog's scalping knife. Elk Dog, Powaqa, and the small band on horseback slowly and proudly pass Glass.

The concluding series of images in their power, depth, authenticity, and tangibility confirm the value and importance of Iñárittu's commitment to actual filming on location. The film creates a crucial balance between digital media and classic direction and filming. As Lawrenson says, "While much of *The Revenant*, then, was dependent on relatively new digital technology, there is still something defiantly old-fashioned about Iñárittu's insistence on real locations and on-camera spectacle. In an era when so many filmmakers are required to shoot logically demanding sequences in green-screen studios, Iñárittu took what he says was a 'very difficult' decision to stand his ground."[18]

Also, giving up Fitzgerald alive to raging river waters, the wilderness, and the Arikara constitutes something of a conclusion to the revision of the Western involved in *The Revenant*. Fitzgerald's body becomes a kind of gift and ritual of respect and reappropriation for the Native Americans for all that has been taken from them by foreign European invaders. Glass gives him to the river and environment as a token of recognition of the violence and the desecration that have been done to the land and its peoples. Such gestures certainly constitute a degree of departure from the conventional and traditional Western formulaic portrayals of Native Americans and the environment.

Regarding the art form of the Western film, a kind of intertextuality occurs frequently in *The Revenant* to such a degree that the film becomes an ongoing internal visualized history of the classic Western. As previously noted, a key element in the film of a Arikara chief's search for his daughter, who was captured by French trappers, transforms the classic John Ford–John Wayne Western paradigm of the captivity narrative into a new perspective and story that could be termed "The Ree Searchers." The amazing computer-generated attack by a mother grizzly bear on Glass suggests a film title of "Dances with Bears." The opening of the film and other sequences of hunting and struggling could be dubbed "The Last of the Puritans" with Glass displacing Hawkeye and the Pawnees continuing the tragic history of Mohican abandonment and devastation. Interior shots of the depressing and oppressive conditions of the white man's crowded frontier fort could have been set up by Clint Eastwood.

Thus, Iñárritu suggests considerable self-awareness of the significance of his art form in rendering the multiple interlaced narratives of his film. He demonstrates great respect for his art and for his stories and ultimately for the quest for meaning and value that both art and narrative convey. A form of intertexuality also persists with the final long take, close-up of Glass staring into the camera with a piercing look that captures Glass's persistent quest for understanding and meaning that resonates with the famous ending of François Truffaut's *The 400 Blows* (1959). The freeze frame puts into place and maintains the suspension and interruption of time that enables the drama

Figure 5.2 *The Revenant*: Searching for meaning and understanding

of the emergence of finite being in tension with the infinite. The look animates Levinas's notion of a time of "A deference of the immemorial to the unforeseeable" (*GDT*: 19). DiCaprio and Iñárritu suspend time in anticipation of venturing again into the uncertain and unknowable but armed with a new vision of finding meaning in the relationship to the other.

Iñárritu takes the Western into new aesthetic, cultural, and historical territory with *The Revenant*'s drama of metaphysical incommensurability. It goes into this new territory in part through its exploration of the metaphysics, ethics, and aesthetics of time and the image in its own art form. With all the power, passion, and beauty of the visual intelligence, imagination, and creativity of *The Revenant*'s rendering of the awesome mystery and wonder of Western spaces and landscapes, a sense of wonder in the film comes from life itself and the infinite gap between the desire to grasp and understand experience and the ultimate failure of the effort. He creates a postmodern vision of the American myth of the New World of Garden of Eden for the new man, the American Adam. All of the struggles, adventures, dangers, and triumphs in Glass's experience and journey still leave him wondering why and about meaning. He cannot bring back his dead son Hawk or his wife. Unlike Fitzgerald, he cannot simply accept such conditions of existence and take life on its own terms with God as a squirrel. Unlike Hikuc, he cannot find comfort in leaving it all in God's hands. As in the dream and the concluding images of the film, Glass can only continue searching for hope, love, and meaning.

Thus, Iñárritu transforms the Western into a rich and unforgettable visual expatiation on time and death, love and loss. Iñárritu and DiCaprio take Glass on the final painful steps of his journey. Especially as accentuated and highlighted by delayed cinema, the concentration on images in relation to the overall thrust of the film's trajectory parallels and sustains existential presence and awakening, not to final and ultimate truths but in the experience of one's own being and engagement with the life of others. As Mulvey writes in another context, "The shock of recognition, the philosophical coming into being, the materialization of presence, is at one and the same time, social and historical a recognition that conjures up a history of economic and cultural oppression."[19]

Moreover, in its final images, *The Revenant* not only articulates emerging existential presence and the violence and death of the image and time, the film also accentuates the inexorable force and place of Nancy's concept of the otherness of existence in existential presence. The powerful exchange of glances between Glass and Powaqa and Elk Dog as they ride past and the voice and beckoning image of reassurance and love of Glass's wife at the end dramatize the necessity of time and space for the other to achieve singular existential presence.

NOTES

1. See Laura Mulvey, *Death 24x a Second: Stillness and the Moving Image* (London: Reaktion Books, 2006), pp. 16, 66.

2. Jean-Luc Nancy, *The Ground of the Image*, trans. Jeff Fort (New York: Fordham University Press, 2005), pp. 24–25; emphasis in the original. All future references to this work will be to this edition and will be included parenthetically in the text as *GI*.

3. See Jonathan Romney, "Alejandro González Iñárritu: 'When you see The Revenant you will say "Wow,"'" *The Guardian*, January 3, 2016, pp. 2–16, http"//www.the guardian.com/film/2016/jan/03-alejandro-gonzalez-interview-the-revenant

4. See Richard Brody, "The Suffocating Solemnity of 'The Revenant,'" *The New Yorker*, January 14, 2016, http://www.newyorker.com/culture/richard-brody

5. For a discussion of *The Searchers* in the context of the Puritan captivity narrative in America see my *Hollywood Renaissance: The Cinema of Democracy in the Era of Ford, Capra, and Stevens* (Cambridge: Cambridge University Press, 1998), pp. 25–55.

6. Nancy, *Corpus*, trans. Richard A. Rand (New York: Fordham University Press, 2008), pp. 81, 128.

7. See Thomas Cole, "An Essay on American Scenery" (1835), in *Essays on American Scenery*, http://www.scun/-ta3584/Cole.htm

8. See Wai-chee Dimock, *Empire for Liberty: Melville and the Poetics of Individualism* (Princeton: Princeton University Press, 1989), p. 9.

9. See Richard Slotkin, *Regeneration through Violence: The Mythology of the American Frontier, 1600–1860* (Middletown: Wesleyan University Press, 1973).

10. Dimock, *Empire for Liberty*, p. 15. See also Jean-Luc Nancy, *The Experience of Freedom*, trans. Bridget McDonald, foreword Peter Fenves (Stanford: Stanford University Press, 1988).

11. Julia Kristeva, *The Incredible Need to Believe*, trans. Beverley Brie Brahic (New York: Columbia University Press, 2009), p. 3; emphasis in the original.

12. Jonathan Romney, "Alejandro González Iñárritu: 'When you see The Revenant you will say 'Wow,'" *The Guardian*, January 3, pp. 2–16, http"//www.the guardian.com/film/2016/jan/03-alejandro-gonzalez-interview-the-revenant

13. Edward Lawrenson, "Call of the Wild," *Sight & Sound* 6, vol. 1 (January 2016), pp. 22–26.

14. Julia Kristeva, *Intimate Revolt: The Powers and Limits of Psychoanalysis*, trans. Jeanine Herman (New York: Columbia University Press, 2002), pp. 28, 38.

15. Ibid., p. 38.

16. Kristeva, *The Incredible Need to Believe*, pp. 30–31.

17. See Catherine Clément and Julia Kristeva, *The Feminine and the Sacred*, trans. Jane Marie Todd (New York: Columbia University Press, 2001), pp. 26–27.

18. See Lawrenson, "Call of the Wild," *Sight & Sound* 6, vol. 1 (January 2016), pp. 22–26.

19. See Laura Mulvey, "*Imitation of Life:* New Forms of Spectatorship," *The New Review of Film and Television Studies*, vol. 15, no. 4 (September 2017): 477.

Epilogue – Time, Spacing, and the Body in Martin Scorsese's *The Age of Innocence* (1993)

Critics and commentators tended to see *Silence* (2016) as a kind of culmination of the themes of redemption, faith, and violence that have pervaded Martin Scorsese's films over several decades. In an article on "The Passion of Martin Scorsese" in *The New York Times Magazine* that preceded the release of the film, Paul Elie writes, "In his new film, 'Silence,' Martin Scorsese returns to a subject that has animated his entire life's work and that also sparked his career's greatest controversy: the nature of faith." Scorsese said so himself. He told Elie, "I don't know if there's redemption, but there is such a thing as trying to get it right. But how do you do it? The right way to live has to do with selflessness. I believe that. But how does one act that out? I don't think you practice it consciously. It has to be something that develops in you—maybe through a lot of mistakes."[1]

In her review of *Silence,* Manohla Dargis, also in *The New York Times,* similarly notes thematic continuity in Scorsese's filmography. She says that "Mr. Scorsese's work has long involved struggles of faith of one kind or another," including early films such as *Mean Streets* (1973) to the more recent *The Wolf of Wall Street* (2013). Dargis writes, "Martin Scorsese's 'Silence' is a story of faith and anguish. It tells of a Portuguese Jesuit priest, Father Rodrigues, who in 1643 heads into the dark of Japan, where Christians are being persecuted—boiled alive, immolated and crucified. Rodrigues (Andrew Garfield) sets out to help keep the church alive in Japan, a mission that perhaps inevitably leads to God."[2] Other Scorsese films that have been seen as stories of faith, redemption, and religious conflict often include *Taxi Driver* (1976), *Raging Bull* (1980), *The Last Temptation of Christ* (1988), *Cape Fear* (1991), *Kundun* (1997), and *George Harrison: Living in the Material World* (2011).

To film critics, *The Age of Innocence* (1993) not only did not seem to belong on any such list of Scorsese films of faith and redemption, it did not even seem like a Scorsese film. Thus, Vincent Canby opened his review by emphasizing the strangeness of even associating Scorsese with Edith Wharton, the acclaimed author of several classic American novels generally deemed stylistic masterpieces that reflect her elite upper-class background and life of the late nineteenth to the mid-twentieth centuries. Canby wrote, "Taking 'The Age of Innocence,' Edith Wharton's sad and elegantly funny novel about New York's highest society in the 1870's, Martin Scorsese has made a gorgeously uncharacteristic Scorsese film. It would be difficult to imagine anything further removed from the director's canon than Wharton's Pulitzer Prize-winning page-turner, not even 'The Last Temptation of Christ.'"[3]

Similarly, Roger Ebert wrote, "Since so many of Scorsese's films have grown out of the streets of modern New York City, out of the Italian American subculture of his youth, the announcement that he would film Edith Wharton's *The Age of Innocence* struck many people as astonishing—as surprising, say, as if Abel Ferrara had announced a film by Henry James. It is only when you see the film, and realize what it is about, that you understand how this material is quintessentially Scorsese."[4]

Also, before *The Age of Innocence* was released, writer Francine Prose wrote, "Much anticipation has focused on how the bloody-minded, paranoid jitter of Mr. Scorsese's previous work ('Taxi Driver,' 'Raging Bull,' 'Goodfellas') would adjust to the statelier rhythms of an atmosphere so rarefied that a woman crossing a party to talk to a man could throw the whole gathering into social shock."[5] Interestingly, Prose's comments came in her multi-illustrated article about the film that ran for three pages in the Sunday film section of *The New York Times*.[6] The newspaper in fact treated the movie as an important cultural event in itself, not only for film but for New York City. In a subsequent edition, the newspaper also ran an interesting article with several photographs and images that showed how locations for settings in the novel in New York City and the area were presented and created for the film.[7]

Upon viewing *The Age of Innocence*, Prose to her surprise found herself "looking for reasons why this seemingly unlikely director was the obvious choice to do it." Noting that the "film is so faithful to the novel," she recognized connections in it to themes in Scorsese's other works. She writes, "Passion, especially repressed passion, has often been Mr. Scorsese's subject. And the organized suppression of unruly desire is the villain blighting 'The Age of Innocence.'" As Prose explains, the hero Newland Archer (Daniel Day-Lewis) gets engaged to May Welland (Winona Ryder), "the angelic blank slate of a girl his society wants him to marry," but "[i]nconveniently Newland falls in love with Countess Ellen Olenska (Michelle Pfeiffer), an interesting, independent woman with a complicated romantic past and a shaky position in

Newland's rigidly codified tribe—a tribe that smoothly closes ranks to keep the lovers apart."[8]

In addition to resonant themes of passion, repression, and latent violence, and tribal codes of social order and behavior, redemption as a motivating drive also connects *The Age of Innocence* to the overall Scorsese canon. What Scorsese explained to Paul Elie regarding his recent *Silence* also applies in a different way to his interpretation of *The Age of Innocence*. He told Elie, "My brother's keeper—it's my brother's keeper!" Scorsese continues, "And it goes beyond your brother. Are we responsible for other people? What is our obligation, when somebody does something that is so upsetting?" He continues to fire off questions. "Do you really have to do it because they're a brother, or you're related, or you made vows of marriage? What is the right thing to do for the other person, and for yourself?"[9]

Such questions of moral and ethical ambiguity and uncertainty suffuse *The Age of Innocence*. They suggest a search for faith and redemption of a more secular sort than the religious and church patterns of expression in some of his other films. In the context of the prominence of redemption and faith in Scorsese's work, it seems significant that Scorsese uses the word "soul" in an interview with Gavin Smith to describe the cost to Newland Archer of his loss of Ellen. He says Archer's "soul goes with her" as she exits from a veranda in Boston.[10] In the *Age of Innocence*, the word "soul" means the search for answers to the questions of ethics that plague Scorsese and that he raises about responsibility to others. Soul describes the body's quest for meaning. The word suggests the need to balance drive with responsibility. Soul means existential awakening and coming to presence in relation to others. It falls into what philosopher Emmanuel Levinas terms "the secularization of the sacred."[11]

Accordingly, as Prose intimates, in *The Age of Innocence*, Scorsese dramatizes and expresses his themes through the assiduously detailed development of narrative and character that closely adhere to the language and structure of the original novel that was written in 1920 but set in the New York of the 1870s. He convincingly captures the drama of moral and ethical crisis for the three main characters in the film and novel.

For some critics, Scorsese's *The Age of Innocence* succeeds artistically as a period piece and costume melodrama about morally ambiguous relationships.[12] Discussing his intention and motivation behind the film, Scorsese says, "With *The Age of Innocence*, I wanted to find a way of making something literary." In a tone, mimicking the language of the novel, he adds, "and Americans are cowed by the tyranny of that word—and also filmic."[13]

Nevertheless, Scorsese insists, "'What I wanted to do as much as possible was to recreate for a viewing audience the experience I had reading the book.'"[14] To achieve his ambition "to have some of the literary experience along with the visual experience of the picture," Scorsese says, "we decided to use a voice-over narration from the book, in which the narrator seems to be standing apart and observing events" (*SOS*: 185). Scorsese co-wrote the screenplay for the film with Jay Cocks, who gave him a copy of the book.[15] As Tom Shone says, "For two years, Scorsese and Cocks worked on the structure. Cocks coming over once or twice a week to hash it out, although they ended up making few changes to the book, and even kept the idea of a non-diegetic narrator for the story, almost as if the voice of society itself were speaking up. The executives at Columbia were confused. "'Who is the narrator?'" they wanted to know. "'Who cares,'" said Scorsese and chose Joanne Woodward—a key casting decision, for it would be Woodward's languid voice, reading Wharton's lapidary prose, that held the picture together."[16]

"OVERTURE AND EPIGRAPH"

It can be argued, however, that Scorsese accomplishes much more than such a successful rendering of the novel in his film version of *The Age of Innocence*. Scorsese takes *The Age of Innocence* to a realm of metaphysical examination and articulation that goes beyond the drama of his film and may even exceed his accomplishments in his recognized classics of the street and the mob. The search for ethical meaning and understanding that Scorsese so poignantly articulates to Elie becomes an exploration in *The Age of Innocence* of the relationship of time and existential presence to the ethical responsibility for the other. On the screen, the spacing of bodies in relationship to the frame, image, and other bodies manifests a coming or emergence of being in time. As Jean-Luc Nancy writes, "We will have to ponder the spacing of time—of *time*, that is, *as a body*."[17]

In an essay on the novel, celebrated writer John Updike says, "*The Age of Innocence*, beneath its fine surface, holds an abyss—the abyss of time, and the tragedy of human transcience."[18] Scorsese not only puts Updike's insight on the screen; he makes his film out of the elements of time, loss, despair, and infinite emptiness that Updike sees as the existential genius of the novel. Scorsese films and edits *The Age of Innocence* through his own form of what Laura Mulvey later termed "delayed cinema."[19] The timing and rhythm, the stalling and movement of his filming and editing make *The Age of Innocence* into a drama of emerging existential presence and the awaking of the ethical imperative of the relationship to the other.

As Deborah Thomas suggests, the opening credits and scene of Scorsese's *The Age of Innocence* project a vibrant flow of visual images and sounds that foreshadow the film's ultimate artistic and cultural significance. Similarly, in her prescient review, Kathleen Murphy says, "The credit sequence stands as overture and epigraph to *The Age of Innocence*: Graceful lines of cursive writing are echoed in the luxurious curves of rose petals unfolding–in accelerating slow motion—again and again, those natural intricacies then repeated in the static, half-concealing artifice of lace." She maintains that "these images" convey "the complex modes and rhythms of revelation that inform this film. Indeed, they are the sensual stuff the movie's made of—speaking forms or figures of speech." She adds that "more than once" Scorsese "demonstrates the increasingly heady mixed-media progressions of an engaged imagination."[20]

In the opening of *The Age of Innocence,* credits such as *A Martin Scorsese Film* first appear in white print against a black background. As the credits continue—*Daniel Day-Lewis* in white lettering—fancy, purplish cursive but rather undecipherable writing appears on a blackish background. With more credits on the screen, the writing becomes reddish. Then slowly from behind the writing, the first unfolding of light-reddish rose petals appears. The unfolding petals surge through the darkness, pushing the credits for secondary performers such as Geraldine Chaplin (Mrs. Welland) and Mary Beth Hurt (Regina Beaufort) to the left and right of the screen. As Murphy indicates, image after image of different roses with changing colors open, unfold, and overlap into other emerging rose petals. The varying speeds of the overlapping slow-motion imagery of the flowers in conjunction with the camera's visual concentration on the inner depths of the flowers as the core center of their generative unfolding all suggest the visual rhythms of emerging life and being. This steady rhythmic propagation of flowery life continues against a black background that contrasts with the rushed acceleration of the opening of white roses. The purity of the aggressively vital white roses soon fades into a frame filled with deep bloody redness.

As Murphy suggests, the lace covering of the bursting roses contributes a paradoxical contradiction to the imagery. The lace intensifies the natural femininity and sensuality of the flowers while also suggesting some control and constriction of the implied sexual significance of the flowers. The fetishistic lace intensifies the desire it inhibits and represses.

The rough redness fades into the grainy whiteness of a flowery lace with white spikes and embroidered flowers that bring back dimly lit cursive writing as the background for a credit pronouncing Scorsese as director. The music of Elmer Bernstein soon bridges over to the off-screen singing of Margaret (Linda Faye Farkas) in Act III of Charles Gounod's opera *Faust.* The opening credit sequence and the subsequent opera scene indicate extraordinarily close coordination and collaboration between Scorsese and cinematographer Michael Ballhaus, production designer Dante Ferretti, and film editor Thelma Schoonover.

The opening credit sequence establishes the tension of the ambiguous relationship between indecipherable but attractive cursive writing and unfolding flowers that keep exploding with life and beauty only to fade out to other flowers. The lace that dresses and contains the flowers insinuates mediation between the sensuality of the flowers and the solidity of the writing. As my student Qianhui (Loro) Pi suggests, the lace operates in a way like language. The lace connects to and covers the exposure of the flowers while also interceding to impede access to the immediate and direct experience of the flowers.

Scorsese in different contexts speaks of the flowers as a basic expression of the film's characters. He says, "While there was a great deal of sensuality in their lives, they didn't appear to be overly sensual, so it seemed the flowers were expressive of their emotions" (*SOS*: 189). Asked by Gavin Smith about "the significance of opening on the flowers and [why] then the camera moves up to the opera singer's face," Scorsese simply answered, "Well, it was the flowers. He loves me, he loves me not. I knew that the first image had to be flowers, that's for sure" (cited in Smith: 21).

Nancy's theory of "exscription" proffers another way to think about the flowers and the writing in the opening sequence of *The Age of Innocence* in their relationship to time, existence, and camera movement in the scene. Nancy argues that "writing *exscribes* meaning every bit as much as it inscribes significations." He says, "It exscribes meaning or, in other words, it shows that what matters . . . is *outside* the text, takes place outside writing." In other words, for Nancy, inscriptions define and categorize experience while exscription concerns existential experience outside of the text and signification. Nancy says, "Writing, reading, I exscribe the 'thing itself'—'existence,' the 'real'—which *is* only when it is exscribed, and whose *being* alone is what is at stake in inscription. By inscribing significations, we exscribe the presence of what withdraws from all significations, being itself (life, passions, matter . . .). The being of existence is not unpresentable: it presents itself exscribed."[21] For Nancy, it can be suggested that the difference between inscription and exscription entails the difference between securing presence for the immanently real and emerging presence of immediate existential experience.

Accordingly, Scorsese immediately implants into the opening sequences of his film the philosophical and ethical imperative of *The Age of Innocence*'s engagement with existential urgency, reality, and time. A background of fancy and delicate but unclear cursive writing contrasts with emerging life in the form of the flowing and surging images of unfolding beautiful rose petals. The fancy writing suggests the formality of rigid class, social, and temporal structures as opposed to the flowering openings of new life.

The writing in the credits sequence forms a background to the stream of flowers. The writing insinuates the tension between conventional naming and language structures in the search for meaning and the spontaneity and authenticity of existential engagement. As Julia Kristeva writes, "Our gift of speech, of situating ourselves in time for another, could exist nowhere except beyond an abyss."[22] Nancy also writes, "In writing, the real is not represented; it presents unheard-of violence and restraint, the surprise and freedom of being in exscription, where writing at every instant discharges itself, unburdens itself, empties itself of itself" (*BP*: 339).

As though affirming the insights of Nancy and Kristeva, the screenplay, which generally copies the text of the novel, describes the complexity and abyss of language. The narrator of *The Age of Innocence* says, "They all lived in a kind of hieroglyphic world. The real thing was never said or done or even thought, but only represented by a set of arbitrary signs. These signs were not always subtle, and all the more significant for that. The refusals were more than a simple snubbing. They were an eradication." The eradication about which the narrator speaks, of course, refers to the refusal of New York society to attend a dinner for Ellen Olenska. This rejection amounts to the obliteration of her existence, a death sentence communicated with discreet indirection by writings on personal cards of regrets, writings no doubt similar to the cursive writing in the credit sequence. Scorsese brilliantly conveys that moment of devastation with a dissolve to a darkened kitchen barren of any of the life and activity that originally went into the preparation for the dinner that would not occur.

Returning to the beginning of the film, an extended arm over yellow daisies introduces a human element into the abstraction of the credit sequence of flowers, movement, cursive writing, and music. Scorsese executes a kind of seamless transition from the flowers of the credit sequence to asters or daisies on the stage of the Academy of Music opera house as the character Margaret sings in Gounod's *Faust*. Here, too, Scorsese has a simple explanation for insisting on historic and literary authenticity in his construction of the opera scene. He says,

> In Edith Wharton's novel there is an opera, a performance of Gounod's *Faust*. Apparently, *Faust* was performed every year, and everyone went to see not the opera but each other, and that's why in the film we wind up past the singers on the opera audience at the end. Choosing the scene involving the picking of flowers, and her singing that he loves me, he loves me not, has a great deal to do with the rest of the picture. When I read the novel, I thought this was a wonderful piece to begin the film. After the opera, we go to the ball, so that the first twenty minutes of the film you have a complete presentation of the way these people lived, with all the rules and the possibilities of embarrassment and the politeness— but politeness covering the cynicism and gossip of the time. (*SOS*: 182)

Commenting on the opera, Robert Casillo maintains, "There is some resemblance between the situation in the opera and that portrayed in the film and novel, as Ellen Olenska like Margaret is a figure of scandal, social ostracism, and punishment, although she too is basically innocent."[23] For Scorsese, more than establishing character consistency between the opera's heroine and Ellen, the greater challenge involved getting "a visual counterpart to the power of the music, again by listening to the music and envisioning the camera moves" (Smith: 21).

The hand and arm that extend into the frame filled with yellow daisies on the opera stage immediately arouses interest in the unseen person reaching for the flowers. Clear and informative lettering inscribed across the frame replaces the more personal cursive writing in the credits. The enframed words in bold print assertively announce the time and place of the scene: "New York, the 1870s." The frame holds the time like a stop-watch in contrast to the fluidity of time in the overlapping flower imagery and changing colors of the opening sequence.

Emerging being becomes the stalled presence of a temporarily severed arm and hand. The synecdochical gesture of showing a part for the whole person intimates that the camera and the looks of the opera scene will divide and separate people rather than bring them together. The camera pulls back to reveal Margaret's "extravagantly painted face" (*S&C*: 1). The camera's action signals the move of the film to the realm of masks and artifice and fragmentation.

From a slight high-angle shot above Margaret, the camera concentrates on her face as she continues singing. It then moves toward her in a kind of swooping gesture from above as though targeting her face. As the moving camera gets level with her face, Scorsese seems ready to enter the dark cavity of her wide-open mouth. The camera then holds on her face in a medium close-up. With a delayed frame, the concentration on the deep inner blackness of the mouth more readily recalls the focus on the deep inner spaces of the bursting flowers in the previous credits scene. The sensuality of both images leaves much room for transporting the metaphysical dynamic of the credits sequence to the time and space of the body on the opera stage.

Holding the frame to still Margaret's movement and her singing exposes a kind of vampirish or ghoulish expressiveness to her masked face. Longish white teeth over the dark gap suggest an incipient violence and dangerous appetite. The inner void of Margaret's open mouth intimates the possibility for illumination by Nancy's theory of "the *black hole* of an absence of matter." Nancy writes that the "body forms very precisely what astrophysicists call a *black hole*: a star whose dimension is such that its gravity withholds its own light, a star that extinguishes and collapses on its own into itself, opening, in the universe at the center of the star and its extraordinary density" (*C*: 75; emphasis in the original).

For Nancy, the body becomes a "wound" of self-consumption, a thing of "infinite intussusception, the *proper* devouring itself, all the way to the void at its center—in truth deeper, even, than the center, deeper than any trace of spacing" (*C*: 75; emphasis in the original). The delayed movement of the framed abyss of darkness of the singer's mouth injects stalled time and death into the frozen frame. For Nancy, equating the mouth with the tomb—"the opening, the tomb or the mouth" (*C*: 15)—relates the mouth as a source of speech to the void at the center of language. Margaret's mouth in the operatic performance in *The Age of Innocence* speaks worlds of suggested meaning beyond the dramas on and off stage.

Thus, the suspension over the abyss of time and language compels grasping for objects, rigid rules, codes of behavior and thought, and inscribed truths for stability and security. Later in the film the narrator describes Archer as content with such support systems. She notes, "Archer had gradually reverted to his old inherited ideas about marriage. It was less trouble to conform with tradition."

At the opera, Scorsese's camera cross-fades to deep red that turns out to be the backing of a theater seat. The red seat offsets the blackness of a tuxedo. The camera shows only part of the body of the man wearing the tuxedo. The camera then catches the rich whiteness of a gardenia in the man's lapel. The camera tilts up to reveal the face of Daniel Day-Lewis's Newland Archer.

The movement of the camera on Archer mimics the movement on the stage with Margaret. As on the stage, the camera on Archer shifts slightly, in this instance to the left from the gardenia shot and up to Archer's face in close-up. It treats both Margaret and Archer as performers who require filming with studied care and attention to develop character and meaning.

Holding these shots in delayed cinema broadens the time and the cinematic image to make the implicit connection between Margaret and Archer, bringing them together through comparable camera movements on their different stages of performance. As though to emphasize the significant linkage of their different performances on different stages, Scorsese has the camera cut to the opera stage to race over the expanse of stage footlights, an action that highlights the theatrical nature of the events before the camera.

The existential question raised in the credit sequence of attempting to break from the written text for "what matters" outside the text also manifests itself in the immediate appearance of Margaret's and Archer's bodies. Nancy's idea of the body as a "black hole" of the void, absence, and nothingness relates to language and writing.

In such a context of language and writing, Nancy sees the body as "being stretched, exasperated, torn between the unnameable and the unnameable: all the stranger for being more intimate" (*C*: 73). Obviously, the use of flowers by Margaret and Archer and throughout the entirety of the film reinforces the theme of the inherent paradox of naming, recalling Juliet's "What's in a name/ A rose by any other word would smell as sweet." Later in the film and novel, Ellen and Archer exchange comments about "labels," another form of naming. She asks, "Is New York such a labyrinth? I thought it was so straight up and down, like Fifth Avenue, with all the cross-streets numbered and big honest labels on everything." Archer responds, "Everything is labeled. But everybody is not."

At the opera, Archer like Margaret appears heavily costumed in his formal tuxedo that identifies him as a member New York's upper-class social, cultural, and economic elite. Following the novel, the film emphasizes the performance and appearance aspect for the elite of attending the opera. Through overlapping dissolves and tight close-ups, the camera reveals objects of fashion, style, and ornamentation all designed to demonstrate and prove the ostentatious wealth, power, and cultivated taste and style of the rich and powerful. Such objects include "high collars, flowing ties, beautiful beading on dresses, jewelry on necks and wrists, men's cufflinks against immaculate white cotton shirts, and shoes . . . women's heels, men's black patent leather pumps" (*C&S*: 1). Pans, dissolves, accelerated montage, and the interesting technique of "double framing" all emphasize, as Scorsese suggests, purposeful exhibitionism as the primary reason for attending the opera. The use of opera glasses by two salacious, malicious, and hypocritical male members of the elite, Larry Lefferts (Richard E. Grant) and Sillerton Jackson (Alec McCowen), to observe the entrance of Ellen Olenska into an opera box with Mrs. Welland (Geraldine Chaplin) and May accentuates the voyeurism and sense of general performance at the opera.

Interestingly, the aesthetics of the opera scene, meaning the exuberance and energy of the music and the creative vitality of the cinematography, contrasts with the sense of rigidity and restriction of the audience at the opera as they observe, judge, and evaluate one another. Scorsese films them so that the wealth, luxury, and ostentation of their lifestyle make them lifeless. Situated in close proximity to each other, they remain apart. The intimacy of what Nancy deems shared time and space or the "otherness of existence" poses a potential existential challenge to the rules and codes that sustain the artifice and inauthenticity of their lives.

The upper-class elite of the film lives to protect itself from the void, thereby condemning themselves to precisely the deep hole of self-consumption and obliteration that Nancy describes. As shot and portrayed by Scorsese, the New York elite experiences time as the space for the entrenched essentials of their lives. They thrive on maintaining isolated bodies and self-centered identities.

TWO FILMS: THE VISUAL AND NARRATIVE

As demonstrated in the opening credits and opera sequences of *The Age of Innocence*, Scorsese turns the film into an innovative work that experiments with time and space and with visual image and language. Scorsese directs the melodrama of Ellen's and Newland's unconsummated love and his suffocating marriage to May into an existential drama of emerging being and the demands of the ethical imperative of the relationship to the other.

In many ways, *The Age of Innocence* becomes a story of two films—the visual and the narrative. In his interview with Gavin Smith, Scorsese readily agrees with Smith's suggestion that he remains "*torn between strict narrative and more digressive impulses.*" He told Smith that he and iconic and controversial director Elia Kazan "were trying to tell a narrative story differently" by departing from conventional narrative structures with new cinematic ways of telling a story (Smith: 20). The narrative of the novel and the Scorsese and Cocks screenplay follow a linear, empirically descript, rigorously economical and tight language that gains added filmic authority through Joanne Woodward's nuanced, subtle, and ironic voice-over. The visual narrative challenges conventional temporal regimes to explore nonlinear, spatio-temporal relationships and possibilities.

Before *The Age of Innocence,* probably Scorsese's most successful experience with this two-track structure of the visual and the narrative occurred with *Goodfellas* (1990), a New York film based on Nicholas Pileggi's book *Wiseguy* (1985) about Henry Hill, a gangster who became a witness against the mob and went into the criminal protection program. Gilberto Perez's analysis of the structure of the film also could apply to *The Age of Innocence*. Perez describes the structure in terms of the division between the "enacted scene" and the voice-over narration. Both propel the story. Perez writes, "The narrative of *Goodfellas* is an extraordinary formal achievement, of the kind that would deserve being hailed as pathbreaking avant-garde experimentation except that it was done in work of popular art."[24]

Scorsese comes even closer with *The Age of Innocence* to making such an original work that could qualify as an avant-garde achievement. Scorsese described the visual track of the film in terms of "imagery" (Smith: 21). Significantly, George P. Castellitto discusses imagery and imagism in the film in a way that helps sets the stage for seeing *The Age of Innocence* in a Mulveyesque context of delayed cinema that enables greater appreciation for the film's visual narrative of time and loss, the existential encounter and the body, and the ethical demand in relation to the other. Delayed cinema facilitates an approach to the film that employs the perspectives and insights of such thinkers as Nancy, Levinas, and Kristeva to help interpret the cinematic image with greater depth and detail.

Castellitto argues that Scorsese in *The Age of Innocence* and other films develops his cinematic images as a form of literary modernism dubbed "the Imagist movement" as advanced in the poetry of William Carlos Williams and Wallace Stevens. He proposes that Scorsese's style of "freezing" images and objects in "freeze-frames" impels a "rhythm" and "suspension" of "movement" and "stasis" that echo the poetry of Williams and Stevens. He says, "Scorsese's technique of 'freezing' objects generates a particular method of cinematic exposition in which characters and objects are portrayed in a moment between movement and non-movement; this 'moment' is the bridge between potential behavior and stasis."[25] He proposes that Scorsese's modernistic visual art and intelligence inform and elucidate his images with substantive thematic content and meaning. He writes, "Each of the scenes in one of his films is a systematized frame of suspended images, much like a single, imagistic poem, that serves to create a visual impression that extends to a thematic and narrative blend."[26] Castellitto also repeats a famous line from the Stevens canon—"no idea about the thing but the thing itself"—that resonates with Nancy's argument that the essence of existence is its own existence.[27]

Indeed, as Castellitto suggests, Scorsese makes his frames and images into dynamic fields of changing relationships of spacious temporality in which bodies and faces fade and emerge, making their own original time and space for new life and death. Bodies and faces create new relationships in time and space to achieve emerging existential presence. Scorsese's rhythms of filming and editing facial and body structures and movements insinuate new life into surging and fading images and moments.

Delayed cinema, as explained and executed by Mulvey, takes Castellitto's important insights to another place for potential critical analysis and interpretation of Scorsese's work. Scorsese's filming and editing often replicate Mulvey's dynamic of delayed cinema. Shifting and fluid spatio-temporal relationships of the image and movement restructure the making of existential presence and the awakening of the ethical imperative. Thus, Mulvey's project of delayed cinema informs Scorsese's art of existential intensity in the encounter with the ethical demand for responsibility for the other and redemption.

Mulvey's delayed cinema dramatizes and illuminates the void of lost time and the passing of life that expresses itself in *The Age of Innocence* as desire and regret. The film articulates that struggle with time in terms of the existential crisis that intensifies the demand for responsibility. Delayed cinema's potential for creative involvement with the fluidities of time and space in film resonates with the insights into time, space, and the body of Nancy, Levinas, and Kristeva.

NANCY AND LEVINAS: TIME AND THE BODY

Interestingly, Jacques Derrida's conjunction of Nancy and Levinas especially suggests their relevance to discussions of the time and ethics of the body and self in *The Age of Innocence*. Linking Nancy and Levinas, Derrida proposes for Levinas "a virtual dialogue with Jean-Luc Nancy," emphasizing Nancy's work on the "*corpus*" or body. For Derrida, imagining this dialogue enables him "to dream a little in reading two thinkers, two friends."[28]

A dialogue between Nancy and Levinas could include the distinction between them about language and writing concerning Nancy's theory of inscription and exscription as opposed to Levinas's notion of the "Saying" and the "Said." Levinas places his terms in the context of his overall first philosophy of ethics. He writes, "I am for the other in a relationship of deaconship; I am in service to the other. In other words, the relationship of responsibility with another signifies as Saying. The Saying, prior to any language that conveys information or content, prior to language as a Said, is exposure to that obligation for which no one can replace me, and which strips the subject right down to his passivity as a hostage" (*GDT*: 161). The Saying places a great burden of responsibility upon the subject for the other. For Levinas, the Saying opens to infinity. Levinas writes, "The subject as hostage is a referral to a past that was never present, to an immemorial past, that of its preoriginal affection by another" (*GDT*: 162). The ethical relationship of the Saying gives access to the infinite. He writes, "From this relationship, the Infinite rises up gloriously" (*GDT*: 163). The experience of the Saying occurs with the power and immediacy of an epiphany.

While Levinas's phenomenology contrasts with Nancy's radical existentialism of the otherness of existence, both share a focus on the body. Levinas writes, "Only a subject that eats can be for-the-other, or can signify. Signification, the–one-for-the-other, has meaning only among beings of flesh and blood."[29] For both thinkers, writing and text in relationship to the body proves central for fulfilling their ethical and existential purposes.

Thus, Nancy regards "the modern body," as we have seen, as "*exscribed* in advance from all writing." Nancy writes, "We have to begin by getting through, and by means of the *exscription* of our body: its being inscribed–outside, its being placed *outside the text* as the most *proper* movement of its text; the text *itself* being abandoned, left at its limit" (*C*: 11; emphasis in the original). The body as exscribed breaks from the textual boundaries of prescribed definitions of being and scripts of inherited conventions and socially approved forms of behavior and thought. It opens place and the spacious for existence. Seeing bodies as "places of existence," Nancy says that "they are *open* space . . . a space more properly *spacious* than spatial what could also be called a *place*." Such space "makes room for the fact that the essence of existence is to be without essence. That's why the *ontology of the body* is ontology itself" (*C*: 15; emphasis in the original). Nancy maintains the "ontological body" needs further study.

Body as exscribed outside text opens space for time and emerging presence. Thinking about time and the history "yet to come—because it is *coming*," Nancy, we recall, writes, "Because it is *coming*, it also *spaces*. We will have to ponder the spacing of time—of *time*, that is, *as a body*" (*C*: 43; emphasis in the original).

Spacing of time as a body positions Nancy in proximity to Levinas on rethinking death in terms of time, meaning, and the body. Levinas, as noted elsewhere in this study, proposes "to think death on the basis of time rather than time on the basis of death" (*GDT*: 106). Levinas emphasizes a temporality open to infinity rather than the assumption of time as "annihilation" and closing upon death. He writes, "Time is not the limitation of being but its relationship with infinity. Death is not annihilation but the question that is necessary for this relationship with infinity, or time, to be produced" (*GDT*: 19).

For Nancy, the ontological body as being carries death with it. Death inheres in the body. Nancy writes, "The body is the being of existence. *How best to take death seriously?* But also: *How are we to explain that existence isn't 'for' death,* but that 'death' is the body of existence, a very different thing." Taking death "*seriously*" presumably means seeing it as part of life that compels finding the exterior space for existence. He writes, "In the span of its lifetime, the body is also a dead body, the body of a dead person, this dead person I am when alive. Dead or alive, neither dead nor alive, I *am* the opening, the tomb or the mouth, the one inside the other" (*C*: 15; emphasis in the original). For Nancy, the mouth as tomb and death and as the "black hole" of an abyss resonates with the resounding vocal emanations of an aria sung by impressive soprano Linda Faye Farkas in the role of Margaret from Gounod's *Faust*. The abyss presents a challenge for life to the existential body. The "*seriously*" dead body becomes the ontological body for life.

Thus, for Levinas and Nancy, death requires engagement in terms either of the relationship to the infinite or for opening space and place for the ontological or existential body to build on new life with the passing of the old. For Levinas, death suggests access to the infinite. Nancy in turn argues that death compels exscription from the text to the experience of existential space outside the text. Resisting death and the vulnerabilities of the body motivates the attempt to inoculate the body against the contagion of death with objects and things that artificially boost the sense of empowerment, status, and privilege. Scorsese suggests that people fleeing death bury themselves under a false armor of jewelry and fashion and other objects that ultimately weigh them down, squeezing the life and death out of them—people like those in the opera boxes in the opening of *The Age of Innocence*.

THE DIVIDED BODY AND SELF: EXISTENCE AND *ZEITLOS*

Scorsese does not make a clean and easy break and exit from the stage of the Academy of Music in *The Age of Innocence*. Instead, he executes a complex maneuver of cuts, overlapping images, and sweeping pans to move the action from the opera stage with Margaret and Faust (Michael Rees Davis) to the other opera of looks and spectacle and conspicuous ostentation taking place in and between the opera boxes looming above the theater that are occupied by the city's social, economic, and cultural elites. Director Scorsese's camera in two different moves pulls back from the stage to focus on Archer and the white gardenia in his tuxedo lapel marking the beginning of the other drama in the audience. Archer enters the box with Larry Lefferts and Sillerton Jackson who share opera glasses to observe a box across the theater from them with May, Ellen, and Mrs. Welland (Geraldine Chaplin). Interestingly, as the camera pans over the gloves, bracelets, and other jewelry, it does not show faces, emphasizing the importance of such items for establishing identity and prominence. He mixes shots of the operatic performance with the social performance in the boxes.

Scorsese also carefully constructed an exceptionally original shot that conveys the sensation of seeing through Lefferts's opera glasses as Lefferts scans the theater. Smith described the shot as a "*flickering, strobe editing effect where you pan across the audience.*" Scorsese explained that "we fell upon the idea of exposing one frame at a time, stop action, and then printing that frame three times and then dissolving between each shot so that each three frames was a dissolve." He said, "That took about a year to figure out" (Smith: 21; emphasis in the original).

More than just an extremely inventive "camera move" that worked as "a kind of stop-action photography" (*SOS*: 186, 187) the binoculars shot comments on the temporal and spatial complexities and possibilities of the "look." As Mulvey intimates, a temporal dimension occurs with any of the three looks she describes: camera, diegetic characters, and the viewer or spectator (*D24*: 190, 183). From a Levinasian perspective, time inexorably relates to the other. He argues that "time is not the achievement of an isolated and lone subject, but . . . it is the very relationship of the subject with the Other."[30] The frantic hyperactivity of the camera with its pulsating mixture of perspectives and imagistic flashes slows to a low-angle shot of the box with Lefferts and Jackson as they continue to peer in snobbish dismay and disapproval over Ellen's presence in the box with May and Mrs. Welland, her aunt. The camera shows Archer deep in the darkness at the back of the box looking frozen as death as Lefferts says, "Parading her at the opera like that. Sitting her next to May Welland. It's all very odd." Alluding to Ellen's marriage to Count Olenska and her separation and possible divorce amidst scandal, Jackson mumbles, "Well, she's had such an odd life."

Delayed cinema helps reveal the slightest movement of Archer's eyes toward the opera box across from him with the women of his past, present, and future life. Then, without saying a word but with the slightest flash of his eyes and barest movement of his chin in Jackson's direction, Archer's stone-cold expression and his physical rigidity turn his whole body into a space of silent resistance. As he rises from his seat in the back of the box to exit without a word, Archer literally takes a step into what will be his new life. Day-Lewis's expression of Archer's restrained exasperation with the gossipy men places Archer in a transitional state in both the past and the future, giving the moment a sense of emerging presence. He leaves the box as though he had never been there.

In the following scene, Scorsese literally confirms the existential significance of Archer's physical departure from one opera box filled with gossipy, sneering men to the women's box on the opposite side of the theater. The camera follows Archer through glass doors that open to a staircase.

Amazingly, the physical body splits apart. One Archer fades off to the left as a kind of ghostly figure and absence. The second Archer makes his way upstairs. Delayed and slowed cinema objectively document Scorsese's decision to break Archer's body into two parts. The divided body clearly suggests a divided psyche. The divided body even more clearly and pertinently highlights the deathly discarding of one exterior physical frame of being for another. Archer advances up the stairs and toward the ladies' opera box with a sense of calm assurance and being. The divided physical body enacts the notion of time as a body creating new time and the potential for a new existential body.

A point-of-view shot from Archer's perspective suggests a coherent, unified subjective position as he enters the box. The camera from his perspective centers on May's bouquet of lilies-of-the-valley. The camera then tilts up to May's face. She beams a smile of joyful adoration toward Archer. The screenplay describes her as "radiant." May's mother, Mrs. Welland, as played by Geraldine Chaplin, greets Archer before introducing him to Ellen seated next to her. Describing Ellen, the screenplay says, "Her face is unconventional, but it is magic" (*S&C*: 3).

The camera movement and images in close-up of May and Ellen project a much greater contrast of faces and beauty than the screenplay suggests. A cinematic vision of extraordinary intelligence and creativity imagined Winona Ryder as May and Michelle Pfeiffer as Ellen as two powerful forces of great passion for love, presence, and authority. The differences between the two women intensify their strengths in their competition for Archer's attention and affection. Archer's subjective look upon them immediately provokes responses from each that taken together visually forecast the multilayered conflicts and tensions that will make up the rest of the film. As in the opening sequences of the film, camera movement, filming, and editing will place the scene in another temporal and spatial dimension.

The thin, tightly structured facial and physical intensity of Ryder's May projects a quality of almost adolescent innocence, charm, and vulnerability.

In contrast, Pfeiffer's golden voluptuousness conveys a siren's command and power. A striking counter-movement occurs in the atmosphere of the ladies' opera box when Archer first acknowledges and then, at May's innocent suggestion, returns to Ellen to be in closer conversation with her. Brilliantly, one "shush" from her mother startles May to be quiet and instantly transmogrifies her smile into stony adolescent submission, leaving the scene in Ellen's hands. Sitting next to May, Mrs. Welland stays fixed in her own polite silence with the back of her head to the camera. She sits in frozen attention to the opera on stage while another opera of passion, emotion, and irresolvable conflict starts behind and next to her between Archer and Ellen.

Oblivious to the impending disaster around her, Mrs. Welland's silence abstracts her from the scene, placing the verbal and visual intercourse between Ellen and Archer into its own spatio-temporal dimension. The banter and reverse shots between Archer and May set a tone and mood for them of giggly flirtatious affection. Archer and Ellen become involved in their personal drama that removes them from the tight society of the box and transfixes them in their own sphere of emerging emotional and mental connection.

Accordingly, in the opening moments of *The Age of Innocence,* Scorsese once again conveys a reimagined reality of time and space. Scorsese and his crew carefully constructed the scene to put Ellen and Archer in their own little world. Thus, soon after his entry into the box, Ellen holds her hand out for Archer in a playful gesture of command. In a brilliant shot worthy of study with delayed cinema, Ellen's hand and fingers extend from the left foreground of the frame through the straight line of her arm to her fully lit shining face with its beautifully engaging smile in the center right of the frame. In that shot sequence, Ellen suddenly glances down questioningly at her hand in Archer's hand as though wondering what next to do with him. Teasing and cautiously flirting with Archer about her memories of their past playfulness as children, Ellen easily maintains command of the situation, waving her fan over the opera audience below the box. Laughingly and charmingly, she says, "I remember we played together. Being here again makes me remember so much . . . I see everybody the same way, dressed in knickerbockers and pantalettes."

As Archer in the scene responds to her by moving closer, Ellen continues to draw his attention to their past as a way of establishing their new relationship for the present and the future. She says, "You were horrid. You kissed me once behind a door. But it was your cousin Vandy, the one who never looked at me, I was in love with." Her remark suggests the power of "the look" for control and direction of a situation. Trying to find a way to deal with the avalanche of nuance and innuendo in Ellen's speech and gestures, Archer says simply, "Yes, you have been away a very long time." At this point, with a great flourish of her "large fan of eagle feathers" (*S&C*: 4), Ellen says, "Oh, centuries and centuries. So long I'm sure I'm dead and buried, and this dear old place is heaven."

Spoken with a sense of irony and sarcasm, Ellen's words return the film to the drama of death and the dark abyss of passing and lost time. As though to accentuate the significance of Ellen's words and their implication for the future of the film's three leading figures, a resounding drum roll from the orchestra of the opera thunders over and through the action on the opera stage and the drama in the opera box.

The drum also signals a crucial shift in the structure of the film itself. It marks the beginning of the voice-over narration. The camera moves from the opera box and stage to another box with Mrs. Julius (Regina) Beaufort. The mellifluous voice of Joanne Woodward pronounces a new temporal authority and regime for the film. A linear temporal narrative will parallel the vagaries of the visual narrative with the camera's penchant for playing with spatial and temporal fluidity. The narrator reports; "It invariably happened, as everything happened in those days, in the same way. As usual, Mrs. Julius Beaufort appeared just before the Jewel Song and, again as usual, rose at the end of the third act and disappeared. New York then knew that, a half-hour later, her annual opera ball would begin."

Accordingly, the narrative like the social structure of the elite, will organize and advance the values of ritual, repetition, stability, and orderliness, all of which Ellen Olenska eschews and oppugns as evidenced by her background and lifestyle. Woodward's voice-over and the camera confirm the priority the elite places upon an orderly temporal regime as a sign of and the means for their control over events and history. The voice-over also confirms the greater significance given to the spectacle of the audience's self-promotion at the opera over the actual musical occasion itself. The camera shows Mrs. Beaufort leaving the Academy of Music to enter one of the many carriages lined up on the street. Woodward reports, "Carriages waited at the curb for the entire performance. It was widely known in New York, but never acknowledged, that Americans want to get away from amusement even more quickly than they want to get to it."

Interestingly, Scorsese's camera and the narrative voice-over turn the opera ball, one of the elite's major rituals of temporal order and social privilege, into an explosive instance of creation. The camera cuts to the Beaufort house and its ballroom. A long straight shot of the ballroom shows a large room in darkness and without any signs of life. A large bag covers the great chandelier that hangs over the room. Shuttered windows keep out the light. The voice-over describes the room and provides the background about the ball and about Regina and Julius Beaufort. Explaining what "was regrettable in the Beaufort past," Woodward reports that "Regina Beaufort came from an old South Carolina family, but her husband Julius, who passed for an Englishman, was known to have dissipated habits, a bitter tongue and mysterious antecedents. His marriage assured him a social position, but not necessarily respect."

A cross-fade covers the screen in deep black. And then suddenly, the blackness breaks into extraordinary life and energy. Dancers burst through to the exuberant music of the orchestra. They dance in structured formations to music that has almost a military or martial resonance and beat. The explosion of life out of the darkness in effect constitutes a new birth to presence and life at the hands of an implied creator, namely Scorsese the director. The Beaufort ballroom explosion of life enacts Nancy's assertion that "the body's not an image-*of*. But it's the *coming to presence*, like an image coming on a movie or a TV screen—coming *from* nowhere behind the screen, *being* the spacing of this screen, existing as its extension" (*C*: 63; emphasis in the original).

The coming to presence on the screen, the creation of life out of the darkness of nothingness presents questions for the scene and the film about the meaning of creation for the created bodies as well as the question of the existence of a creator. Nancy writes, "Bodies thus created, which is to say, *coming*, and whose coming spaces the *here*, the *there*, every time." The coming to presence of such bodies as spaces for existence in our times insinuates the need for and reliance upon others. He writes, "Bodies demand, yet again, their creation. Not an incarnation inflating the spiritual life of the sign, but a birthing and a sharing of bodies" (*C*: 89, 83; emphasis in the original). He emphasizes the meaning and perpetuation of life through other bodies. He says that "our world creates the great number of bodies, creates itself as the world of bodies" (*C*: 89). He also notes the significance of the absence of a creator. He writes, "A creator contains, retains his creation, and relates it to himself. But the creation of the world of bodies doesn't return to anything or anyone" (*C*: 107). Nancy's discussion of created bodies and creators carries over and enlightens the theme of emerging presence in *The Age of Innocence*.

In *The Age of Innocence*, the voice-over narrator counters the abyss of language and time with a prose style of accuracy and clarity. The rigorous precision of the prose matches the choreographed regularity of the dancers at the Beaufort ball. As Scorsese says of the voice-over narration, "The gracefulness of the prose has a kind of scathing, ironic violence to it" (*SOS*: 185). The narrator functions as an omniscient all-knowing power. She guides and controls the story, providing information and background on people and events. The narrator establishes an orderly temporal regime of the past and present with a sense of being able to forecast the future with considerable accuracy. She describes Archer as a man who enjoys challenging "conformity" and "convention" but ultimately upholds "family and tradition" to maintain "a world balanced so precariously that its harmony could be shattered by a whisper." A world of such balance and symmetry can be made accessible by the narrator's clear and precise descriptive language. With economical and concrete detail, she introduces and explains how people such as Lawrence Lefferts, old Sillerton Jackson, and the rake Julius Beaufort all fit into and function in this world.

In contrast to the orderly linear temporality of the narrative voice, Scorsese's camera at the Beaufort ball moves and works according to a very different temporal order. Although it deliberately pauses to exhibit the figures mentioned by the narrator, the camera's basic movement suggests a certain visual randomness and opportunism. It sways and swoons, establishing a rhythm with the music of the ballroom orchestra. The frame fills and empties and fills and empties again. The camera follows Archer but he seems detached—like a lost object bouncing between and against other created bodies in flux before the camera. Dancers swirl and turn around him as the camera continues from his perspective through the ballroom. The filming follows the pattern of rhythm and suspension that Castellito describes. Interestingly, one frozen image incorporates into the film frame a painting of people at a party that replicates the actual Beaufort ballroom event. Painting and filmic image duplicate each other. The painting in a way trivializes the ballroom people. It makes them a bit ordinary. Scripted, these people lack being.

Thus, Scorsese says, "Paintings were so important; like movies to us today" (Smith: 26). Throughout the film, Scorsese indicates a fascination with the contrast between the static framing of painting as opposed to the mobile framing of film. So, in pausing at the painting of a gala social event that mirrors the Beaufort party, Scorsese highlights the power of film as an art form in time of moving images. The exchange and interaction between film image and painting constitute a kind of meta-commentary on the visual narrative itself as operating in a temporal regime that differs from the linearity of the narrative voice-over. The rhythms, fluidities, freezes, pauses, and suspensions of flow and movement of the visual insinuate the nonlinear aspect of the visual narrative.

Paintings also figure prominently in a later scene at the home of Mrs. Manson Mingott (Miriam Margolyes), May's grandmother. A surfeit of paintings covers the wall space of the mansion. When the camera moves up the stairs, the progression of paintings on the wall especially makes the point of framing as opposed to the moving image. One painting in particular, John Vandelyn's *The Death of Jane McCrea*, shows two bare-chested Indians scalping a white woman. The conspicuous place of the painting suggests its importance in predicting the violence of a different kind that will be inflicted not only upon Ellen but upon May as well over the relationship of each to Archer and to each other.

At the Beaumont ball, after moving through the various drawing rooms of the mansion in a psychic zone of his own space and time that resembles what Julia Kristeva calls the Freudian timeless or *Zeitlos,* Archer finds May with her friends talking about her engagement.[31] The camera shoots him in a straight medium shot as he gestures with pleasure and even pride in seeing May, an image that recalls his stance and look upon greeting May at the opera. May's straight linear narrative tends to capture Archer and keep him steady on the straight and narrow path of the narrative. The camera frames her like a stilled image of a painting on a wall.

In contrast, Scorsese tends to see and develop Ellen in terms of the visual narrative that plays with time and space. Scorsese goes through Archer's consciousness and imagination to depict Ellen's reaction to the regrets that New York society sent to the Archers to decline their invitation to a dinner party in Ellen's honor. Returning to the spatio-temporal motifs at the beginning of the film, Scorsese dramatizes Archer's mental envisioning of the emotional and psychological costs to Ellen of such rejection. Cursive writing again provides a background, this time for the free-flowing movement of notes of regret regarding the dinner. The movement of the notes compares to the flowers blossoming in the beginning of the film. The rhythm and timing of the notes change in Archer's mind and imagination. Both the flower and rejection sequences in the film contrast the signification of writing with the passing of time and existential loss over an abyss of nothingness. As Archer and Ellen perceive it, the rejections constitute not just a denial in writing but, as previously noted, an "eradication" of Ellen's existence. The notes simply reject her—but the film art of the scene wipes out her existential being.

Projecting his emotional involvement into the scene of regrets and rejection, Archer envisions Ellen by herself before a blazing fireplace. The camera shows her left side in a medium high-angle shot. Dissolves go to her right side when she suddenly sharply turns her face to look with extraordinary intensity into the camera. With eyes blazing, she fades into an extraordinary cross-fade of red that creates the impression of calmly burning in hell.

Similarly, the camera becomes innovative when it sweeps Ellen across a room in her blazing red dress at the party given in her honor by Henry and Louisa van der Luyden. It then leads her toward Archer sitting by himself. Later, when she opens yellow roses sent to her by Archer, she becomes part of a cross-fade into yellow. At a performance of the play *The Shaughraun*, Regina Beaufort beckons to Archer sitting by himself in May's absence in the orchestra to join her and Julius, Jackson, and Ellen in their box suspended above the audience. The scene repeats the moment in the women's box at the opera when Archer and Ellen achieve a sense of isolation even in the midst of other people. At the play, Scorsese encloses Archer and Ellen in a classic iris to create and protect their private, personal time and space. Murphy notes that "the two are magically irised into a cone of perfect silence and intimacy, the world well lost" (Murphy: 14). They remain in their own sphere separated from the people who occupy the theater box with them.

Writing and the body come together with Ellen's note to Archer inviting him to see her at the van der Luydens' country home on the Hudson River while May remains in St. Augustine for the winter with her ailing mother. The film cuts to a shot replete with implied sexuality showing Ellen "bundled in warm fur" (*S&C*: 47) as she directly addresses Archer. Fur enwraps her neck and covers her head.

The tactile sensuousness of the physicality of the fur accentuates the sexual implication of their rendezvous. The lighting on her face stresses the soft sensuousness of her cheeks. Images of her face and body intermingle and overlap with the discursive writing of her note to him. Ellen recites the words in her letter, "'I feel so safe here. I wish that you were with us.'" Archer jumps at the chance to be alone in the country with Ellen.

The camera cuts and tilts down from the open Hudson River country sky to Archer in his winter outfit looking in the direction of the camera into the distance. A cut from his point of view to a shot across snow and ice shows a momentarily unidentifiable figure in deep background situated in a meager space between large trees with ragged and frosty brush and overgrowth on the left and right of the screen leading directly to the person in the distance.

Freezing the frame enables seeing the scene as a kind of Freudian dream scene with symbolism and imagery of both the fear and desire for sexual contact. Ellen stands as distant from Archer but enticingly desirable over bitingly frozen terrain that suggestively insinuates the enticement and the pain of intimacy. Another cut brings Ellen and Archer together in images that overlap. She continues to wear fur around her neck, but the coat has changed to a sensuously red cloak.

Ellen provocatively introduces the thought "that women here are so blessed they never feel need," but when Archer asks, "What sort of need?" she draws back, saying, "Please don't ask me. I don't speak your language," continuing the theme of the implied relation of language and meaning to the physical body. They enter an old house with a single log and the embers of a fire glowing warmly in the fireplace. Archer tosses a log onto the fire that bursts with a heat and force to feed the flames. The moment recalls a Freudian "simile" of "female sexual parts" and orgasm that declares "pine shavings can be kindled in order to set a log of harder wood on fire."[32] Fueling the unconscious connections of fire to sexuality, the camera cuts to Archer as he walks from the fire with his back to Ellen and toward a window as she says that she "can't feel unhappy when you're here." In the scene, as he stands by the window with his eyes closed, she rises and goes to him, hugging him passionately. The contortions of his face exhibit the dreamy intensity of his desire for her. When he turns back, Ellen sits by the fire and it becomes apparent that the contact was imaginary and manifests his unrealized wish and desire for her.

The scene in the film comes directly from the novel that introduces crucial themes and elements into the visual and voice-over narratives. Wharton

writes, "For a long moment she was silent; and in that moment Archer imagined her, almost heard her, stealing up behind him to throw her light arms
about his neck. While he waited, soul and body throbbing with the miracle to
come, his eyes mechanically received the image of a heavily-coated man with
his fur collar turned up who was advancing along the path to the house. The
man was Julius Beaufort."[33] Wharton thereby inserts into the text the idea of
fusing body and soul through love only to have such melding undone by the
emasculating intervention of Julius Beaufort.

The images of the scene on Scorsese's screen also evoke a kind of Freudian
distortion and nightmare. Ellen honestly protests that "I didn't know he was
here," but Archer with obvious jealousy and anger operatically moves from her
to open the door for Beaufort. Entering the door and house, Beaufort physically
dominates the scene and image, casting Archer aside into a diminished figure
of impotent adolescent rage. Freezing the image emphasizes its nightmarish
quality. Archer stands in the background reduced in size by an open door that
itself seems like a shrunken entry to a kind of miniature house. Scorsese then
cuts away from the country scene to Archer isolated in his study still smarting
over his humiliation by Beaufort who mocked him for "rusticating."

Wharton, however, informs and enlightens the scene with a brilliant
account of existential and psychological significance that proves important
for understanding the situation in both the novel and the film. She writes of
Beaufort, "His way of ignoring people whose presence inconvenienced him
actually gave them, if they were sensitive to it, a feeling of invisibility, of nonexistence. Archer, as the three strolled back through the park, was aware of this
odd sense of disembodiment; and humbling as it was to his vanity it gave him
the ghostly advantage of observing unobserved."[34] Wharton's words help to
explain the important shift in direction and emphasis for the film that occurs
after the scene in the country.

BODY AND SOUL

From the very beginning of *The Age of Innocence* in the opera sequence, masks
and performance help to define the contours of meaning and significance.
Masks often present the individual subject's public and social face and appearance. Wharton's "disembodiment" insinuates the creation of a secret or false
self and ideal that requires a false front and calculated performance. Macbeth
says, "False face must hide what the false heart doth know" (1.7.82). The
masks in the film at the opera and at the theater for *The Shaughraun* and masks
that form the facial expressions of those in the audience and at social gather-
ings of the elite manifest such disembodiment of divided selves. The mask
describes or characterizes Archer's stony face and rigid posture in the men's

box at the opera; at dinner with his mother, sister, and Jackson; looking for May amidst the dancers at the Beaufort ball; and with the attorney Letterblair (Norman Lloyd). Mostly, the division of his body into two parts as he goes up the stairs at the opera house dramatizes Archer's divided nature that necessitates the recourse to a false front.

Archer's masks and disembodiment express the self's search for a thriving soul and mind to gain the body's existential being. Archer's masks and disembodiment incorporate in his physical body the abyss of lost time and death. His struggle for the ontological body gets defined and expressed in his conflicting relationships with Ellen and May. His body in relation to the bodies of Ellen and May becomes the field for the existential struggle of *The Age of Innocence.* Relationships with Ellen and May become the context for his existential journey. Archer's relationship to lost time and death manifests itself in his drama with Ellen and May.

In Archer's relationships with two women the struggle for existential engagement becomes inexorably linked to the drama of the ethical imperative of responsibility to the other that extends the ontological body to the time of the other. Both Levinas and Nancy in their different ways consider the relationship to the other as a condition for the existential and ethical subject. Thus, what Wharton describes as "soul and heart throbbing" intimates the beginning of an effort to find body and soul together for the encounter with time and death. Ellen and May project two radically different unions of body and soul. Scorsese's filming stresses Ellen's free spirit and imagination as "a miracle to come" as opposed to May's structured and formal temporal regime of duty, loyalty, and higher purpose.

Interestingly, both Ellen and May at different crucial moments in *The Age of Innocence* directly face and speak to the camera in addressing Archer while Archer does not speak in such a manner. At such moments, Ellen and May speak with a moral authority that contrasts with Archer's frequent reticence and ambiguity in confronting ultimate issues of ethical authority and choice. They argue to Archer about doing the right and ethical thing above self-interest and personal happiness. Simply put, the seemingly innocent and unknowledgeable May proves to be the expert in archery in contrast to Archer's passivity while the provocative Ellen epitomizes moral and ethical freedom in choosing self-sacrifice.

Regarding the melding of body and soul, for English poet and priest John Donne, achieving and securing the unity of body and soul was a lifetime challenge and hope. In 1619, Donne preached, "In the constitution and making of a natural man, the body is not the man, nor the soul is not the man, but the union of these two makes up the man." This "deepest and most passionately held belief," according to Donne scholar Ramie Targoff, "was the defining bond of his life." As Targoff notes, "This question of how body and soul relate to each other had plagued philosophers and theologians since ancient times."[35]

Four centuries after Donne preached and wrote about it, the question of the union of the body and soul remains a central concern to the philosophers in this study of time and presence in cinema. Levinas, as we have seen, considers the body and soul in a phenomenological context of his first philosophy of an ethics greater than being. Nancy sees the body and soul as inseparable in an existential relation to time and space that collapses interior and exterior boundaries in pursuit of perpetually emerging being and presence. Julia Kristeva makes a postmodern Freudian and feminist argument for the importance of a revivified soul through her work, but especially in her book on "the maladies of the soul."[36]

Levinas engages this question of the body and soul in various phases of his work. He writes, "The body does not happen as an accident to the soul. Shall we say that it is the insertion of a soul in extension?" He confesses that "this metaphor solves nothing" but requires continued study and examination for the meaning, representation, and operation of the soul "in the extension of the body."[37] For Levinas, the soul needs the body in its engagement with the other. He writes, "Human subjectivity is of flesh and blood" (*GDT*: 188). The body makes not only physical but also spiritual and ethical contact possible.

The perplexities of bridging and melding body and soul cohere for Levinas in the context of ethical responsibility for the other. He writes, "But approached on the basis of responsibility for the other man, the psyche of the subject is the one-for-the-other, the one having to give to the other, and thus the one having hands for giving" (*GDT*: 188).

Levinas's "hands for giving" extend the subject's body and soul to the other. The hands indicate the importance that Levinas places upon "the touch" and "the caress" as extensions of the soul in relation to the vitality and purpose of the body (see *TI*: 256).

Levinas's allusion to "hands for giving" also resonates with Derrida's linkage of his "two friends" Levinas and Nancy since hands for "stroking" intimate connection through the caress and touch with the idea of hands for "stroking" for the caress and touch. In this vein, Derrida felt "tempted" to compare "Levinassean Eros" and the "Nancean psyche."[38] Another possible comparison between the two thinkers concerns Levinas's union of body and soul and Nancy's theme of the "soul" as part of the stretching and tearing of the body.

Seeing the soul in the ontological body's confrontation with death, Nancy writes, "The *soul* is the form of a body, and therefore a body itself (*psyche extended*)." He perceives the soul as indispensable to the body. He writes, "In the soul the body *comes*, in the spirit it is *taken away*" (*C*: 76, 77; emphasis in the original). Nancy returns to Aristotle to argue "the soul is the primal *entelechy* of a natural organized body," picking up as well on Donne's idea of the "making of a natural man." Nancy writes, "'Entelechy' means being accomplished with regard to its end (*telos*). Entelechy is a thing's being completely achieved" (*C*: 127–128; emphasis in the original). Nancy summarizes entelechy as "the one takes place through the other" (*C*: 128).

Continuing, however, to follow Wharton's lead in depicting the complexity and depth of her characters in *The Age of Innocence,* Scorsese films and portrays both Ellen and May as exceeding a simple dichotomy between the body and the soul. They each engage body and soul in their different ethical and psychological spheres in ways that compel difficult maneuvering for Archer on his own path toward a form of redemption.

Thus, Scorsese cuts from Archer's humiliating disappointment and failure with Ellen at the hands of Beaufort at the Hudson country retreat to his isolation in his study with, as the narrator reports, the taste of "cinders in his mouth" and the feeling of "being buried alive under his future." Scorsese then cuts to a medium close-up of Ellen in profile at her table as she writes to Archer. With her long golden blond hair down in ringlets and a somewhat distraught appearance, her voice-over narrates the writing that appears on the screen. Interestingly, in her somewhat anxious state, Ellen does not directly speak or even look to the camera. She says and writes, "Newland. Come late tomorrow. I must explain to you," but he tears up the note and goes to his prospective future with May.

From his perspective, the camera cuts to an elevated extreme long shot of the carefully designed gardens in St. Augustine, Florida where May and her mother spend the winter. The shot shows a straight path through a perfectly symmetrically balanced formal garden. Rows of roses, hydrangeas, and irises maintain the balanced landscape on each side of the pathway. Significantly, the screenplay notes that this long shot and "scene should match Archer's meeting Ellen previously" (*S&C*: 51). The small figure of May in the distance of the shot in her white dress and in the green garden indeed contrasts with the unruly winter roughness of the Hudson scene with Ellen. May's physical appearance reinforces the contrast with the sensuousness and spontaneity of Ellen's appearance in both the country house and at her writing table. May sits in a formal garden in a formal dress with her hair parted down the middle and pulled back tightly in perfect order.

Scorsese's style of filming the St. Augustine Garden scene also contrasts significantly with the Hudson country house scene. Consistent with the division in the film between the "imagism" of the visual narrative and the linearity of the voice-over narrative, Ellen's scene includes Archer's fantasy and the subsequent manipulation of time and space, while May's scene in the garden happens with close-ups and shot-reverse shots in a tightly structured dramatic order.

In the garden scene, May questions Archer's commitment to her, including hinting at her awareness of Ellen by suggesting that Archer may wish to "fulfill" his "pledge" to another "even by her getting a divorce." Establishing her position on the moral high ground, May says, "I couldn't have my happiness made out of a wrong to somebody else. We couldn't build a life on a foundation like that." Ellen and May both advocate for others as opposed to just themselves. Characteristically, Ellen tends to speak in terms of emotions and values while May thinks systematically with metaphors of building and construction and planning a life.

Archer's response also proves significant. He insistently maintains to May, "There is no one between us, May. There is nothing between us." The "nothing" suggests some ambiguity if not blatant deception on Archer's part. Substantively nothing means no obstacle or impediment to their marriage stands between them. Nothing also could mean nothing of value between them. It also suggests nothing in the existential and metaphysical sense as in the void and the abyss of meaning and language between them. Later in the film at the Beaufort lawn party, May wins at the Newport Archery Club contest, while the narrator voice-over intimates, "But what if all her calm, her niceness were just a negation, a curtain dropped in front of an emptiness? Archer felt he had never lifted that curtain."

For sure, the scene behind May's curtain, opens to the "real" world of the powerful who control events before the curtain. May plays a commanding role in both places before and behind the curtain, thereby suggesting her own double identity and divided self in the film. Thus, her power of, as the narrator said, "negation" serves her social position. The power of negation in this sense recalls George Steiner's idea of the "generative nothingness at the heart of being." Steiner relates this nothingness to language and being. He argues "if being is to be thought in depth" then "a new kind of language must be found."[39] May relies on and employs the old kind of language of writing, inscription, and the Said that keeps her world together and that secures her place in that world. She strives to keep body and soul together with the language she inherited that she uses as artfully as her bow and arrow to strike down those who would endanger her position and family.

Ellen and Archer in contrast with their artistic sensibilities, tastes, and interests discuss a new language for a new life that can provide meaning and understanding to their relationship. Ellen, we recall, protests to Archer that "I don't speak your language" while Archer at another point responds to the idea of Ellen as his "mistress" saying, "I want . . . somehow I want to get away with you. Find a world where words like that won't exist." To this Ellen responds, "Oh my dear where is that country? Have you ever been there? Is there anywhere we can be happy behind the backs of people who trust us?"

Instead, throughout their relationship, Ellen proffers a language of ethical demand and responsibility that resonates with May's words. In the drawing room of her house, she tells Archer, "Don't make love to me. Too many people have done that." She speaks to him in a familiar language of ethics and sacrifice, reminding him that to a considerable extent she learned that language from him. She says, "Didn't you talk to me—here in this room—about sacrifice and sparing scandal because my family was going to be your family? And I did what you asked me. For May's sake. And for yours." She further reminds Archer how he had set the example for caring for others. She says, "You hated happiness brought by disloyalty and cruelty and indifference. I'd never known that before and it's better than anything I've known."

In the scene, Ellen and Archer first speak heatedly to each other and then embrace with passion. In the near darkness of Ellen's room, Scorsese again directs attention to a burning log in her fireplace that helps to light the room so that the scene radically contrasts with the bright daylight of the earlier garden setting between Archer and May. Breaking from their passionate embrace on her couch, Ellen stands apart from him, imploring Archer to follow the example he originally set. The camera holds and captures the compressed tension of the emotion of Ellen's speech to Archer.

As Ellen tells Archer that his example was better than anything she had experienced before, Scorsese's visual narrative again transforms a scene with its reconstruction of time and space to insinuate a sphere of experience in a different dimension of love. Ellen's speech at a distance of a few feet from Archer on the couch suddenly changes to a voice-over. Dissolves and overlapping images move her to the couch. Delaying the frame and image shows her back to the camera and the front of her dress to the camera with Archer face down suspended between the two images. The frame and images become suspended in time and space with her approach to and presence on the couch.

The camera follows Archer down past the bottom and hem of the dress to her feet. As she says, "I'd never known that before, and it's better than anything I've known," he kisses her satin shoe that points out from beneath her beautiful dress. Archer's kiss upon the shoe takes the temporal dimension of the scene to another sphere of a lost time of fetishization.

With his face and torso in her lap, she says, "Newland. You couldn't be happy if it meant being cruel. If we act any other way, I'll be making you act against what I love in you most. And I can't go back to that way of thinking. Don't you see? I can't love you unless I give you up."

Ellen then rests her head on Archer's back with her arms and hands embracing his back and shoulders. With another dissolve, the camera moves back, emphasizing his sense of collapse onto her. The dissolves and overlapping imagery create the tangible sense of the intimacy of the two lovers enwrapped in each other.

Then in another brilliant dissolve, the camera catches a maid's hands

Figure E.1 Michelle Pfeiffer in *The Age of Innocence*

passing a small silver tray with a note on it to Ellen's hand. Her hands open the letter and the camera tilts up to Ellen's expressionless face and then back to her arm and hand, extending the letter to Archer who reads it as the camera tilts up to his face. The hands in the sequence resonate not only with the use of Margaret's hand in the opera at the beginning of the film as a synecdochical part of the whole but also for its ironic resonance with Levinas's giving hands.

A voice-over then bridges to a medium shot of May in bright light with enormous pink and white rhododendrons that cover the entirety of the background behind her. The camera zooms in on May as she recites the message on her handwritten letter that informs Ellen even before Archer about the agreement to an early marriage. Scorsese's concentration on flowers and on May's mouth and lips again returns the film to the blossoming flowers and the black hole of the soprano's open mouth in the film's operatic opening. For Archer and Ellen, May's mouth opens to the void of lost time and death. The camera goes from medium close-up to extreme close-up for May to announce "Only a month" until the wedding. The camera moves closely on her as she adds, "I will telegraph Newland. I'm too happy for words and love you dearly. Your grateful cousin May." The camera then moves from a close-up of May's bright eyes and joyful expression to the crumpled message in Archer's hand and a close-up of his face that reveals his impotence, despair, and anguish.

As though to emphasize at this point in the film the significance of the camera and the visual narrative to *The Age of Innocence*, Scorsese cuts to a photographer's studio for May's wedding photos and a dissolve from Archer's face to May "posing in wedding dress, as seen upside down in the VIEWING GLASS of an old camera" (*S&C*: 64). Scorsese also dissolves to the photographer, who happens to be Scorsese himself. With considerable irony, the narrator voice-over notes that May and Newland will spend their honeymoon in the same country house where Archer and Ellen met.

Continuing the motif of hands, on her honeymoon May gets her hands sculptured. Also on the honeymoon, the narrator voice-over indicates Archer's continuing ignorance of his wife's hidden powers to act and influence events on her own, saying, "There was no use trying to emancipate a wife who hadn't the dimmest notice that she was not free." In addition, regarding Ellen, the narrator reports, "As for the madness with Madame Olenska, Archer trained himself to remember it as the last of his discarded experiments. She remained in his memory simply as the most plaintive and poignant of a line of ghosts."

The association of Ellen with a ghost keeps her alive in a manner similar to Bazin's notion of the photograph itself as "embalmed time."[40] She exists as a kind of ghost for much of the film. Toward the end of *The Age of Innocence* in Paris with his son Ted, Archer finally seems to gain greater insight into the significance of Ellen as the emblem of the passing of time and life. The narrator voice-over reports, "Whenever he thought of Ellen Olenska, it had been abstractly, serenely, like an imaginary loved one in a book or picture. She had become the complete vision of all that he had missed."

A crucial image and scene at Newport, R.I. anticipates Archer's insights by many years. Leaving his wife May with her grandmother Mrs. Mingott, he goes, at Mrs. Mingott's suggestion, to find Ellen after a maid informs the group that Ellen, who was visiting from nearby Portsmouth, has stepped out. The narrator says that since his marriage to May, Archer had heard stories of Ellen "with detachment, as if listening to reminiscences of someone long dead." As Archer moves closer to a vision of Ellen at Newport by the sea, the narrator continues, "But the past had come again into the present, as in those newly discovered caverns in Tuscany where children had lit bunches of straw and seen old images staring from the wall."

In the Newport boat scene, Scorsese's imagery and filming make the passing of time part of the film's artistic and visual structure. Turning a corner on his path to the sea, Archer sees Ellen on the pier looking out to the sea with her back to him. A long shot shows a sailboat gliding "between Lime Rock lighthouse and the shore" (*S&C*: 72). The narrator reports, "He gave himself a single chance. She must turn before the sailboat crosses the Lime Rock light. Then he would go to her" (*S&C*: 72). The screenplay directions state: "He looks to the boat. It glides out on the receding tide between the lighthouse and the shore. He looks at Ellen: she seems to be drawn into the sunset. Back to the boat: it PASSES the lighthouse. Water SPARKLES between the stern and the last reef of the island. Back to Ellen. She has not turned" (*S&C*: 72).

A sense of profound sadness and loss accompanies the passing of the boat and scene as Archer turns his back away from Ellen. The sense of loss impels Archer to seek out Ellen one more time at Newport and Portsmouth only to collapse into the fetishization over what he mistakenly thinks is her parasol. He holds the parasol with a passion comparable to his kiss upon Ellen's shoe.

Resuming his pursuit of Ellen up to the major social event of his and May's first dinner party, Archer finds himself forced to face some realities. The screenplay describes Archer as sitting at his dinner in "suspended animation" (*S&C*: 110), a phrase that could describe Scorsese's film art and style of temporal rhythms, fluctuations, and variations in *The Age of Innocence*. The dinner scene also describes the social elite of New York in a language of violence that often has been used to characterize the gangs, mobsters, and street people of Scorsese's well-known other New York films. The narrator sees "all the harmless-looking people at the table as a band of quiet conspirators" who place Archer and Ellen at "the center of their conspiracy." Archer finally comes to understand that, as the narrator voice-over reports, "the whole tribe had rallied around his wife," making him "a prisoner in the center of an armed camp." The screenplay notes that the "careful social choreography" at the dinner was designed to keep Ellen and Archer apart (*S&C*: 114). Most important, the narrator voice-over says, Archer realizes finally that "New York believed him to be Madame Olenska's lover . . . And he understood for the first time, that his wife shared the belief." At the conclusion of the dinner, the most elite of the New York families escort Ellen to the door, making sure to keep her from Archer.

May's pregnancy seals Archer's fate. With that news that May had been "right" in telling Ellen of her pregnancy before its certainty, the camera pans his studio, advancing the time forward by several decades. The narrator says, "It was the room in which most of the real things of his life had happened." The narrator quickly summarizes the major family events of his life in the room, including the births and triumphs of his children and concluding with May's death. In the room, he takes a call from his son Ted (Robert Sean Leonard) to join him on a business trip to Paris. And in Paris, Ted tells Archer that May had informed him about Ellen. Ted asks him how he could "resist seeing the woman you almost threw everything over for. Only you didn't." Ted explains about May, "The day before she died. She asked to see me alone, remember? She said she knew we were safe with you, and always would be. Because once, when she asked you to, you gave up the thing you wanted most." In stunned silence for a second, almost in a whisper so that it may not register with Ted and remain a secret, Archer says, "She never asked me."

Scorsese's *The Age of Innocence* ends with some little controversy with Archer's decision not to accompany Ted upstairs to visit Ellen in her Paris apartment. Archer says, "Just say I'm old-fashioned. That should be enough." Going to visit Ellen, Ted leaves Archer by himself on a bench below her window. The camera tilts up from Archer's point of view to the window. The window moves and suddenly sunlight flashes off of it with an intensity strong enough to make Archer slightly squirm. Scorsese for the final time in the film employs rhythmic dissolves that disturb linear temporality. The camera dissolves back to the past through several decades to revisit Newport and the lighthouse and the sailboat moving over and through the sun's reflections on the water. This time Ellen turns to face the camera in all her radiant beauty and flashes a vivacious, captivating smile as the camera moves closer. Back at the Rue du Bac, Archer looks up teary-eyed at the window again as a servant closes Ellen's window. Archer rises and walks with his back to the camera along a little street and disappears from the street and the frame.

About the ending of *The Age of Innocence*, Jay Cocks told Scorsese that "audiences never forgave" the failure of Day-Lewis and Pfeiffer to consummate the relationship between Ellen and Archer.[41] Scorsese, however, has repeatedly defended his decision to stay with Wharton's ending to the novel. Describing Archer as a "'stand-up guy'—a man of principle who would not abandon his wife and children," Scorsese says, "When he really wanted something, he gave it up because of his children. That's very interesting to me. I don't know if I or a lot of other people could do the same, but I know that even today there are many who would. It's about making a decision in life and sticking to it, making do with what you have" (*SOS*: 194).

Whatever aesthetic, ethical, and moral criteria Scorsese uses to explain his decision for the ending of *The Age of Innocence*, keeping Archer and Ellen apart in Paris maintains the focus of the film on time, loss, and despair as opposed to allowing it to become primarily a romantic and sexual melodrama. Moreover, denying a romantic, sexual conclusion to *The Age of Innocence* sustains the film's Levinasian ethical project of the priority of the other that May, Ellen, and Archer to varying degrees ultimately proclaim and strive to practice. Instead of acceding to the desire for an artificial and conventional ending to the film that hides its existential encounter with the void of language and meaning, Scorsese offers a cinematic masterpiece of not only desire but of time and the search for being "in depth." He makes us uncomfortable in a time of pathological self-centeredness, disconnection, and technological manipulation by proposing that the death we carry in our bodies demands recognizing the body's inescapable connection to the soul. With Levinas, Nancy, and Kristeva, he visualizes the soul as the extension of the body, making the union of the body and soul a crucial part of the journey toward existential presence and ethical subjectivity. The commingling of body and soul opens the possibility for a temporal dimension of death and love on the basis of time instead of time on the basis of the annihilation of death. Levinas, Nancy, and Kristeva on time help inform Scorsese's art in *The Age of Innocence.*

Archer does indeed get, as Anthony Lane says, "the life crushed out of him" but only for a time.[42] As Scorsese argues, Archer eventually gains more in the way of dignity, maturity, and love, precisely those things that both Ellen and May knew he would lose by satisfying his impulses.

Thus, being too old fashioned to visit Ellen in Paris means more than adhering to old values and beliefs. It suggests an ability to live in different temporalities. In her review of *The Age of Innocence*, Murphy associates Newland Archer with the mythical American Adam who begins history over again in a New World Garden—but Archer, she says, gets "neatly unmanned by a snake-in-the-grass Eve" (Murphy: 12). Archer's American Adam accedes to two Eves, to both Ellen's and May's enervating arguments for the necessity to live and even thrive in real time with language. Given the chance to speak again with Ellen in Paris, Archer declines. Like Melville's Billy Budd, he gestures toward the abyss and chooses silence. When Scorsese films an aging Archer as disappearing outside the frame, it can be argued that he steps with the aid of his cane into infinity.

NOTES

1. See Paul Elie, "The Passion of Martin Scorsese," *The New York Times Magazine*, November 27, 2016, pp. 44, 46.
2. Manohla Dargis, "When Questions and Prayers Go Unanswered," *The New York Times*, December 23, 2016, p. C10.
3. Vincent Canby, "Grand Passions and Good Manners," *The New York Times*, September 17, 1993, p. B1.
4. Roger Ebert, *Scorsese by Ebert*, foreword by Martin Scorsese (Chicago: University of Chicago Press, 2008), p. 139.
5. Francine Prose, "In 'Age of Innocence,' Eternal Questions," Arts & Leisure, *The Sunday New York Times*, September 12, 1993, p. 29.
6. Ibid., pp. 29, 36, 37.
7. See Christopher Gray, "Recreating 'The Age of Innocence' in Brick and Paint," Arts & Leisure, *The Sunday New York Times*, October 24, 1993, p. 11.
8. Prose, "In 'Age of Innocence,' Eternal Questions," p. 29.
9. Elie, "The Passion of Martin Scorsese," pp. 47–48.
10. See Gavin Smith, "Martin Scorsese Interviewed by Gavin Smith," *Film Comment*, vol. 29, no. 6 (November–December 1993): 16. Future references to this interview will be cited parenthetically in the text as Smith.
11. Emmanuel Levinas, *God, Death, and Time*, trans. Bettina Bergo (Stanford: Stanford University Press, 1993), p. 163. All future references to this work will be to this edition and will be included parenthetically in the text as *GDT*.
12. See, for example, Julie Salamon, "Film: Scorsese's Opulent 'Age of Innocence,'" Leisure

& Arts, *The Wall Street Journal*, September 16, 1993, p. A18 and Anthony Lane, "Gilded Pleasure," *The New Yorker*, September 13, 1993, pp. 121–123 who disputes the idea of the film as a "costume piece." For a coherent and solid argument against the success of the film as an interpretation of the novel, see, Linda Costanza Cahir, "The Perils of Politeness in a New Age: Edith Wharton, Martin Scorsese, and *The Age of Innocence*," *Edith Wharton Review*, vol. 10, no. 2 (Fall 1993): 12–14, 19.

13. *Scorsese on Scorsese*, eds. Ian Christie and David Thompson, rev. edn (New York: Farrar, Straus and Giroux, 2003), p. 185. All future references to this work will be to this edition and will be included parenthetically in the text as *SOS*.

14. Tom Shone, *Martin Scorsese: A Retrospective* (New York: Abrams, 2014), p. 161.

15. See Martin Scorsese and Jay Cocks, *The Age of Innocence: Screenplay and Notes* (New York: Newmarket Press, 1995). All future references to this work will be to this text and will be cited parenthetically in the text as *S&C*.

16. Shone, *Martin Scorsese: A Retrospective*, pp. 162–163.

17. Jean-Luc Nancy, *Corpus*, trans. Richard A. Rand (New York: Fordham University Press, 2008), p. 43; emphasis in the original. All future references to this work will be to this edition and will be included in the text as *C*.

18. John Updike, "Archer's Way," *The New York Review of Books*, November 30, 1995, p. 18.

19. See Laura Mulvey, *Death 24x a Second: Stillness and the Moving Image* (London: Reaktion, 2006), passim. All further references to this work will be to this edition and will be included parenthetically in the text as *D24*.

20. See Deborah Thomas, "*The Age of Innocence*: Martin Scorsese, 1993," *CineAction*, vol. 62 (December 2003): 22–24; see also, Kathleen Murphy, "Artist of the Beautiful," *Film Comment*, vol. 29, no. 6 (November–December 1993): 12. All future references to this review will be to this text and will be cited parenthetically as Murphy.

21. See Nancy, *The Birth to Presence*, trans. Brian Holmes et al. (Stanford: Stanford University Press, 1993), pp. 338, 338–339; emphasis in the original. All future references to this work will be to this edition and will be included parenthetically in the text as *BP*.

22. Julia Kristeva, *Black Sun: Depression and Melancholia*, trans. Leon S. Roudiez (New York: Columbia University Press, 1989), p. 42.

23. Robert Casillo, "Mobsters and Bluebloods: Scorsese's *The Age of Innocence* in the Perspective of his Italian American Films," in *A Companion to Martin Scorsese*, ed. Aaron Baker (London: Wiley Blackwell, 2015); http://www.blackwellreference.com.proxy.library.vanderbilt.edu/subscription, last accessed October 24, 2017, p. 20.

24. Gilberto Perez, *The Material Ghost: Films and Their Medium* (Baltimore and London: Johns Hopkins University Press, 1998), pp. 255–256.

25. See George P. Castellitto, "Imagism and Martin Scorsese: Images Suspended and Extended," *Literature/Film Quarterly*, vol. 26, no. 1 (1998): 26, 23.

26. Ibid., p. 28.

27. See Wallace Stevens, "Not Ideas About the Thing but the Thing Itself," in *The Collected Poems of Wallace Stevens* (New York: Alfred A. Knopf, 1964), p. 534.

28. Jacques Derrida, *On Touching—Jean-Luc Nancy*, trans. Christine Irizarry (Stanford: Stanford University Press, 2005), pp. 83, 84. All future references to this work will be to this edition and will be included parenthetically in the text as *T*. Derrida, p. 84 writes, "One is tempted then to proceed 'as if,' to pretend, in a brief *tableau vivant*, to couple the Levinassian Eros (Nancy never names Eros, I think, outside of the text titled 'Psyche') and the Nancean Psyche (Levinas never names Psyche, I think)."

29. Emmanuel Levinas, *Otherwise Than Being or Beyond Essence*, trans. Alphonso Lingis (Pittsburgh: Duquesne University Press, 1998), p. 74.

30. Emmanuel Levinas, *Time and the Other*, trans. Richard A. Cohen (Pittsburgh: Duquesne University Press, 1987), p. 39. See my *Levinas and the Cinema of Redemption: Time, Ethics, and the Feminine* (New York: Columbia University Press, 2010), pp. 9–14 for an expanded discussion of this idea.

31. See Julia Kristeva, *Intimate Revolt: The Powers and Limits of Psychoanalysis*, trans., Jeanine Herman (New York: Columbia University Press, 2002), p. 12. All future references to this work will be to this edition and will be included parenthetically in the text as *IR*.

32. See Sigmund Freud, *Three Essays on the Theory of Sexuality*, trans. James Strachey (New York: Basic Books, 1962), p. 87.

33. See Edith Wharton, *The Age of Innocence* (1920; rpt. New York: Modern Library/ Random House, 1948), pp. 133–134.

34. Ibid., p. 134.

35. Ramie Targoff, *John Donne: Body and Soul* (Chicago: University of Chicago Press, 2009), p. 1. For the Donne quote see *The Sermons of John Donne*, eds. George R. Potter and Evelyn M. Simpson, 10 vols. (Berkeley: University of California Press, 1953–62), vol. 2, pp. 261–262.

36. Kristeva deems an active soul as a resource for the revivification of modern psychic life. She passionately propounds a rebirth of the soul as necessary for modern man to find and create representations of the self and society that can overcome the narcissism of the "new maladies of the soul" that modern media, technology, and consumerism cultivate. She writes, "Modern man is losing his soul, but he does not know it, for the psychic apparatus is what registers representations and their meaningful values for the subject." She maintains in *New Maladies of the Soul* (New York: Columbia University Press, 1995), pp. 6–8 that under current conditions "psychic life is blocked, inhibited, and destroyed."

37. See Emmanuel Levinas, *Totality and Infinity: An Essay on Exteriority*, trans. Alphonso Lingis (Pittsburgh: Duquesne University Press, 1969), p. 168.

38. Derrrida, *On Touching*, p. 84.

39. George Steiner, *Martin Heidegger* (Chicago: University of Chicago Press, 1989), p. 115.

40. See André Bazin, "The Ontology of the Photographic Image," in *What is Cinema?* ed. and trans. Hugh Gray, 2 vols. (Berkeley: University of California Press, 1967), vol. I, p. 14.

41. Shone, *Martin Scorsese: A Retrospective*, p. 164.

42. Anthony Lane, "Gilded Pleasure," *The New Yorker*, September 13, 1993, p. 122.

Index

Age of Innocence, The, 153–85
Allen, Woody, 49, 74
Alvarez, Irineo, 121
Amores Perros, 106, 129
Antonucci, Vittorio, 43
Anzaldúa, Gloria, 103–5
Arendt, Hannah, 39
Aristotle, 177
Armendáriz, Aitor Ibarrola, 104
Arriaga, Guillermo, 104, 106–7, 128
Arthur, Jean, 16–17
atheism, 22–3

Babel, 106, 129
Ballhaus, Michael, 157
Baranda, Cecilia, 69
Bauche, Vanessa, 10, 113
Bazin, André, 8, 110, 119, 128, 182
Bergman, Ingmar, 74, 146
Bicycle Thieves, 35–54
Big City, The, 82
Big Sleep, The, 8
Birdman, 129
Blanco, Roxanna, 57, 65
body, 2, 10, 17, 22–3, 28n, 52, 56–60, 63, 68,
    70, 73–4, 83, 85, 88–90, 118, 140, 155,
    160–1, 164–6, 168, 171, 175–8, 184; *see
    also* nudity
Bogart, Humphrey, 8–9, 122
Bondanella, Peter, 36
border patrol, 111–14, 116–17; *see also la
    frontera*

Broadway Danny Rose, 49
Brody, Richard, 134, 138

Campero, René, 121
Canby, Vincent, 154
Cape Fear, 153
Capra, Frank, 15–16
Carell, Lianella, 42
Caron, Laurent, 93
Carter, Matthew, 103–4, 106, 120
Casillo, Robert, 159
Castellitto, George P., 163–4
Cedillo, Julio Cesar, 109
Chaplin, Geraldine, 157, 162, 167–8
Chiari, Giulio, 46
Clift, Montgomery, 10, 25
Cloud, Arthur Red, 132
Cocks, Jay, 156, 163, 184
Cole, Thomas, 140–1
Collins, Lorna, 40
Cooper, Sarah, 25, 80, 82–3, 87–9, 92, 96
Cornil, Christelle, 86
Cotillard, Marion, 78–97
crucifixion, 146, 148

Dardenne, Jean-Pierre and Luc, 36–8,
    78–97
Dargis, Manohla, 104, 153
Davis, Michael Rees, 167
Day-Lewis, Daniel, 10, 154, 157, 161, 168,
    184
De Sica, Vittorio, 33–54, 79

death, 46, 60, 87–8, 90, 101, 109–11, 116–17,
    119, 121, 130, 144, 161, 166, 181, 185
    mask, 65, 109–11, 116, 119, 130, 146
delayed cinema, 1–11, 15, 19, 24–5, 33–54,
    56, 61, 64, 66–7, 70, 74, 83, 121, 127–9,
    142, 145, 148, 156, 163–4, 167–9
Denis, Claire, 14
Derrida, Jacques, 101, 106, 129, 164–5, 177
Diaz, Emilia, 73
DiCaprio, Leonardo, 127, 132, 139–40,
    150–1
digital media, 1, 6–7, 9, 24–5, 128, 149
divided selves, 10, 71, 140, 166, 168, 175, 179
Doane, Mary Ann, 5, 27n
Donne, John, 176–8
Dorati, Ida Bracci, 49
Dove, Grace, 151

Eastwood, Clint, 149
Ebert, Roger, 108, 154
Elie, Paul, 153, 155
Emerson, Ralph Waldo, 141
ethical imperative, 3, 5–6, 19, 23, 25, 33,
    37–8, 41, 71, 74, 76, 103, 156, 163–4,
    176
    responsibility, 17, 20–1, 38, 45, 58, 179–80
Etulain, Richard, 103
Evidence of Film, The, 14
existentialism, 2, 5, 11–13, 19, 33, 80

Farber, Manny, 8
Farkas, Linda Faye, 157, 166
Farrow, Mia, 49
Ferrari, Federico, 58–60
Ferretti, Dante, 157
Ford, John, 11, 134, 149
400 Blows, The, 149
French art cinema, 78, 80
Freud, Sigmund
    dream analysis, 22, 174–5
    uncanny, 1, 7
    unconscious, 6, 7, 22
    zeitlos, 3, 22–3, 25, 102, 147, 172
frontier (American), 102–4, 127, 129, 133,
    137–9 141–2, 149; *see also* West
    (American)

Garfield, Andrew, 153
Gentile, Julieta, 60

*George Harrison: Living in the Material
    World*, 153
ghostly presence, 9, 50, 168, 175, 182
Girlfriend Experience, The, 10
Gleeson, Domhnall, 133
Godard, Jean-Luc, 7, 74
Goodfellas, 154, 163
Goodluck, Forrest, 132
Gordon, Robert S. C., 39–40, 43, 46–7,
    49
Gourmet, Olivier, 93
Grant, Richard E., 162, 167
Grønstad, Asbjørn, 2
Grossman, Vasily, 71
Gumbrecht, Hans Ulrich, 2–6, 9, 11, 27n
    chronotope, 3, 27n
Guzzini, Néstor, 73

Hamidou, Ben, 90
Hardy, Tom, 133, 135–6, 138–9
Hawks, Howard, 8, 9
Heidegger, Martin, 13, 15, 87
Helm, Levon, 118
Howard, Duane, 134, 148
Hurt, Mary Beth, 157, 170
Huston, John, 122

Iannone, Pasquale, 38
Iñárritu, Alejandro González, 106, 127–51
It's a Wonderful Life, 19

Jazz Singer, The, 10
Jefferson, Thomas, 141
Jolson, Al, 10
Jones, January, 111, 115
Jones, Tommy Lee, 10, 101–24, 127

kairos, 3, 20, 23–5, 120, 147
Kaplan, E. Ann, 82
Kavka, Martin, 21
Kazan, Elia, 163
Keough, Riley, 10
Kiarostami, Abbas, 14, 34
Koto, Serge, 94
Kristeva, Julia, 3, 19, 22–4, 79, 90, 102, 105,
    107, 113, 120, 143, 147, 158–9, 163–4,
    172, 177, 184–5, 187n
    grace 22–4, 147
Kundun, 153

La Demora, 36–8, 56–76
la frontera, 103–5, 108–9, 112
La Promesse, 82
La Rocca, Gianni, 86
La Vie en Rose, 81
Lane, Anthony, 84, 185
Last Temptation of Christ, The, 153–4
L'avventura, 10
Lawrenson, Edward, 144, 149
Le Petit Soldat, 7
L'enfant—The Child, 80
Leo, Melissa, 111
Leonard, Robert Sean, 183
Levinas, Emmanuel, 3, 19–21, 45–6, 70–2,
    74, 79–80, 83, 85–97, 101, 105–8, 117,
    119–20, 124, 129, 150, 155, 163–7,
    176–7, 181, 184–5
  co-presence, 91–2; *see also* Nancy, Jean-
    Luc
  eros, 177, 186n
  face, 74, 119–20
Lilla, Mark, 20
Limerick, Patricia, 103
Lloyd, Norman, 176
Lubezki, Emmanuel, 127, 131
Lyotard, Jean-François, 11

McCowen, Alec, 162, 167
Maggiorani, Lamberto, 41–2
Magomedgadzhiev, Timur, 91
Man with a Movie Camera, 7
Margolyes, Miriam, 172
mask, 65, 74, 109–11, 116, 119, 130, 146, 160,
    175–6; *see also* death mask
Mean Streets, 153
Menges, Chris, 108
mise en scène, 34–8, 41–2, 44, 47–8, 50, 53,
    58, 61–3, 67, 74, 76, 78–80, 82, 89, 96,
    102, 132
Misfits, The, 10, 25
Moby-Dick, 111
Monroe, Marilyn, 10, 25
Morgenstern, Joe, 80–1, 84
Mosley, Philip, 37, 80
motherhood, 23–4, 45
Mr. Smith Goes to Washington, 15–19, 25
Mulvey, Laura, 1–3, 5–11, 14–15, 24, 34, 47,
    83–4, 110, 121, 127–8, 151, 156, 163–4,
    167; *see also* delayed cinema

Murphy, Kathleen, 156–7, 173, 185
Murray, Jonathan, 86
music, 4, 43, 91–2, 157, 160, 162

Nakehk'o, Melaw, 134
Nancy, Jean-Luc, 2, 4–6, 9–19, 26, 33–7,
    39–40, 47, 58–60, 70–1, 79–80, 91–2,
    97, 108, 110, 119–21, 129–30, 140, 142,
    144, 151, 156, 158–66, 171, 176–8,
    184–5
  birth to presence, 4, 11
  co-presence, 6, 13, 17, 35, 43, 91–2
  entelechy, 17, 140, 178
  exscription, 158–9, 165–6
  free space of time, 16, 18, 33, 34, 36, 58,
    79, 142; *see also* spacious temporality
  otherness, 4, 6, 13, 15–16, 19–20, 33–9, 92,
    97, 165
  togetherness, 2, 4, 6, 13, 19, 33–4, 97
Negative Space, 8
neo-realism, 34–41, 58, 78–81, 96
Neyrat, Frédéric, 11
nudity, 56, 58–60, 62, 68, 70–1, 85, 89–90

O'Connor, Flannery, 108–9
Olin, Lena, 10

paternity, 23–4, 45, 50, 75, 124
Pepper, Barry, 10, 25, 111, 122–3
Perez, Gilberto, 163
Pernas, Oscar, 65
Petit, Chris, 8
Pfeiffer, Michelle, 154, 168–9, 184
photograph, 7–9, 109–11, 119, 121, 128, 182
Pi, Qianhui, 158
Pileggi, Nicholas, 163
Plá, Rodrigo, 36–8, 56, 58–9, 61–2, 64–5, 69,
    74, 76
Poulter, Will, 133, 139
Prose, Francine, 154–5
Punke, Michael, 127

Raging Bull, 153–4
Ray, Satyajit, 82
redemption, 17, 47, 50, 116, 121, 124, 153–5,
    164, 178
Renoir, Jean, 36
Revenant, The, 127–51
Rodriguez, Mel, 113

Rohter, Larry, 82, 84
Romney, Jonathan, 132, 143
Rongione, Fabrizio, 86
Rosetta, 80
Ryder, Winona, 154, 168

Sallée, Catherine, 81, 86
Saltamerenda, Gino, 44
Santello, Laura, 58
Sartre, Jean-Paul, 11
Schoonover, Thelma, 157
Scorsese, Martin, 153–85
Scott, A. O., 80–1, 84
Searchers, The, 11, 25, 134
Secco, María, 58
Segovia, Fecundo, 61
Segovia, Thiago, 61
Shone, Tom, 156
Silence, 153, 155
Simon, Scott, 104, 107
Smith, Gavin, 155, 158, 163, 167
Smith, Mark L., 127
Sornin, Batiste, 93
spacious temporality, 16, 33–9, 41, 43–4,
    47–8, 50–1, 53, 58, 61, 64, 67, 79,
    89–90, 142, 164
Staiola, Enzio, 44
star-power, 11, 83
Steiner, George, 2, 4–6, 11, 13, 15, 26, 179
Stevens, Wallace, 163–4
Suárez, Cecilia, 110
Stewart, James, 15, 17, 25
Svilova, Elizaveta, 8

Targoff, Ramie, 176
Tarkovsky, Andrei, 5
Taxi Driver, 153–4
Thomas, Deborah, 156
Thoreau, Henry David, 140–1
Three Burials of Melquiades Estrada, The, 10,
    25, 101–24, 127–8
Tillich, Paul, 3, 19–20, 23, 120

time
    diachronic time, 3, 20–1, 101, 105, 107–8,
        117, 139
    temporal dimension, 16, 17, 19, 60, 167–9,
        180, 185
    temporal regime, 3, 6, 12, 19, 20–3, 25, 46,
        61, 140, 148, 170–2, 176
transcendence, 4, 5, 20–1, 25, 26, 101, 119,
    120, 124
Transcendentalism, 141
Treasure of the Sierra Madre, The, 122
Truffaut, François, 149
Turner, Frederick Jackson, 103
21 Grams, 106, 128
Two Days, One Night, 36–8, 78–97

Unbearable Lightness of Being, The, 10
Updike, John, 156
urban space, 39–44, 46–7, 70

Vallarino, Carlos, 57
Vandelyn, John, 172
Vertov, Dziga, 7–8, 11
Vitti, Monica, 10

Wagstaff, Christopher, 40, 43, 49
Wayne, John, 11, 25, 134, 149
Welles, Orson, 36
West (American)
    genre, 101, 104, 127, 141, 149–51
    hero, 134
    landscape, 108, 138, 141, 151
    Westerners, 138–9
Wharton, Edith, 154, 156, 159, 174–6, 178,
    184
Williams, William Carlos, 163–4
Wolf of Wall Street, The, 153
Woodward, Joanne, 156, 163, 170

Yoakam, Dwight, 111

Zavatini, Cesare, 79

EU Authorised Representative:

Easy Access System Europe Mustamäe tee 50, 10621 Tallinn, Estonia

gpsr.requests@easproject.com

Printed and bound by CPI Group (UK) Ltd, Croydon, CR0 4YY

26/05/2025

01882802-0001